15-00

Folk Literature
of the British Isles

Readings for librarians,
teachers, and those who work
with children and young adults

edited by
ELOISE SPEED NORTON

The Scarecrow Press, Inc.
Metuchen, N.J. & London
1978

Library of Congress Cataloging in Publication Data

Main entry under title:

Folk literature of the British Isles.

    Bibliography: p.
    Includes index.
    1. Folk literature, British--History and criticism--
Addresses, essays, lectures. 2. Folk literature,
British--Bibliography. 3. Folk literature, English--
History and criticism--Addresses, essays, lectures.
I. Norton, Eloise Speed, 1928-
GR141.F62   398.2'0941   78-10324
ISBN 0-8108-1177-4

Dedicated to the

Members of the Mississippi
University for Women,
1976, Study Tour,

Folk Literature of the British Isles

INTRODUCTION

The purpose of this book is two-fold. It is an attempt to show that study tours can have substance and focus and benefit not only those who participate but others as well. Secondly, it is an attempt to draw attention to an area of ethnic folk literature that those who work with children and young adults in the United States should know more thoroughly than they do at present. The current interest in heritage, whatever it might be, has presented an interesting challenge and entree for librarians. British folk literature is an important area to consider. A search of the literature reveals a definite shortage of material about British folk literature for the librarians and others who work with children and young adults.

This book is a compilation of essays, articles, research and bibliographies that I feel should be shared with others interested in the subject of folk literature of the British Isles for children and young adults. Some are lectures given to a study tour I directed, Summer 1976, from different points in the British Isles as we visited folklore societies and other places important in folk literature. On my study tours, I make a bibliography of selected materials on the theme of the study tour. I mail this list when they enroll for the tour. The participants prepare themselves as time and interest permit. I have included this bibliography and other bibliographies prepared for this group. I pass articles and books around while we are traveling, in airports and on buses, and for bedtime reading. I have included some of these as reprints. The original research was done by colleagues and myself in close consultation with one another after the study tour. We have learned a great deal from the experience and are happy to share all these resources with you.

Eloise S. Norton

ACKNOWLEDGMENTS

Since this book was attempted because of a Study Tour in Folk Literature of the British Isles, which Mississippi University for Women allowed me to direct, I am greatly indebted to this institution. The student workers in the Department of Library Science have been my chief source of strength and encouragement. Lynn Williams, Kathy Downes, Regina Moore, Becky Buchanan, Debora Ditsworth, Elena Pang have all typed, proofed, checked, rechecked, and compiled data. It has been our book all the way. Our thanks to Bob Stahl, School of Education, MUW, who advised us on the design for Mrs. Sumrall's and my article. In his defense, we took some of his advice and wished we had taken more.

Last but not least, the advice and support of those who contributed the original material at little or no monetary reward should not be overlooked. Thank you, Mollie Hunter and Katharine Briggs for your sound counsel to a first offender. Our discussions were very valuable to me. I will cherish them.

CONTENTS

PART I

GENERAL

FOLKLORE IN ENGLISH LITERATURE

Katharine M. Briggs

Uncertain what ground to cover here, I have decided on a rapid survey of the whole field with special reference to children's books when they become relevant, that is when fictional books began to be written specially for children, which was not until the 18th century. Some of the earliest information about our folk belief is to be found in the writings of the medieval chroniclers and historians.

Even before medieval times Nennius, writing in 679, gives us our introduction into the great legendary "Matter of Britain" in his mention of "The Warrior Arthur" in Historia Britonum. He is called a warrior, not a king, and the 12 battles listed range over England and Northern Scotland. Professor Collingwood, in his Roman Britain, thinks it likely that Arthur was an actual warrior who led a picked band, armed and deployed in the Roman manner, which had almost been forgotten, to the aid of any king who was overrun by invading Saxons. Already by Nennius' time Arthur had become a legendary character, for in the last of the battles, Mount Badon, Arthur is reported as having slain 960 men. "No one laid them low save he." No hero of legend could do more. Besides this Nennius mentions the mark of the feet of Cabal, Arthur's favorite hound, imprinted on a piece of Welsh tradition. The Tale of Cuhlwch and Oluen from the Red Book of Hergest, which was included by Lady Charlotte Guest in The Mabinogion, shows Arthur as a mythological character. In this story we have a god-like king

This talk was given to visiting Librarians of Mississippi University for Women in the Library of the Folklore Society in London, August, 1976. Dr. Briggs is a past president of the Folk-lore Society, honorary life member of the American Folklore Society. Copyright © by Katharine M. Briggs, 1978.

surrounded by a lesser pantheon of knights with special magical skills, very much in the style of some of the early
Irish folk tales.

In 1125, in his Gesta Regum Anglorum, William of
Malmesbury, a serious and scholarly historian, wrote, "He
is the Arthur about whom the Britons rave in empty words,
but who in truth is worthy to be the subject not of deceitful
tales and dreams but of true history." The dreams which
he mentions were of the second coming of Arthur, for 12
years before a riot had broken out in Bodmin Church because some visitors from Laon had mocked the Cornishmen
for believing that Arthur was still alive and would return to
help his countrymen. It is clear that the legend was fully
alive, but it owes its extraordinary literary importance to
Geoffrey of Monmouth's Historia Britonum, which combined
the traditions of Merlin and of Arthur in such a way that the
literary world of the time was taken by storm and the "Matter of Britain" swept through England, France, and Italy,
and even invaded Germany.

The first delight in tales of battle and adventure was
built up by the French prosewriters and the poets into the
complicated and delicate structure of Chivalry. The social
and psychological background is examined and reconstructed
in The Allegory of Love by C. S. Lewis, a study which is
still almost indispensable to a full appreciation of the subject. An earlier work on the narrative is E. K. Chambers'
Arthur of Britain. Some valuable recent books are F. H.
Treharne's The Glastonbury Legends and Geoffrey Ashe's In
Search of Camelot, both in paperback. Examples of the Romances which show the development of the Arthurian legends
are those Marie de France, Christian de Troyes and the
Lanzelet, an interesting translation of a lost French original
into German, and, of course, Thomas Malory's collection of
this material. The Middle English poem of Sir Lanval is to
be found in Carew Hazlitt's Illustrations of the Fairy Mythology of Shakespeare, which contains many extracts of fairy
material from various works.

Scattered about among the writings of the medieval
chroniclers and historians are a small number of fairy anecdotes and pieces of folk belief which give us some indication
of the long pedigree of much of our more modern folklore.
Ralph of Coggeshall tells the curious and interesting story of
the Green Children, a mysterious couple who claimed to
come from St. Martin's Land, an underground country where

there was neither sun nor moon but a perpetual twilight, and where the inhabitants fed on beans--traditionally the food of the death--although it is to be noted that they also kept flocks and herds. He also gives the story of Malekin, a house-haunting fairy who claimed to have been a human, stolen by the fairies from her mother, and a circumstantial account of a merman or wild man of the sea. William of Newbridge confirms the story of the Green Children, and also gives a specimen of the many tales of a drinking cup stolen from the fairies.

Of the medieval historians, Gervase of Tilbury gives us an example of the fairy midwife story and the blinding of the seeing eye, of a fairy banquet and a stolen horn, of some tiny domestic fairies, the Portunes who visit farmhouses at night, and of the Grant, a bogey-beast creature rather like the Picktree Brag. All these anecdotes are quoted by Keightley in The Fairy Mythology. Walter Map, the friend of Geoffrey of Monmouth, in his De Nugis Curialium, tells several important stories, as for instance of King Herla, who was invited into Fairyland, and returned after three hundred years instead of three days, so that he and his following ride till the Day of Judgment because they know that if they dismount they will crumble into dust. There is also the story of Wild Edric, an early example of the Fairy Wife, with the taboo attached to the marriage, and a Melusine story from Brittany. It will be seen how many of our familiar legends come from these early days.

In the Celtic areas we have the early legends, the remnants of the Celtic mythology, the Bardic traditions of accurate oral transmission which preserved the ancient beliefs like flies in amber. Lady Wilde, in her Ancient Legends, Mystic Charms and Superstitions of Ireland, gives a vivid and poetic description of the discipline of the Bardic training; those who are anxious to study the subject in depth will find Professor Eugene O'Curry's Lectures on the Manuscript Materials of Ancient Irish History a mine of information. The Four Ancient Books of Wales by W. S. Skene is a very valuable work on the subject. The translation of The Mabinogion by Gwyn Jones and Thomas Jones is a scholarly and delightful modern work. J. F. Campbell's Popular Tales of the West Highlands and Carmichael's Carmina Gadelica, though they were orally collected in the 19th century, give a very good idea of the ancient background against which they were set.

With the advance in printing, the publication of books
and the rise of the popular press in chapbooks, broadsides
and pamphlets, we learn more about the popular traditions
and we find equivalents of children's literature. The first
books produced for children were designed purely for instruction. Caxton's Babees Book was a handbook for the training
of pages. Claudius Hollibund's English Schoolmaster was a
lively and entertaining conversation book in French. The
chapbooks, however, designed to be read by the newly literate classes, were equally attractive to children. The Mad
Pranks and Merry Jests of Robin Goodfellow tells us now a
good deal about the fairy beliefs of this period, but would be
as great a delight to boys and girls as to serving-men and
maids. "Jack the Giant-Killer," "Jack and the Beanstalk,"
the adventures of St. George and of the other six Champions
of Christendom, "The Birth and Adventures of Tom Thumb,"
"The Miraculous History of Fortunatus," "The King's Daughter of Colchester," and many more which have been familiar
to us from childhood were eagerly devoured by children 400
years ago. The dramatists and poets who came up from the
country to make their fortunes in London brought country beliefs with them, and if they were too sophisticated to share
the fears and credulities of their country neighbors they felt
themselves free to use these beliefs for ornament and delight.
This freedom gave us A Midsummer Night's Dream, and
Drayton's fairy poetry, Lyly's fairies and those in the Maydes
Metamorphosis, and later on, those in Ben Jonson's masques
and Herrick's fairy poetry. Towards the end of the 17th
century we were invaded by the French fairy tales, which set
the pattern for our literary fairy tales for 200 years. They
first brought the fairy godmother into fashion.

The 17th century was remarkable for the Antiquaries,
the forerunners of the Folklorists--Aubrey, Glavil, Ashmole,
Camden, Kirk, Bovet, De Loyer--who explored popular beliefs of all kinds and wrote books on all subjects from Archaeology to Calendar Customs. It was the age of long didactic poems, Drayton's Polyolbion, Browne's Britannia's
Pastorels, Heywood's Hierarchy of the Blessed Angels, of an
increasing awareness of local history, to be seen in Camden's
Britannia, and Carew's Survey of Cornwall and the translators
both from the classics and from contemporary literature,
Philemon Holland, Silvester and a host of others. The Age
of Speculation preceded the Age of Reason, and all beliefs,
traditions, practices, natural phenomena and ancient monuments were worthy of investigation. It was a time, too, of
extravagant sects and wild theories; in reaction against it the

18th century concentrated on order, neatness, symmetry and the Social Man rather than the Enthusiast. Education and training became of great importance and the first fictional books for children were directed to that end.

In most of the 18th century the fairies were used as instruments to point a moral, as they were in the later stories of Le Cabinet des Fées, but before the end of the century the first stirrings of the Romantic Revival brought reality and emotion back to folklore. One of its forerunners was Thomas Gray with his researches into Scandinavian mythology and his revival of the Welsh legends in "The Bard." William Collins' primly named "Ode on the Popular Superstitions of the Highlands of Scotland" records real Scottish fairy beliefs and customs: the tribute of food left out for the fairies, the dreaded elf-shot which destroyed men and cattle, and the kelpie, which makes his first appearance in poetic form in this poem.

With the writings of Walter Scott, however, the Romantic Revival is fully established. His poems and novels are full of traditional matter and his Minstrelsy of the Scottish Border, particularly the essay on fairies which it contains, proves his wide knowledge of folk tradition, even at that early age, which is further reinforced by Demonology and Witchcraft. His older contemporary, Burns, breathed the air of tradition in the same way. Hogg, Cunningham, and Cromek all had a first-hand knowledge of tradition, though it must be noted in their work that they were all embellishers, and could not leave the plain, unvarnished tale to do its work; in fact, sometimes they embroidered their theme so much that the original story was almost lost under the heap of ornament. Even Crofton Croker, who did such good work collecting the Irish tales and legends and gave us some stories that could not be surpassed, found it difficult to refrain from a sprightly humor that touches jocularity at times.

As the 19th century went on, the standard of accuracy left little to be desired and William Henderson's Folk of the Northern Countries might be called a model of a collector's notebook. By the time the Folklore Society was founded in 1878, a larger number of books on folklore and of collections of tales, legends and anecdotes in oral circulation had already been published, and those writers of children's books who wished to draw their material from traditional sources were well equipped to do so.

As I have already said, the 18th century children's

books were bent on edification, and all independent existence
is denied to their fairies.   A good example is to be found in
The Governess, a pleasant but intensely moral story written
by Sarah Fielding, the sister of the novelist.   An allegorical
fairy story about a very wicked giant and a good man and
amiable dwarf is read to Mrs. Teachum's little company,
and Mrs. Teachum hastens to point out to them that the fairy-
story and magical elements in the tale are to be interpreted
in a strictly allegorical sense and that these stories are of
no use unless the moral is extracted and practiced.

In the 19th century, however, such writers as Mrs.
Ewing and Charlotte Yonge wrote tales with morals indeed,
but not fanatically centered round edification, and firmly
based on folk beliefs or folk stories.   In "The Brownies, "
for instance, the original legend of the brownie of Trout's
Farm is told by the old grandmother just as any story might
have been told in a chimney corner by any old woman who
firmly believed in the fairies.   In the same way, Charlotte
Yonge's story A Reputed Changeling is an accurate account
of the belief which made many children's lives a misery to
them.   Peregrine Oakshott, a rejected child, whose treatment turns him into an autistic one, has one chance of regeneration after another taken from him and is the victim of
the superstitions of his time.

Beside these well studied tales, still with their moralistic background, a crop of fairy tales and fantasies sprang
up.   One of the best and most striking of these is Jean Ingelow's Mopsa the Fairy.   No child could feel that he was being
got at by this.   It has the authentic atmosphere of fairyland.
George Macdonald's stories are splendid pieces of folklore,
though it is not possible for him to ignore a moral issue.
No story should do so; the important thing is that the tale
should not be twisted to edification.   The purest in atmosphere is George Macdonald's early book, Phantastes, but The
Princess and the Goblin and The Princess and Curdie are full
of appeal for most children.   It is a tough, heroic world we
enter, with none of the flaccid automatic machinery of the
18th century stories.

Since those days supernatural tales for children have
gone through many phases.   At the beginning of the 20th
century a wave of sentiment flowed over children's literature.
There was a plethora of pretty-pretty, airy, gauzy fairies
with a facile solution to every problem.   Before that we had
had the parody of the fairy-tale, often witty and delightful,

based on the sophisticated French fairy tales of Perrault and Madame d'Aulnoy. Thackeray's Rose and the Ring was the first of these and one of the most successful. Another excellent example is Prince Prigio by Andrew Lang, who was certainly fitted by width of knowledge and an impish humor to parody the whole range of fairy tales. The parody did not kill the saccharine fairy tale, however, and neither did Kipling's headlong attack in Puck of Pook's Hill. It continued to limp on until the outbreak of the Second World War. However, there were many rivals. There was the school of Hans Andersen, for instance, with its leaning towards whimsy and its touch of tragic irony. Oscar Wilde's Happy Prince was an early example; the stories chosen by Louey Chisholm for The Enchanted Land and Laurence Houseman's Moonshine and Clover were among many others. There were also fairy stories for grown-up people: Maurice Hewlett's Lore of Proserpine, with its ruthless fairies, creatures of another creation; de la Mare's fairies in Broomsticks and his strange fairy play, Crossings; Clemence Dane's The Moon is Feminine, founded on the fairy anecdotes in the Medieval Chronicles; Hope Mirrilees' Lud-in-the-Mist, which has been lately reprinted.

In the middle of the Second World War came J. R. R. Tolkien with The Hobbit and lesser but delightful works like Farmer Giles of Ham. These were followed by the Narnia books of C. S. Lewis, and then came the heroic trilogy, The Lord of the Rings. This seems to have killed trivialities, though it is not a book intended for children. The fantastic children's books of our day are full of meat. Ursula Le Guin's trilogy on The Wizard of Earthsea, Alan Garner's tales with their carefully researched and thought-out folklore, and Nicholas Stuart Gray's reshaping of folktales--these writings are full of meat, and Stuart Gray's in particular deserve to become classics. Nor are Penelope Lively's variations on folklore themes to be despised. And there are many more; in fact we may say that both folklore studies and the creative work springing from the knowledge of these studies are in a flourishing state at present and promise a rich harvest in the future.

Katharine Briggs' Works

The Anatomy of Puck. London: Routledge and Kegan Paul, 1959.

The Anatomy of Puck. New York: Arno Press, 1978.

A Dictionary of British Folk-Tales in the English Language,
        Parts A and B.   4 vol.   London: Routledge and Ke-
        gan Paul, 1970-71.

A Dictionary of Fairies.   Alan Lane, October 1976.

An Encyclopedia of Fairies.   New York: Pantheon Books,
        27th January 1977.

The Fairies in Tradition and Literature.   London: Routledge
        and Kegan Paul, 1967.

The Folklore of the Cotswolds.   London: Batsford, 1974.

Folktales of England (with Ruth L. Tongue).   Chicago: Uni-
        versity of Chicago Press, 1965.

Folktales of England.   London: Routledge and Kegan Paul,
        1965.

Hobberdy Dick.   London: Eyre and Spottiswoode, 1953.

Hobberdy Dick.   Oxford, England: The Alden Press, 1969.

Hobberdy Dick.   Baltimore: Puffin Books, 1972.

Hobberdy Dick.   New York: Greenwillow, 1977.

Kate Crackernuts.   Oxford, England: The Alden Press,
        1963.

The Last of the Astrologers; The Autobiography of William
        Lilly.   F. L. S. Mistletoe Books I, 1974.   (edited by
        Katharine Briggs)

Pale Hecate's Team.   London: Routledge and Kegan Paul,
        1962.

Pale Hecate's Team.   New York: Arno Press, 1978.

The Personnel of Fairyland.   Oxford, England: The Alden
        Press, 1953 and 1969.

The Personnel of Fairyland.   Detroit: Gale, 1971.   Reprint
        of 1953 edition.

FAIRIES IN CHILDREN'S BOOKS

Katharine M. Briggs

Children became very important people in the twentieth century. Children are, of course, important in all centuries because they are the custodians of the future, but the attitude towards them changes with the period. In the twentieth century they became financially important. Special clothes were designed for them, not just small versions of what grown-up people were wearing; the shops were flooded with toys and models, very costly ones or those that were comparatively cheap and expendable, and above all the press was flooded with books specially designed to meet their tastes and to give them delight. Sometimes, it seems that the books were too specially designed. Everything was made easy, the children's minds were never stretched, they never experienced the delightful conquest of a new idea, or rolled a long word gustfully around their palates. This was, perhaps, especially true in the early years of this century, though the tendency may go in vertical waves rather than exactly by date.

I am writing here of the presentation of fairies in children's literature. Children now have a tremendous amount of material to choose from if they can be helped to find the kind of thing that is congenial to them, and can be trained to read perceptively and not to get into the habit of allowing a soft stream of language to flow over their mental surfaces.

In early medieval times the proportion of people who could read was relatively small. A man who could pick out a few passages of scripture was counted as a clerk, and could claim the legal immunities that belonged to a churchman.

This lecture was prepared for a visit to Mississippi University for Women, Columbus, MS, October 1977. Copyright © by Katharine M. Briggs, 1978.

Aristocratic children were carefully trained for the position they had to hold, in courtly manners, etiquette, music and dancing; in all the expertise of war for the boys, in needlework and the direction of a grand household for the girls, but they were not necessarily highly literate, though it is hard to believe that Marie de France, for instance, could not write.   Before the time of printing, books were rare and extremely precious and only specially fortunate children would have access to them.   Fairy tradition would come to most children orally, from stories told about the fire or from readings from romances or the songs sung by minstrels. Those who were brought up in monasteries would learn to write and would hear legends of the saints, but they would not be likely to hear much about fairies from those unless they happened to stumble on the Legend of St. Collen and his encounters with the Fairy King on Glastonbury Tor.

There are occurrences of fairies in the early monkish chronicles, for example, Ralphe of Coggeshall's account of Malekin, a little captive in Fairyland, and of the Green Children who came out of a cave near Wolfpits in Suffolk, and William of Newbridge's story of the Fairy Banquet and the fairy goblet stolen by a human visitor; but children would not have access to such sources, nor is it likely that a child would have an opportunity of browsing through Giraldus Cambrensis, Gervase of Tilbury or Walter Mapes, though he might be rather more likely to see Geoffrey of Monmouth's History of Britain, which first brought the Arthurian Legends into fashion.   These early romances would be the books which a child in a courtly household would be most likely to hear recited or even to read for himself.

We can get a very good idea of the kind of fairy literature available to a medieval reader from Carew Hazlett's little book, Fairy Tales, Legends and Romances Illustrating Shakespeare and Other Early English Writers, published in London in 1875.   This contains Joseph Ritson's Fairy Tales (1831) and G. O. Halliwell-Phillips' Illustrations of the Fairy Mythology of a Midsummer Night's Dream (1845).   Among these we find The Romance of Sir Launfal, an early Arthurian Medieval Romance, translated from the writings of Marie de France, about the love of a mortal knight for a fairy princess, who imposes the usual fairy injunction of secrecy on him; it is an early example of the Fairy Wife story with its accompaniment of a broken taboo.   There is also the beautiful Romance of King Orfeo, in which Pluto is turned into a king of fairyland and Orpheus successfully rescues Eurydice--called in

the poem, Dame Meroudys. Here again, we have an early
fairy tale of rescue from fairyland, of which a familiar example is the Ballad of Young Tanilin. We have, too, an
early romance of Thomas and the Fairy Queen, less vivid
than the ballad but more detailed. After this, we come to
the beginning of the 16th century with Lord Berner's translation of Sir Hoon of Bordeaux, published about 1540, though
the only surviving edition is that of 1601. Halliwell-Phillips
has chosen his extract skillfully here, for the book is a long
one, but here it covers Hoon's first meeting with Oberon,
the Fairy King, and Oberon's account of his birth and descent
(he was the son of Julius Caesar and the Fairy Lady of the
hidden isle of Chafalone) and of the gifts given to him by the
fairies who visited his mother at his birth. One fairy, however, was offended and cursed him with dwarfish size. Here
we have an early instance of what was later to become the
motif of the fairies at the christening and the curse of the
one who was offended. We have also the first appearance of
Oberon, as King of the Fairies.

We have reached the age now when Caxton set up the
first printing press in England and when literacy became
much more common. The 16th century was the period of a
great upsurge in education, largely by private bequest from
wealthy citizens. The Oxford Reformers, Colet, More,
Elyot, Cheke and Ascham, were deeply and fervently convinced of the value of education to the private citizen and to
the State, and their conviction impressed itself on all thinking
men of their period. A paper on "Education and Apprentice-
ship" by H. M. Curtis which appears in Shakespeare in His
Own Age--originally volume 17 of The Shakespeare Survey--
examines the whole educational position in Shakespeare's England and emphasizes the great surge forward in educational
opportunities during that period. Westminster, Merchant Tay-
lors', Harrow, Charterhouse were all founded at that time
and a great number of market towns, such as Stratford, were
newly endowed with grammar schools, where the sons of poor
men could obtain a free education. In ten counties examined
by W. K. Jordan in Philanthropy in England, 1480-1660 (1959),
it could be said of eight counties that every country boy lived
within twelve miles of a grammar school and that every small
town and large village contained some place of education.
The education of the grammar schools was almost entirely
classical, but every grammar schoolboy had gone first to a
"petty school" where he learnt to read and write his cate-
chism and creed, with some training in the fundamentals of
the christian faith. The pupils might even be taught the ele-

ments of Latin, summed up in The Primer.   This petty
school was commonly attended by girls as well as boys.
Attendance began at the age of four or five, and the boys
moved on to the grammar schools at seven or eight.   It will
be seen that the scholars produced by these schools were
well able to continue their own education even if they did not
go to university.

Educational books were not entirely lacking.   One of
the first books produced by Caxton was The Babees Book,
but this, like most other books written for children in the
next few centuries, was intended for instruction rather than
delight; its purpose was to teach young pages all that they
would need to know about the intricacy of waiting at table and
all the other duties of a page.   For light reading, however,
there was a wealth of chapbooks which were carried round by
pedlars and could be borrowed from the servants, or even
bought by the young master himself, if he was in funds.
Carew Hazlitt gives us a very good specimen of a fairy chap-
book, Robin Goodfellow, His Mad Prankes and Merry Jests.
The date of the surviving edition is 1628 but there is little
doubt that it is an early work.   In this tale, Robin is the
child of King Oberon and a mortal country girl.   He is a
very mischievous little boy and when his mother threatens to
whip him, he runs away and takes service with various masters.   On his travels, he falls asleep by the roadside; when
he wakes, he finds a scroll beside him telling him that he is
Oberon's son and giving him fairy powers of shape-shifting
and receiving everything for which he wishes.   After this, he
goes from place to place and plays various pranks until he is
received by Oberon into fairyland.   It is in no way a distinguished work, but it incorporates, in the account of the fairies
he meets, a number of the folk traditions of the time.

Carew Hazlitt's remarkable little compendium of fairy
literature goes on to give examples of the miniature fairies
which came into fashion toward the end of Elizabeth the
First's reign and kept their popularity all through the next
century.   In Drayton's Nymphidia the fairies have lost the
dignity which they preserved through A Midsummer Night's
Dream.   Their control of human destiny and of the seasons
has left them, and, in spite of its liveliness, the whole af-
fair is a court intrigue in minuscule.   With Herrick, as with
Drayton, all the delight is in littleness, but this miniature
world might well endear itself to children; little Robert Louis
Stevenson, who enjoyed a miniature fairy world, might well
have got much pleasure out of "A Beggar's Petition to Queen
Mab":

Please your Grace, from out your store
Give an almes to one that's poor,
That your mickle may have more.
Black I've grown from want of meat,
Give me then an ant to eat
Or the cleft eare of a mouse
Over-sow'cd in drinke of souce,
Or, Sweet Lady, reach to me
The Abdomen of a bee,
Or command a cricket's hip,
Or his huckson to my scrip.
Give for bread a little bit
Of a pease that got to shit,
And my full thanks take for it
Floure of fuzballs that's too good
For a man in needyhood.
But the meal of milldust can
Well content a craving man.
Any orts the elves refuse
Well will serve the beggar's use.
But if this may seem too much
For an almes they give me such
Little bits, that nestle there
In the pris'ner's pannier,
That a blessing light upon
You and the Mighty Oberon
That your plenty last till when
I return your almes again.

This is taking the fairies with entire want of serious-
ness.   What fairy needs to beg from a fairy when he can extract the foyson out of mortal food?   Yet in some of Herrick's poems he shows awareness of real fairy tradition.   As,
for instance, in:

If ye will with Mab find grace,
Set each platter in his place,
Rake the fier in and get
Water in ere sun be sett,
Wash your pailes and clense your dairies,
Sluts are loathsome to the fairies,
Sweep your house, Who doth not so,
Mab will pinch her by the toe.

This is in the straight line of folk tradition.   The fer-
tility fairies have a strict concern for neatness and order and
many will punish slattens by worse than pinching.

The small fairies were fashionable until the middle of
the 17th century, when they became as small as microbes in
"The Duchess of Newcastle," Poems and Fancies (1653):

> Who knows, but in the braine may dwell
> Little small Fairies, who can tell?
> And by their several actions they may make
> Those formes and figures, we for fancy take.
> And when we sleep, those visions, dreams we call
> By their industry may be raised all,
> And all the objects, which through senses get,
> Within the braine they may in order set,
> And some pack up, as Merchants do each thing
> Which out sometimes they to the memory bring.
> Thus, besides our own imaginations,
> Fairies in our braine beget inventions.
> If so, the eye's the sea they traffic in
> And on salt watery teares their ship doth swim
> But if a teare doth breake, as it doth fall,
> Or wip'd away, they may a shipwrack call.

The Duchess of Newcastle was considered rather a
figure of fun in her time but, nevertheless, the picture of
the small fairy tended to usurp the heroic one in literary
tradition. It had an authentic place in folklore but the Elizabethan literary fashions for the small fairy tended to give it
a larger place than it originally held.

It was from these poems and from the chapbooks and
broadsides that children had to find food for their imaginations. Until the 18th century everything written for them was
directed exclusively to their instruction.

In 1709, Richard Steele published an article in the Tat-
ler about the literature enjoyed by his little godson, who
seems to have concentrated his reading entirely upon chapbooks. Apparently, he was anxious to deal with accepted
facts, for he had lately abandoned Aesop's fables as too fanciful and was concentrating on The Adventures of Don Belli-
anis of Greece, Guy of Warwick, The Seven Champions and
"other historians of that age." Guy of Warwick and other
chapbooks, like Sir Bevis of Southampton, will be found in
The Old Story Books of England collected by W. J. Thoms.
The supernatural creatures contained in these stories are
giants and dragons, not fairies, but the boy's sister Betty
preferred fairies. She "deals chiefly in fairies and sprites,"
Steele says, "and sometimes in a winter's night will terrify

the maids with her accounts until they are afraid to go to
bed. " She seems to have derived her knowledge from reading, not tradition, for her mother is quoted as saying that
she was a better scholar than her brother.

Two years before Steele's article, the first translation of Madame D'Aulnois's Fairy Stories was published in
England, and it is just possible that Betty might have known
them. Perrault's Contes du Temps Passé was not published
until 1697, under the name of P. Darmancour.

This was Pierre Perrault d'Arrmancour, the eldest
son of Charles Perrault and a boy of 18 at that time. It
was claimed that these stories were folk-tales told him by
his governess and written down by him. They are on folk
themes, much polished and suited to the taste of a witty and
sophisticated court. They had an immediate success.
During Charles Perrault's lifetime they were accepted as
written by his son, but after Charles Perrault's death they
were increasingly ascribed to him. According to Percy
Muir's analysis of the situation in his English Children's
Books (pp. 39-40), this was an unwarrantable assumption.
This highly successful book had no successor, for Pierre
Perrault died in 1700. When Samber's translation came out
in England in 1729 it made an immediate conquest of the
English nurseries, and traditional English fairy tales were
pushed into the background. In any case, they had only appeared in scattered chapbooks. D'Aulnois and Perrault introduced the fairy godmother into England. After this, in
literary fairy stories the fairy godmother, the fairies at the
christening, and the offended wicked fairy make a recurrent
theme. It is no wonder that they were popular, for in the
16th and 17th centuries, the Puritan writers dealt hardly with
the fairies and treated the best of them as devils. William
Warner, for instance, in Albion's England, develops a theory
that Robin Goodfellow did no work about the house at all, but
got the housewife up in her sleep to do it all:

> Ho, Ho, Ho, Ho, needs must I laugh such fooleries
> to name,
> And at my crummed messe of milke each night
> from maid or dame,
> To do their chares, as they supposed, when in
> their deadest sleepe,
> I pull'd them out their beds and made themselves
> their houses sweep,
> How clattered I among their pots and pans, as

dreamed they?
My hempen, hampen sentence, when some tender
   foole would lay
Me shirt or slop, them greeved for I then would
   go away.

Evidently, Warner knew the fairy traditions, but condemned them, as most of the other Puritans did.   There
was a kind of hangover from their disapproval into the 18th
century, and when the booksellers of that period began to
commission books expressly for children, their aim was
strictly educational, as it had been in earlier times.   Such
fairies as appeared in the 18th-century children's literature
were after the pattern of the fairy godmothers who were bent
on the edification of their protegées.   An example is "The
Fairy Gifts" by Comte de Caylus (which will be found in Andrew Lang's Green Fairy Book), in which a good fairy who
educates a number of princesses and offers each of them the
choice of a fairy gift at the end of her stay, sends round the
youngest to observe the effects of the gifts before making her
choice.   As a result of her observations of her former com-
panions she chooses nothing but a quiet spirit, which proves
the best gift of all.

The 18th-century fairy stories are parodies of this,
being interpreted allegorically.   Even these were soon frowned
upon.   The odious Mrs. Trimmer rewrote Sarah Fielding's
rather pleasant book The Governess in 1820, removing all the
fairy stories but one, although they were carefully explained
as moral allegories.   Through nearly the whole of the 18th
century, the children's stories became almost painfully mat-
ter-of-fact and utilitarian, though Maria Edgeworth's lively
mind and strong interest in human nature gave lasting charm
even to a book so unattractively named as The Parent's As-
sistant.   However, in the best of these books, we look in
vain for fairies.

In the 19th century, though a moral was still accept-
able, the stories were less twisted towards didacticism, and
the Romantic Revival stimulated an interest in real traditional fairies; they ceased to be dummy figures.   The publication of Grimm's Household Tales in 1812 aroused an interest
in native traditional fairy tales throughout Europe and, indeed, as far afield as Japan.   In the Celtic areas of Ireland,
Wales, the Highlands of Scotland and Cornwall the traditions
had never died, but they now became the subject of research.
In lowland Scotland and England, there were still fairy beliefs

to be collected, though not such an articulated and organized
tradition.   In Ireland, Crofton Croker, who was in correspondence with the Grimm Brothers, was early in the field
with his Fairy Legends of Ireland.   In Scotland, Walter Scott,
Hogg, Cunningham, Cromek, J. F. Campbell and many others
crystallized and diffused the knowledge with varying degrees
of accuracy.   In Wales, Charlotte Guest translated the ancient
books of Wales under the title of the Mabinogion.   Hunt and
Bottrell made contact with the last of the Cornish Droll-Tel-
lers.   The spirit of Irish scholarship awoke and Douglas
Hyde, Lady Wilde and Yeats began the great work which is
still continuing.   In England, the spirit of the 17th century
antiquaries seemed to revive itself.   Researches, which grew
more and more accurate and scholarly, were pursued all over
the British Isles.   Scholars of all countries corresponded and
exchanged their views and at length, in 1878, the Folklore
Society was founded.

While all this activity was going on, writers on fairylore had no longer an excuse for ignorance about the nature
and character of the fairies; indeed, we are often amazed by
the amount of knowledge shown by the 19th-century writers of
literary fairy tales.

One of the most interesting facets of the study of literature is the interplay between folk tradition and creative
work.   Traditional knowledge rises up to inform and inspire
creative literature, and this in its turn sinks down into folklore and enriches it.   In the 19th-century uprush of writing
for children, two factors were combined.   The first was a
strong interest in oral tradition, which grew out of the Romantic Revival, and the second, which perhaps sprang from
the same soil, was a sense of the importance of childhood
and of the individual soul of each child.   Already this was
foreshadowed in some of the 17th-century writings, in Tra-
herne and Vaughan, and in a few of the theophrastic characters, but in the 16th and again in the 18th century, children
were often treated as malleable material which it was the
responsibility of their parents and teachers to press into a
desirable mould.   The whole attitude to children was changed
by the end of the 19th century.

I wish there were time here to indulge in an exploration of such delightful novels of domestic life as Charlotte
Yonge's Pillars of the House and The Daisy Chain or J. H.
Ewing's Six to Sixteen, perhaps the best book for girls ever
written.   But there is nothing of fairies about these books,

though the authors of them were well grounded in folklore.
So let us talk about one of the early 19th-century books which
might be better known than it is, Granny's Wonderful Chair
by F. E. Brown, a blind Irish girl brought up in great pover-
ty in an Irish cabin surrounded by a great number of brothers
and sisters, who managed somehow to educate herself and to
make her living by literature, even paying for the education
of a younger sister to act as her amanuensis.   She wrote
historical novels, but the book by which she will be remembered is this collection of fairy stories, held together by a
slender but engaging plot, which was published in 1857.
There is a certain simple dignity about the style which re-
minds one of a folk story-teller, as if the silver bough had
been tinkled and we had been hushed to listen.

Another book of special quality was written in 1869,
Jean Ingelow's Mopsa the Fairy.   There is no trace of en-
gineered morals here.   We are in a wild, fairy world, in-
tricate but free, where you may do whatever you can do.
Jack travels from one fairyland to another, each rather different in nature and conditions.   Hidden but inexorable behind the fairyland, however, is Old Mother Fate, who must
be obeyed in the end.   It is an invented fairyland, and yet
curiously true to folklore tradition.   For instance, the one-
foot-one fairies cannot cry unless a human mortal cries in
their company.   It is a luxury which they greatly prize.
The book is interspersed with some delightful snatches of
verse.   It is now published in Dent's Children's Classics,
which republished a good many of the Everyman Books, in a
less pleasant form.   George Macdonald's Phantastes (1857)
has something of the atmosphere of Mopsa the Fairy, but it
is a more moral world and a sterner one.   Juliana Horatia
Ewing shows a very sound knowledge of fairylore in three
stories with a naturalistic foundation: The Brownies, Lob-
Lie-by-the-Fire, and Amelia and the Dwarfs.   The stories
are so good that as children we forgave them for their
morals.   As well as these, Mrs. Ewing has a collection of
short invented stories: Old Fashioned Fairy Tales, which
are very like real folk stories in style and are excellent to
tell.   Mrs. Molesworth's book, The Cuckoo Clock, came out
in 1877, not much later than Macdonald's Princess and the
Goblin (1872).

In the beginning of this century, there came a crop
of flaccid fairy stories by Ross Fyleman and Enid Blyton,
with airy-fairies with gauzy clothes and butterfly wings, and
revolting little elves in children's magazines.   Kipling rightly

lashed out at them in Puck of Pook's Hill. It was not long
that they were at their worst. More honest, more substan-
tial fairies came to the fore again in B. B.'s Little Grey
Men (1942) or Croft Dickenson's Borrobil (1944). In the
first, the gnomes are almost like long-lived animals, and
the second is an exploration into the Stone Age and the dangers of primitive magic. Both are down-to-earth and honest-
to-goodness, with no whimsey about them. C. S. Lewis's
Narnia books show a real respect for mythology and folklore,
and are deeply felt and serious books, full of zest for life
and an appreciation of beauty, as well as a very inventive
imagination. The crown of modern children's fairy books is
J. R. R. Tolkien's The Hobbit (1937). It is soundly based
on folklore and where the folklore is invented, it is convinc-
ing; the dangerous and exciting parts are almost too exciting,
the characters are rounded, the scenery is magnificent, the
humor is entertaining and the action has an epic quality.
The whole conception is lifted into another dimension and
adult quality in The Lord of the Rings. Some people, for
one reason or another, are unable to enjoy it. We can only
condole with them; they have missed something.

Books About Children's Books

Cook, Elizabeth. The Ordinary and the Fabulous. An Introduction to Myths, Legends and Fairy Tales. Cambridge University Press, 1969.

Huck, Charlotte S. and Doris A. Young. Children's Literature in the Elementary Schools. New York: Holt,
   Rinehart and Winston, 1961.

Muir, Percy. English Children's Books 1600 to 1900. London: Batsford, 1972.

Opie, Iona and Peter. The Classic Fairy Tale. Oxford University Press, 1974.

St. John, Judith. The Osborne Collection of Early Children's
   Printed Books, 1506-1954, A Catalogue. Toronto:
   Toronto Public Library, 1958.

Tuer, Andrew. Old-Fashioned Children's Books. The Lead-
   enhall Press Limited, 1899.

REFLECTIONS OF A STORYTELLER
--HER NATIVE FOLKTALES

Eileen Colwell

Storytelling is an enjoyable experience, not the least part of one's pleasure being the search for suitable stories to tell. To have to find a story for eager children is an incentive--if one is needed--to delve into the rich fields of literature. It is folk tales, however--the people's stories-- that are the most productive source of tales for telling. After all, these stories have always been <u>told</u> and have been handed down orally from generation to generation. As long as there are storytellers to bring them to life, folk tales will flourish, for they are not just material for scholarly pursuit but spontaneous expressions of the humor, wisdom, and imaginative fantasy of the people.

Each country has its own distinctive folk tales, and while they may be similar in theme, they vary greatly in presentation. This can be seen even in such relatively small countries as those which make up Britain. Each has its own tales with varying supernatural creatures and a different atmosphere, from the Seal People of Scotland to the Boggarts of Lincolnshire in England or the wizards of Wales.

Naturally I have particular favorites for telling from all these areas of my native land, stories which are not only typical of their place of origin, but which appeal to me as a storyteller and to children also. Folk tales were never intended for children, so what is it that appeals to them--their directness, their slapstick humor, the magic that pervades them?

Eileen Colwell is an author, children's librarian retired from Hendon, London, retired lecturer from Loughborough School of Librarianship, Loughborough, England, and still very active as an international speaker, writer, and traveler.

Not only do countries have their varied tales; so do the smaller areas of the countries. It is difficult, therefore, to choose a story from the children's favorites which can be said to be typical of England as a whole. Should it be The Giant of the Wrekin, or The Pedlar of Swaffham, or The Dragon of Shervage Wood or Jack Buttermilk? I have chosen instead the droll of The Three Sillies.1 It is at least typical of the down-to-earth humor of the common people and the capacity of the English to laugh at themselves. It could be told in any dialect, its ridiculous situations and dilemmas can be enjoyed by any child (or adult). The girl and her parents shedding floods of tears over something which may never happen ("while the beer runs out over the floor"), the variety of "sillies" who are apparently so plentiful in the England of the Middle Ages--this is a story which is fun to tell and calls forth bursts of spontaneous laughter.

For Wales, I would choose something quite different. Wales was one of the last refuges of the Celtic race as successive waves of invaders swept into England. It is a land which, with its lofty mountain peaks, its thick forests and barren uplands, has given birth to many stories, from the 13th-century story of the harpist, Einion, who was enchanted by a demon in the form of a beautiful woman, to the homely tale of the brave dog, Gelert, slain mistakenly by his master. There are tales of lake fairies, of spirits of the mountains, of magic, and even of miraculous cow. I have chosen none of these but have preferred a legend of King Arthur, for Wales has many stories of that legendary hero and would seem to be a fitting setting for him. The tale I enjoy telling is called Where Arthur Sleeps2 and Arthur's sleeping place is at Craig y Dinas, deep in the hillside, its silence unbroken for centuries. The teller, a Welshman, Gwyn Jones, has turned his Celtic imagination to a good effect and has used words so skillfully that the lilt of the Welsh tongue can be felt. There are colorful phrases which, while they may not be fully understood by children, please the ear: "A sonorous clamour of bronze" ... "the hooves of the horses effulgent as an autumn moon...." Every child holds his breath in suspense as the thief edges round the bronze bell, touches it inadvertently and hears the dread voices of the three sleeping knights, one "as light as a bird's," another "as dark as a bull," and the third "coldly menacing."

Scotland is a land rich in story and song, especially in the Western Highlands and the islands to the north. The more isolated and remote the region, the more atmospheric

the tales. It is as if mist and rain gave birth to the stories
told in the long winter evenings round the peat fire. My favorite story comes from the Orkney Isles, remote islands
"occupied" for 600 years by Norse raiders, pawned by an im-
pecunious king and then given as dowry with his daughter to
James III of Scotland.

In a group of islands it is natural that many stories
should have the sea as inspiration and background. Giantess-
es grind salt on the bed of the sea, mermaids entice unwary
fishermen to the depths, weird spirits haunt the deserted
shores, ghosts wail at night, islands appear and disappear in
the drifting mist. It is a legend of the seal people that I
like to tell particularly, although to rather older children than
usual, for this is a story of a mother who left her children
to return to the sea. The version I use is by Helen Waddell,
the classical scholar. [3] It has a dream-like atmosphere--the
seal people "who cast no shadow," dancing on the sand in the
moonlight, the young man carrying the beautiful woman from
the sea to his dark cottage with its glowing peat fire. There
is an unforgettable moment of suspense when the seal woman
stands with her seal skin once more in her hands as the story could swing either way. Homely sounds are all about her
and she can hear her children playing in the stack-yard--but
there is another sound, that of the sea surging in the bay,
and it is the sea that calls her. There is a last glimpse of
her floating on the waves and then she dives to her "fairy
palaces at the bottom of the sea where there comes neither
snow nor darkness of night and the waves are as warm as a
river in summer." A sad story perhaps, but one that appeals
for its undertones of love and yearning and loss.

The old Ireland is now Eire but storytelling has no
frontiers. Few countries are as rich in traditional stories
as Ireland and until very recently the professional storytellers, the shanachie, were still practicing their art. Among
Ireland's great tragic stories are The Three Sorrows of
Storytelling and one of them is the tale of The Children of
Lir. [4] This is one of my favorites, a moving story which
arouses compassion even in unsentimental children. The four
children in the story--gentle, loving Fionuala and her three
brothers, so cruelly changed into swans--are tragic figures
not easily forgotten. They are condemned to live for "three
hundred years on the waters of Lake Derryvaragh, for three
hundred years on the Straits of Moyle, for three hundred
years on the Atlantic by Erris and the Isle of Glora." The
sound of their sweet, forlorn singing haunts the story until

at last they regain their own shapes, only to fall to dust.
"Thus was the end of their long and sorrowful journey. "

And so to one county, Cornwall, the strangest of all
the counties of England, for even today it is a land apart.
Cut off from the rest of Britain for centuries, it even had
its own language until the 18th century.   It is surrounded on
three sides by the sea, its steep cliffs are riddled with
caves, its countryside scattered over with ancient dolmens
and great stone circles which have evoked stories of giants
and demons and men so wicked that, like Jan Tregeagle,
they are condemned to everlasting torment--Jan's howls of
rage can still be heard on stormy nights as he tries to
weave ropes from sand.   Even the stories of the numerous
saints are more akin to magic than to the Christian religion.
From Cornwall came one of the great love stories of the
world, Tristan and Iseult, so effectively retold by Rosemary
Sutcliff.   The lost land of Lyonesse lies under the waves at
Land's End and King Arthur is supposed to have lived in his
castle at Tintagel with the enchanter Merlin.   Cornwall, like
Wales, was peopled by the Celts and their native imagination
has colored the local tales.

But Cornwall has gentler spirits too, mermaids, fairy
folk and Knockers.   It is a story of the Knocker, [5] the little
men who were working in the tin mines long before human
beings arrived, that children enjoy.   The hero is a black-
haired, blue-eyed boy of nine.   His father, Chenoweth, ig-
nores the Knockers' demand for a share of the succulent cornish pasty he is eating and so meets bad luck.   But Billy,
brave and sensible, earns the good will of Blue-cap, a Knocker who leads him to a rich lode of tin.   "Blow me!" says
Billy, "Blue-cap deserves his wages!" and Blue-cap gets them
in the form of a large cornish pasty.

Another Cornish favorite with children is the story of
Skillywidden, [6] a strange little being who is captured by a
farmer and held prisoner because he knows where there is a
crock of gold.   The farmer's children love the merry little
fellow, but one day they hear a voice cry sadly, "Oh, my
dear and tender Skillywidden, wherever canst thou be?"   And
as they watch, the little Skillywidden runs to meet his Mammy
and the two disappear "in the whisk of a cow's tale. "

These are only a few of our native folk tales that
children and I have enjoyed together.   Folk tales are the
heritage of children everywhere, particularly those of their

own country.   May there always be storytellers to bring
them to life by their enthusiasm and skill.

Notes

1. Jacobs, Joseph. English Fairy Tales. Putnam (fac-
    simile ed., Schocken, 1967).

2. Colwell, Eileen. A Second Storyteller's Choice. Cro-
    well, 1965.

3. Waddell, Helen. The Princess Splendour and Other Sto-
    ries. Puffin Books.

4. Colwell, Eileen. A Storyteller's Choice. Walck, 1964.

5. Colwell, Eileen. A Second Storyteller's Choice. Cro-
    well, 1965.

6. Colwell, Eileen. Round About and Long Ago. Houghton
    Mifflin, 1974.

Books by, or edited by, Eileen Colwell

Bad Boys. Baltimore: Penguin, 1973.

Books to Begin With. London: Jenkins, 1964.

Eleanor Farjeon: A Monograph. London: Bodley Head,
      1961; New York: Walck, 1962.

First Choice (with other authors). London: Library Associa-
      tion, 1968.

Hallowee'en Acorn. London: Bodley Head, 1967.

How I Became a Librarian. Nashville: Nelson, 1956.

The Little Gray Neck (with James Riordan). Reading, Massa-
      chusetts: Addison-Wesley, 1976.

The Princess Splendour (editor). New York: Longman,
      1969.

Round About and Long Ago: Tales from the English Coun-
      tries. Boston: Houghton Mifflin, 1974.

A Second Storyteller's Choice (editor). London: Bodley
  Head, 1965; New York: Walck, 1965.

A Storyteller's Choice (editor). London: Bodley Head,
  1963; New York: Walck, 1964.

Tales from the Islands. Baltimore: Penguin, 1975.

Tell Me a Story (editor). Baltimore: Penguin, 1962.

Tell Me Another Story (editor). Baltimore: Penguin, 1964.

Time for a Story. Baltimore: Penguin, 1967.

The Youngest Storybook. London: Bodley Head, 1967; New
  York: Watts, 1968.

TRACKING DOWN ELVES IN FOLKLORE

Mary Calhoun

What is the difference between a boggart and a nisse?
A lubberkin and a dwarf? A brownie and a pixie? And why
the differences?

When I set out to plan a series of picture books about
European elves, the first task was to sort out the strands of
their individual characteristics. In studying folklore collected
in the nineteenth century, I found a whole sociology of elfdom
emerging from people's beliefs. Before I was done, I felt I
could take a degree in elfology.

An elf is a fairy is a gnome is a nisse. Even folklorists have not settled on an all-inclusive term for the small
people, speaking only of "fairy tradition." So, arbitrarily, I
call them elves. To me, that classification best calls to
mind the general type of little man with magical powers.

As seen in peasants' tales, elves fall into two groups.
There were the outdoor, "trooping fairies," who flocked together in companies, and there were the household sprites,
who were loners.

The pixies (piskies) of Devon and Cornwall, England,
were an outdoor race. These were little men in tattered
green suits who flitted about in swarms. They might invade
a cottage to tease a lazy housewife, or they might steal into
a barn to thresh corn for a deserving farmer. Generally,
however, they played on the moors, misleading travelers and
guiding them into bogs--thus, the term "pixy-led."

Reprinted by permission from The Horn Book Magazine 45 (June 1969), 278-282. Copyright © 1969 by The Horn
Book, Inc. This interesting article extends beyond the British Isles but has entertaining background information on the
subject.

Their Welsh counterparts were the ellylldon, or portunes, little old men in patched coats who worked on farms,
and who, when hungry, took frogs from their bosoms and
roasted them on coals.   The ellylldon were luring elves.
Their finger-ends could become five spinning lights, leading
belated peasants into marshes and over cliffs, upon which
event the ellylldon would "laugh loudly at the credulity of
mankind. "

Also in Wales lived the coblynau, gnomes who worked
in the mines.   (As did the wichtlein of Bohemia.)   The
gnomes were ugly; but they were good friends to miners,
calling attention to rich lodes of ore by their ghostly tappings.
The coblynau carried tiny hammers, picks and lamps, and
seemed to work busily, flitting about the shafts; but they
never really accomplished anything.

In northern Europe--Germany, Denmark, Scandinavia--
the outdoor elves usually dwelt underground--in mounds,
caves, mines, or mountain depths.   They were variously
called dwarfs, trolls (though a troll might be a big, frightening creature, too), bergmen (hill-people), or huldru-folk (hidden people).   Usually they were rather grumpy, stumpy little
people, but they carried on typical human occupations.   They
married and had children, they baked and brewed, they herded
cattle or they mined minerals.   They had little communication
with mankind, but upon occasion they might indulge in neighborly borrowing and lending--a loaf of bread borrowed from
an obliging man or woman, a bowl lent to a needy human
family for a christening.   They also indulged in a bit of un-
neighborly stealing--of sheaves of wheat from a field, a keg
of beer from a farmhouse, or even a child.

A note of sadness runs through the lore of these stumpy little people.   Many tales describe their last encounter
with men and their leave-taking when the human beings drive
them away.   I tried to convey this relationship in The Thiev-
ing Dwarfs (Morrow).

The house elf is almost always male.   (I found one
exception, a female brownie, Hairy Meg, who lived in the
Scottish Highlands.)   Usually there was just one elf to a
house--one was enough!   These were little old men who
helped or tormented in house and barn.   In return for their
services they wanted only a bowl of porridge left on the
hearth for them.

In this class fall the brownie of Scotland; the boggart
of northern England; other English elves, such as the lubberkin, lob-lie-by-the-fire, and Robin Goodfellow; the bwbach
(pwcca or puck) of Wales; the nisse and the tomte of Denmark, Sweden, and Norway; the follet of northern France (in
Normandy, the lutin or gobelin); the kobold of Germany--
though the kobold might also be a mine elf; and Jack-of-the-
Bowl of Switzerland.   The Irish leprechaun, or clurican, was
a loner, but he was not given to acting the servant in houses
and was more often come upon in the fields.

The character of these sprites differs in shading according to region.   German lore about kobolds is heavily detailed, symbolism is emphasized, and the kobold comes
through as an almost ominous creature in a household.   The
Swiss handmandle, on the other hand, was a gentle, joyous
elf, singing as he led cows away from dangerous precipices.
The nisse seems the most human of the elves, a wrinkled
little man in gray jacket, pointed red hat, and slippers.   For
all his trickery, he craved human friendship and might be
found sitting on a wall crying when he had been mistreated.
The boggart, although he could be seen in various forms,
was least human.   He was a whirling, tempestuous spirit,
much like a poltergeist (knocking ghost), banging on walls
and shouting in the night to wake up the folk.

In Norway, the vattar was not seen at all-but was pre-
sumed to enter the house through the drains, and a comfortable attitude prevailed toward him.   Scalding water was never
thrown down the sink without first warning, "Watch yourself,
good vattar, not to get scalded."

There are so many tales of elves and the details are
so specific that one wonders: Were there actually small
magical people once?

Folklorists have speculated on how the tales arose.
Thomas Keightley in The Fairy Mythology suggests that elf
lore originated with the Gotho-Germanic races, spreading
wherever the Teutonic peoples invaded.   The beliefs were
adopted by the conquered folk and took on local characteristics.
Thus Germany's "Rumplestiltskin" becomes "Tom Tit Tot" in
England.   Keightley says that Mediterranean countries have
few tales of elves, and states that such accounts are found
only in regions invaded by the Visigoths, as in Naples, where
the house spirit, Moniaciello, is remembered.

Other folklorists point out that many of the little people were said to live in mounds, both in northern Europe and in Britain. Maybe, they say, "elves" were shorter, aboriginal folk who hid in caves when invaders came from the east, popping out to trick and torment their conquerors. One nineteenth-century folklorist speculated that the full-sized people of the Fairy Family of Wales, y Tylwth Teg, were in truth Druids hiding from Christian invaders.

Or, elves represent ancestral spirits, say other theorists. In Scotland that seems to be the case with the brownie, in his shaggy brown cloak. A family would have its own personal brownie, who had presided over the fortunes of the farm for hundreds of years. Naturally enough, the dour brownie would resent a bribe.

Most folk, however, seemed unconsciously to regard the elves as godlets. The elves were the keepers of morals; they upheld the virtues. Pixies, for all their piquancy and fun, had a passion for cleanliness and would pinch and slap dirty housewives. The wrinkled old nisse approved of hard work. To help industrious servants, he would labor all night in the barn and kitchen; but he dragged lazy workers down the stairs by their heels. An elf was like a conscience. In tales from Germany the master of the house might find himself psychologically hounded by his kobold.

Perhaps the people naturally had an ambivalent attitude toward the tormenting-helpful elves. Tales divide about equally between schemes for acquiring an elf and ruses to get rid of one.

From Denmark comes a recipe for catching a nisse: First chop down a tree. When the tree crashes, nisses will come running to see what has happened. Sit down on the trunk to visit with the nisses. It may happen that when wedges are driven into the tree, a nisse's coat tail will fall into the cleft. When the wedge is driven out, the tail will be fast and the nisse a prisoner.

However, a resident elf, with his high standards and malicious trickery, could become obnoxious. As a last resort, the peasant would pretend to move away, hoping the elf would then leave the empty house. Variations of this tale are found in England, Wales, Ireland, Germany, and Denmark. One story goes:

A peasant and his wife piled all their household goods in a cart and led the cow out of the barn. Pretending despair, the man said in a loud voice,

"Well, that old boggart is too much for us. We'll have to move away."

As he and his wife and their cartload went down the road, they met a neighbor, who said,

"What, are you moving today?"

And from a tub on the cart came a squeaky voice,

"Aye, neighbor, we're flitting today."

In a German tale the peasant set fire to his barn as he departed, expecting to burn the kobold with it. But as the man looked back at the flaming barn, a voice from the chest on the cart exclaimed,

"It's time we came out! It's time we came out!"

Throughout folklore there were a variety of tricks for getting rid of elves, but none of them worked when an elf wanted to cling to a family. The only time an elf departed was when he was insulted, usually by a gift made in gratitude by the innocent peasant.

Considering the tenacity of elves to families, it is a surprise to me that so few elves came with the settlers to America.

PART II

ENGLAND

SOME FOLKTALES AND LEGENDS FROM NORTHERN ENGLAND

John D. A. Widdowson

Since its heyday at the turn of this century, folklore scholarship in England has suffered a considerable decline, especially as an academic subject.   Nowhere is this fact more noticeable than in the collection and study of folktales. The famous English folktale scholars who flourished in the late nineteenth and early twentieth centuries not only collected tales but also made their contributions to the analysis and classification of traditional narratives elsewhere in Europe and beyond.

Folklore scholarship in England also apparently declined somewhat in prestige following the disenchantment with the theories of the solar mythologists.   This decline was reflected in other branches of folklore study in the country itself until comparatively recent times.   During the past 20 years, however, and especially in the present decade, there has been a remarkable reawakening of both popular and academic interest in folklore in England.   Along with this movement has come a reappraisal of the important contribution which folklore makes in the development of a culture. With the recognition of such academic disciplines as anthropology, sociology, and linguistics has come the realization that the folklorist has a crucial part to play in documenting the traditional cultural heritage.   By observing and analyzing existing traditions he is able to clothe the bare bones of theory with the living reality which is the "personality" of the

Reprinted with permission of the author and the International Reading Association from Folklore and Folktales Around the World, ed. by Ruth Kearney Carlson (IRA, 1972), pp. 118-134.   Dr. Widdowson is the director of the Centre for English Tradition and Language at University of Sheffield, England and is the editor of Lore and Language.

culture itself.   Equally important, he can reach back into
history to trace the development of those traditions which
have helped to mold contemporary culture.

It should not be assumed, however, that there has
been a lack of continuity in English folklore scholarship during the twentieth century.   Much important work has, of
course, continued for many years in other parts of the British Isles, notably through the Irish Folklore Commission,
the School of Scottish Studies, and the Welsh Folk Museum.
Although some aspects of the traditional inheritance received
comparatively little attention, others continued to be studied
in considerable depth and with increasing insight, thus main-
taining important links with earlier work in these fields.
The study of local language, for example, has continued to
expand and develop and has been stimulated greatly in recent
years by the realization that all aspects of linguistic usage,
contemporary and historical are worthy of study.[1]   The investigation of childlore[2] has proved equally fascinating to the
scholar and to the general public.   Studies of custom and
belief[3] have aroused considerable interest over the years,
and both psychologists and sociologists are becoming increasingly aware of these aspects of human behavior, both individual and social.   Folk music, dance, and drama have also
received considerable attention, notably through the work of
the Folk-Lore Society and the English Folk Dance and Song
Society.   Traditional arts, crafts, work techniques, and related aspects of material culture have also continued to
stimulate research and collection, especially on the part of
local museums and particularly those concerned with rural
life.   As Bonser[4] testifies, continuity of research into all
aspects of folklore has been maintained throughout this century through the work of the Folk-Lore Society.   Local societies have also maintained similar research, and individual
scholars and specialists have continued to publish material
on many aspects of folklore.

It is perhaps significant, however, that of all the
branches of folklore scholarship in England, the collection of
folk narrative seems to have been one of the last to claim
attention in the current revival of interest.   This delay may
be due to three principal factors:

1. It is known that comparatively few Märchen appear
to have survived even up to the nineteenth century in
England.

2. It may be felt that the early collectors had already
assembled and described a large number of traditional
narratives; and it was, therefore, unlikely that a substan-
tial number of other narratives, especially Märchen,
would be discovered at this late date.

3. The enormous and far-reaching developments in education, technology, and communication during this century
may suggest that the traditional narrative would survive
rarely, if at all, in contemporary England.

In spite of these factors, however, examples of English traditional narrative have been collected and published
at various times throughout the century, some of them recently.[5] Nor are such objections as these justifiable obstacles in
the collection of contemporary traditional narrative, which,
although perhaps greatly modified since the nineteenth century,
may still be found in abundance and most certainly merits
attention. It is true that one should not expect to find numerous examples of Märchen, but many of the motifs, formulas,
and structural devices of the genre may be characteristic of
many traditional narratives which are to be regarded as
legends or anecdotes rather than true folktales.

Traditional narratives live on in the minds of both
countryman and city dweller; and as Dorson[6] and others have
pointed out, tales are told, often in the shortened form of
anecdotes or jokes, on numerous social occasions when people
meet casually. More frequently the storytelling situation
arises when a larger group gets together at a sporting event,
such as a football match; or perhaps for a drink at "the local" (i. e., the public house), or on more formal social occasions, such as parties and dinners. In the traditional manner the telling of one tale triggers off another; and so the
tales are passed on and modified, like other aspects of folklore, by oral transmission. At times, variants of a given
tale will be mentioned and even discussed; and such introduc-
tory remarks as, "Oh, the one I've heard goes like this..."
or "The Yorkshire version of that is a bit different..." are
common. Stories may vie with one another and with their
own variants in this way, and elements of blason populaire
enter into the situation on occasions when a story is told
against, or alternately in praise of, a given person or place.
A raconteur may often prefix his tale with such questions as
"Have you heard this one?" or "Have you heard the one
about...?" or "Do you know this one?" If most members of
the group have heard the tale or if it is felt to be too well

known to the audience to raise a suitable response, the tale may simply be alluded to and perhaps enjoyed vicariously, as it were. The audience is reminded of the punchline or the point of the tale after brief allusive reminders, such as "You know, it's the one where the Englishman, the Irishman, and the Scotsman are.... " Narratives of this kind pass into and out of print. They may be quoted or retold from a printed version in a jokebook, magazine, newspaper, or even a radio or television script. They may then undergo the processes of oral transmission and may perhaps be found in print again at a later date. Some of them may appear in novels, plays, and short stories and may even serve as the basis for plots. Analyses of children's fiction, for example, frequently reveal quite a remarkable number of resemblances between the stories and traditional narratives in structure, motifs, formulaic qualities, humor, directness, and simplicity.

A major problem in collecting traditional narratives is the ephemeral nature of their variants, which change so rapidly that a given version may be extant for only a brief period of time. The basic structure of the narrative persists, nevertheless, and remains substantially unchanged in spite of considerable modifications of location, nomenclature, and sometimes even motivation and punchline. Versions may be told which have different heroes, different locations, and markedly contrasting styles and yet preserve the essence of the tale, whether it is told in full or abbreviated form.

A second and more difficult problem is the fact that many people may not regard such narratives as in any way significant. Once the stories have been told, they lose their point, in a sense, at least insofar as that particular audience is concerned; the teller thus needs a new audience. This characteristic marks a fundamental difference between the Märchen told as entertainment for adults and its contemporary equivalent, the anecdotal legend. The Märchen would often be told and retold, and the same audience would hear it many times, perhaps even insisting on the accuracy of its restatement on each occasion. Although the majority of present-day stories are told to amuse and entertain, they rely heavily on novelty for effect and shun the tedium of the twice-told tale. This search for novelty inevitably means that new tales are being evolved all the time, albeit often based on the same old types and motifs; and new variants spring up in different places, carrying the tale into perhaps different channels from its original.

Certain basic themes, however, persist in traditional narratives of all kinds. Among the common stock of oral narratives are anecdotes about trades and professions, racial and social groups, and types who are regarded as characteristic of a given group, represented either adversely or otherwise. The fool, the strong man, the boaster, the drunkard, and similar types figure prominently in both the legend and the anecdote in present-day oral narratives in England, as elsewhere. People who typify the real or the supposed characteristics of a tradesman from a given location, such as a Yorkshire farmer, a Sheffield grinder, or a Filey fisherman, are also often found. Stories about preachers continue to be told, and there is an apparently inexhaustible fund of tales and jokes about politicians. Individuals who are in some way unusual in behavior, dress, appearance, physical, or mental makeup--indeed, eccentrics of all kinds--figure strongly in such narratives. A considerable amount of social comment, both bantering and serious, is to be found in them, consequently, which deliberately singles out both groups and individuals and hinges the tale upon them or upon a particular aspect of their behavior, personality, and so on. In this way, tramps, rag-and-bone men, and people with regional accents or foreign pronunciations become the typical butts of such stories.

In the north of England comparatively few anthologies of traditional narratives have appeared this century to supplement the work of the great nineteenth-century collectors. A great wealth of legends and anecdotes, however, remains scattered through numerous books, journals and newspapers, quite apart from those still remembered and told, often in dialect, throughout the region. In spite of the efforts of enthusiastic individual collectors over the years, no systematic attempt has been made to preserve for posterity more than a tiny fraction of the total number of tales which are still so well known and widespread. This condition applies even more to the uncharted profusion of tales and anecdotes in regional standard speech and other varieties of usage.

The establishment of the Institute of Dialect and Folklife Studies at the University of Leeds and, later, the Survey of Language and Folklore at the University of Sheffield has given new impetus to the collection of folklore in the north of England. Although no full-scale investigation of the folktale has been undertaken as yet, a number of tales have already been collected and now form part of the archive of the survey at Sheffield. It is from this archive that the examples of tales in the present study are drawn. They were collected mainly in the East Riding of Yorkshire, but some contrastive material from the West Riding is also included for comparison. It is interesting to note that tales of a similar type, told in the local dialect and with strong local characteristics, are to be found in these two different settings--the small, quiet seaside town and the large urban center. The East Yorkshire tales were collected during the writer's fieldwork in the small fishing town of Filey between 1959 and 1963. The West Yorkshire examples were collected by P. S. Smith and the writer during fieldwork for the survey in the Sheffield area in 1969. The tellers in both regions were for the most part in their fifties to early seventies.

As is often the case with traditional narrative, the examples presented here were all told in regional dialect, and none of the tellers used even a northern regional standard speech as his normal mode of utterance. A major problem in the transcription of dialect narratives is the degree to which the pronunciation may be indicated in normal orthography. Such stories inevitably lose much of their local flavor and also, perhaps, a considerable amount of their forcefulness and freshness when transcribed into standard English. It is possible, nevertheless, to give local flavor by rendering some of the distinctive features of pronunciation in the transcript. For the general reader, however, it is usually necessary to normalize the narrative considerably. While the conventions of spelling may allow certain dialectal features to be presented fairly accurately, other features prove difficult if not impossible to render intelligible, especially for readers unfamiliar with the dialects concerned. Thus, it often happens that an inaccurate and misleading picture of the dialect as a whole is given. In these circumstances it seems best either to render the entire material phonetically or in normal spelling. In the present study, normal orthography is used; therefore, only those obvious features of local usage (such as the distinctive pronunciation of the final sound in syllables ending in ing) which are commonly found in similar transcripts elsewhere have been indicated. Unusual items of vocabulary and usage are in brackets.

The distinction made by folklorists between the folktale proper and the legend poses some problems in the classification of the tales which follow. It is not always easy to separate the legend--a tale regarded as true or told as if true--from other stories which typify the "willing suspension of disbelief" implied by the true folktale. In contrast with the legend, the

folktale is given an unreal or fantastic setting. It may be
set in a world of magic, peopled by ogres or talking animals.
The nearest approach to this kind of tale in the present corpus
of material is a version of the story about how a mouse escapes death twice. In this tale a mouse falls into a vat of
beer at a brewery while reaching over it to get a drink.
The brewery cat offers to rescue the mouse who agrees that
in return the cat can have him to eat. The mouse tricks the
cat, however, and escapes safely to his hole. The story
ends with the well-known punchline about people saying or
promising anything when they are "in drink." This punchline
is typical of the play on words between literal and metaphori-
cal meaning often found in other traditional tales. The story
is well known in the north of England and has many characteristics of the folktale, including of course, the dialogue between two animals:

>Yance [once] there was a little mouse got into
>a house, and he felt very hungry when he got in-
>side so he has a look round to see if there's aught
>[anything] to eat. Presently he comes across a
>door; it was slightly open, so in he pops. There
>was naught on t'floor so he climbs up yan [one] o'
>t'legs that was holdin' (the) shelf up. An' t'first
>thing he come across a piece o' sweetcake. An'
>he has another good go at that. An' then he felt
>dry, so he had a look round to see if there was
>aught to drink, but there was naught [nothing]
>nowhere. So he sholls [slides] down t'leg that
>holded t'shelf up an' scratched a hole into t'next
>door. An' as luck would have it there was another
>hole sown there into t'next door, so he pops out
>an' he'd got into a spot [i. e. place] an' he says,
>"By! There's a rare nice smell in here!" An'
>he'd getten into t'brewery; an' there was two great
>big vats in this brewery, an' there was a lot o'
>steps led up to t'top so you could, see, look inside
>to see what there was in. So (the) little mouse he
>climbs up to t'top an' has a look at t'first one, an'
>that was no good 'cause it was only half full. So
>he thought, 'I'll have a look across at t'other yan
>[one]." When [i. e. well] away he goes across to
>t'other yan. It was nearly full. So he thought,
>"Why, if I reach down I can get a drink here."
>Why, he reached o'er an' just as he was goin' to
>get a drink he tumbled in. There he was in t'beer,
>an' he started swimmin' round an' round. And (the)

sides o' t'vat was that slape [slippery] an' brant
[steep] he couldn't get out.

An' just then t'old brewery cat looked o'er side.
He says to him, he says, "Thou's in a fine mess!
What's thou doin' in there?"

"Why, I tumbled in," he says. "Will thou get
me out?"

"Why," he says, "what will thou give me if I
get thou out?"

"Why," he says, "thou can have me."

So t'old cat says, "Collar hold on my paw, then!"
So he put his paw down an' (the) little mouse col-
lared hold on his paw, an' he ran up his leg an'
onto his back an' down onto t'ladders, an' down as
fast as his little legs could carry him. An' he just
gat into his hole when t'old cat come after him.
"Thou's a fine fellow! Thou said I could have thou,
if I gat thou out!"

The only other tale in the present corpus which de-
mands any suspension of disbelief is one in which a mermaid
appears. Clearly this tale is a legend in that it is told as
if true and comes into the category of supernatural legend by
virtue of the reference to the mermaid. However, even the
supernatural element itself is treated humorously. This story
is retelling of an earlier version remembered as a typical
example from the repertory of a particular great storyteller
in Filey:

He used to tell the tale, thou knows. He says when
he was ... years since, when he was a young man,
he went abroad. He went ... he was abroad, like,
in big ships. An ya [one] day they'd been in a
hurricane or somewhat, an' ... an' they ('d) been
brought up in (the) lee of an island for repairs.
An' (the) sails had been blown out on her, and (the)
spars had broken an' bent, and (he) carried on,
like. They brought up about four days in (the) lee
o' this island--, (a) lagoon sort of a spot. An'
old B____ said he was on watch. (O') course, he
was a great storyteller, like. He said he was on
watch. He heard somebody shoutin'. (He) looked

>all o'er an' couldn't see naught. (He) wandered
>round--still heard somebody. He thought it sounded
>like a woman. He looked o'er (the) side an' he
>said there was a mermaid swimmin' about. He
>says, "Aye," he said, "there was a mermaid.
>Why," he says, "hallo. What do you want, miss-
>is?"
>
>She says, "Do you mind movin'?"
>
>He said, "We can anchor where we like. The
>sea's free!"
>
>She says, "I know you can, but," she says,
>"you've dropped your anchor right outside our lava-
>tory door, an' my father's been fastened in four
>days!"

The supernatural element is also present in an anecdotal version from Sheffield of a tale in which two boys who
are sharing apples they have stolen are overheard in a cemetery. The person who overhears their counting concludes
that Jesus and the Devil are sharing up the dead between
themselves. Versions of this tale are found elsewhere in the
north of England; and although this example is very brief, it
includes the essential elements of both structure and definite
local setting typical of more elaborate versions:

>Aye, when they were in t'churchyard ... two
>kids, aye. Two kids, were it, sharin' ... been
>scrumpin' [stealing] apples an' ... aye, that were
>about Cemetary Road cemetery an' all. You know
>where t'Frog Walk is, where ... you know where
>you go on from Pembroke Street on t'wall there?
>(These) kids (had) been scrumpin' apples, an' they're
>in t'churchyard sharin' 'em. An' this here bloke's
>comin' past sozzled [drunk], an' he hears these kids
>sayin', "One for thee, an' one for me! One for
>thee, an' one for me! like. An' he was sozzled,
>this bloke, an' he goes runnin' home. He says,
>"I've just heard Jesus an' t'Devil sharin' t'dead
>up!"

Although the remainder of the tales in this collection
take the form of local legends or anecdotes, some of them
include motifs which are also found in folktales. An example
is the following anecdotal legend from Sheffield which tells of

an abortive attempt to frighten a drunken man. It parallels
the folktale of "The Youth Who Wanted to Know What Fear
Is.[1]" This version describes an attempt to frighten the man
by having one of the jokers lie in a half-dug grave in the
cemetery through which the drunk always passes on his way
home. The formulaic triple repetition of the groans from
the man in the grave illustrates the persistence of the "rule
of three" common in folktales.

> I hear about one (story) in t'cemetery, when he
> goes ... an' this were true--up at t'Ecclesall
> cemetery. An' this here chap always used to go
> through t'cemetery. They made this here ... they
> knew which way he went, an' they made this
> here ... oh, I know: the bloke there ... an' he
> thought, "Why..."--he knew he went past his here
> place where this grave had been dug, so they
> thought they'd have a joke on him. So a bloke
> goes down--an' it's cold weather, you know, an
> they ... one o' these chaps he goes down this here
> grave, an' he's waitin' for him passin', like. An'
> (o') course they were tryin' to shake him, frighten
> him. He's comin' back, kali sozzled [i.e., blind
> drunk] as he always is. An' this here bloke's
> sayin', "Oh!" he says. "Oh! It's very cold down
> here! Oh! It's very cold down here!" So this
> bloke, he ... he was the drunk they were tryin'
> to frighten; he says, "What's up, old lad? Art
> thou cold?" He says, "Here thou art! I'll cover
> thee up!" He started kickin' t'soil on him (to)
> keep him warm!--They were goin' to frighten him!

Also, contests of various types are featured in folktales, and a parallel motif is found in the story of "The Seeing Match" recorded at Filey. The contest is won by means
of a trick through which one of the contestants is proved to
be telling a lie.

> But ya [one] day he reckoned he had good eye-
> sight, an' he went down to (the) cliff top; him an'
> yan of his old boathands was challengin' yan another
> to a seein' match--how far they could see out to
> sea. They ... they glanced out to sea an' then
> they looked harder an' harder until he saw a very
> small thing, (a) little bit of a dot right out to sea.
> An' he says to B_____, "Can thou see that thing
> out there?"

"Yes."

"What is it?"

He says, "It's old P_____ an' them. They're
shootin' their lines on High Rock." They're, like,
shootin'--they're puttin' 'em into (the) sea, you
see. (He) said, "They're shootin' their lines on
High Rock. Can thou see it?"

"Yes."

"Is thou sure?"

"Yes, I can," he says.

"Why," he says, "can thou see old W_____
givin' P_____ a chew o' baccy?"

He's looked. He says, "Yes."

"Ah, why," he said, "(thou)'s a b_____ liar
then, because he doesn't chew!"

(He) says, "Thou's wrong!"

A brief version of a well-known tale about the man
who, when invited to sample the delights of female company,
chooses instead to avail himself of some kind of food was
recorded from a storyteller at Filey. In this version the
protagonist is a house-painter by trade; and the toothsome
morsel he selects is not cheese, which is a common motif
in similar tales, but the typical Filey delicacy of curd
cheesecake.

They telled me that old G_____ was ... he was
a painter by trade, an' ... he was courtin' a lass
on (the) Crescent [an upper class residential street],
and ... in his younger days, like. And she ...
there was cellar-kitchens to these Crescent houses;
so she took old G_____ down into t'cellar-kitchen
an' walked him through into t'pantry with a candle.
'Now, G_____," she says, "thou can have aught
[anything] thou likes!"

He says, "I think I'll have yan [one] o' them
cheesecakes!"

Legends about professions are common and often point not only to the typical characteristics of the profession in question but also to the idiosyncrasies of the individuals concerned. The following two stories from Filey about local preachers show how both professional and individual characteristics are employed for humorous effect.

> A preacher, the special preacher at a village church, he was comin' one night. And the old lady of the village was livin' with her daughter and she had a very, very bad cold, so she couldn't go. So she says, "Why, thou go," she says. "Thou can tell me what he's like when thou comes back." Well, this preacher was a man who had all his sermon written out, an' he kept lookin' down at it, an' then up at the congregation; then down at it and up at the congregation. So when the young woman got home, t'old woman says, "Well, what sort of a fellow was he?"

> "Why," she says, "he was like an old crow in a tatey-field [potato-field]--two pecks an' then look up!"

> A preacher on the Wolds, he was a fellow that used to get excited when he gat in t'pulpit. An' there was an old farmer used to sit down in t'front seat, cuppin' his ears up so he could hear him. An' half way through t'sermon this here fellow that was preachin' tumbled out onto t'old fellow. He says, "I hope I aint hurten you!"

> "Nay," he says, "it was my fault. I ought to have shifted at first!"

Other tales told may include references to preachers and their families. The following story concerns the meanness of a local preacher's wife and tells how a local "character" succeeds in outwitting her. This additional feature of characterization adds to the effect of the conclusion by implying that a mean person deserves to be taught a lesson. Elements of social comment, such as this, are often found in traditional narratives, sometimes with serious didactic purpose and sometimes, as here, with a lighter, humorous comment upon an aspect of human nature.

> There was one old chap in particular, an old

... he was (the) lifeboat coxswain, old B_____
...When he stopped goin' to sea, he couldn't rest.
He had to be doin' somewhat [something], so he
started to hawk fish round about farms.... However, he used to go round (the) countryside hawkin'
this fish, an' it gat to ba proper feud between him
an' a local preacher's missis--(a) big farmer he
was, but he was a local preacher an' all. An' his
missis was a narrow one! By God, she was a
greedy devil. She was well known for it--wouldn't
buy naught [nothing]. She'd skin a b_____ cat!
However, she used to come out to old (B_____).

It was a long, lonely road to get up to this
farm, an' he used to go up with this old horse an'
flat cart. An' when he gat to this farm, this wife
used to come out, an' she used to look at t'cart
and she always wanted somewhat which there
weren't on (the) cart. Every time old (B_____)--
she had him [i.e., caught him out]. She always
could see somewhat what there weren't on. Well,
ya night he couldn't sleep. He thought, 'I'll do
her [i.e., pay her out]! If it' (the) last thing I do,
I'll do her!" He wasn't really hard up for money,
'cause he left quite a lot o' money when he died,
like, as money went in them days. However, ya
day he went up to this farm. He had everything
what crept an' crawled an' swum in (the) sea on
(the) cart. (The wife comes out. "Now,
(B_____)!"

"Now, missis. "

"You have a rare show!"

"Aye. "

Her eyes is flashin' round his cart. She had
eyes like a ferret an' they were flashin' round his
cart to see what he hadn't on. And she couldn't
find naught. Suddenly she seed [saw] there was no
kippers on (the) cart. He says ... she says to
him, "Huh! You have no kippers on (the) cart,
(B_____)!" Her eyes lit up, like. He says,
"Nay, I aint none on t'cart, lass, " he says.

"Why, " she says, "now I would have had four or

five shillingsworth o' kippers off you if ... if
you'd had any, " she says. "My husband does like
kippers. Now, if you'd had some kippers, " she
(said), "I would have had four or five shillingsworth. "

"By God, " he says, 'I have you this b_____
time, missis" An' he had 'em all stuffed won his
trousers!

It sometimes happens that different versions of the
same story may be found coexisting in an area. The tale
may be transferred to another protagonist, for instance. A
simple story may be elaborated, or alternatively a longer
version may lose much of its elaboration. All references to
the local preacher's wife are absent from the following anecdotal version recorded from another storyteller.

Another funny old fellow there was at Filey, (a)
fellow called B_____ S_____; and that was his
nickname, B_____ S_____. An' he used to go
out gatherin' winkles on (the) Brig [a rocky head-
land on the north side of Filey Bay]. An' he had
winkles an' ... an' he would have a basket on his
arm, and bloaters an' kippers an' (would) go
round. Old women used to say, 'Now then,
B_____! What have you today?"

"Why, some bloaters. "

"Why, aint you any kippers?"

"No, I have no kippers today. "

"Why, " she said, "I wanted bloaters. "

Alright. Old B_____ though next day when he
went round he would cop [catch] 'em, like.
An' ...

"Now then, B_____! Have you any bloaters
today?"

"Yes, I have some bloaters!"

An' he had (the) bloaters under his coat'. He
pulled (the) bloaters out! He made them alright!

The modern farmer comes in for humorous criticism in the following anecdote where an old farmer casts aspersions on modern farming methods.

> This is the old farmer and (the) field o' wots [oats]: ya [one] day on t'Beverley road just outside o'Driffield an' old farmer an' a young fellow were leant o'er a five-barred gate. An' t'old farmer says to t'lad, he says ... he says, "They can't farm nowadays." He says, "Look at them headings [headlands]! They aren't ploughed up." He says, "An look o'er yonder at that field o'wots," he says. "It's that short," he says, "(the) sparrows'll have to kneel down to peck it!"

Shopkeepers, like other tradesmen, may have tales told against them. A humorous comment on a shopkeeper who is not only unscrupulous but also rather self-righteous is found in the following story from Filey.

> However, he used to sell (shrimps) ... he used to take 'em round, an' (the) grocer used to sell 'em in them days. However, this grocer sent round straight away in sike [such] a great hurry. He wanted seven pound o'shrimps off old B____. So B____ takes him seven poun' o'shrimps round--sends 'em round, like, with t'lass. An' however, (it) weren't long afore (the) grocer was round. He says, "Hey! How many shrimp does thou reckon thou's sent me?"

> Old B____ says, "I've sent thou seven pound."

> He says, "Thou hasn't. Thou hasn't!" He says, "I've weighed 'em on proper scales, an'," he says, "there's just o'er six pound." (He) says, "Where's thy scales?"

> He says, "There."

> (He) says, "Where's thy seven pound weight?"

> (He) said, "I aint yan [one]."

> (He) said, "Thou hasn't yan!" He says, "How's thou weighed me seven pound o'shrimps, then?"

> (He) says, "I weighed 'em out with that seven
> pound o' sugar I gat off thou this morning'!"

The isolation of small towns and villages up to the
end of the nineteenth century and beyond gives rise to many
stories about the insularity of such communities. Many
people never left the boundaries of their own parishes, and
the fisherman who had traveled up to a hundred miles or so
of his home port was illustrated in the following two tales
from Filey. In the first, a fisherman goes to London for
the first time and acts as if he were still in his small home
town. In the second, reassurance is given by an old fisherman that "foreign countries," which are in fact just towns
some miles along the East Coast, will come to the country's
assistance in the Boer War.

> His sister was seriously ill in London. He gets
> his pilot trousers on an' his reefer jacket, this
> square-cut hat, 'lastic-sided boots--they were the
> ... they were the thing in them days. An' they
> used to wear hairy hats, most of 'em, when they
> were dressed [i. e. dressed in their best clothes],
> little sealskin hats. However, he got dressed,
> went to London. When he gets out at Kings Cross,
> he went up to (the) policeman. He says, "Can thou
> direct me to our Mary Lizzie's?"

> I'll tell you what ... a story my grandfather
> used to tell about him. When the herrin' fleets
> used to follow the herrin' shoals, like, in them
> days, well they used to meet the Scotch lasses an'
> the Scotchmen comin' down with 'em. Early on in
> t'summer they used to go up as far as 'bout Shields
> .... They used to reckon they'd been to t'end o'
> t'world almost when they used to go to Hartlepools,
> Whitby, Scarborough an' down as far as Lowestoft
> an' Yarmouth at t'back end o' (the) year. An' then
> they used to come back from Lowestoft, like, when
> the herrin' ... when the herrings had left there, do
> you see. That was as far as they went to south-
> ward.... But, however, anybody (who) had been
> as far to northward as Hartlepool an' as far to
> southward as Lowestoff, they' certainly been some-
> where! They'd travelled, accordin' to their ideas!
> However, old M____ was sat on (the) cliff-top seat
> down at t'bottom o' Queen Street ya [one] day, an'

(the) bloke comes down with (the) special papers.
When there was aught [anything] happened, there
used to be a special paper come out in Scarborough,
you see, an' they used to come round here sellin'
'em, shoutin' in (the) street, "Special!" Everybody
has to go--them what could read; there weren't a
lot could read in them days. However, old
M_____ wouldn't buy a paper in any case. "What's
up?" So somebody went an' bought a paper, an'
he read this paper. "By God," he said, "there's a
rum carry-on in (the) world, M_____! We're all
goin' to be killed!"

"Killed?"

"Aye," he says, "an' thou an' all! Thou's goin'
to be killed! Thou'll be in with 'em! (Thou)
doesn't want to think thou'll get out on it! Thou
an' me an' all (the) lot on us, whether you're
Ranters [primitive Methodists] or Wesleyans or ...
we're all goin' to be killed!"

"What ... what's up with thou?" he says.
"What's thou gettin' excited about?"

He says, "War's broken out!"

"Who with?"

He says, "With (the) Boers in South Africa.
An'," he says, "we're all goin' to be killed!"

Old M_____ says, "Thou doesn't want to let
that worry thou." He says, "We shall win, 'cause,"
he says, "all them foreign countries like Hartlepools
an' Lowestoft'll come an' help us!"

The drunken man is a stock type who is the frequent
butt of the humorous story, as already indicated. He appears also in a number of north country versions of the story
in which he imagines that the reflection of the moon in water
is, in fact, a cheese. (Examples of this tale have been collected for the Survey of Language and Folklore from South
Yorkshire and also from Lincolnshire.) Sometimes a story is
given added interest by identifying the drunk with a particular
trade or profession. The Sheffield grinder, for instance, who
by virtue of his work is obliged to slake his thirst frequently,

has become one of the tradesmen with whom such stories
may be identified. In the following tale, a Sheffield grinder
resolves to stop drinking and to save his money for "faith,
hope and charity," but the results of his good resolution
prove to be somewhat different from what he expected.

You ever heard the tale about that ... that chap
the Sheffield grinder? And he used to come home
drunk every ... every Saturday, singin' an' rowtin'
[shouting, bawling] at t'top o' his voice. An' all
t'neighbours were annoyed with him, like, and
played hell about him. An' one Saturday his wife
says, "Hey," she says, 'I wish thou'd learn to
have more sense," she says. "Thou'rt spendin'
all thy money, annoyin' t'neighbours an' all that,"
she says. "An' if thou'd look after it, we could
save a bit."

So anyway he says, 'I'll ... I'll not booze
[drink] any more. I'll start an' save my money."

So, right religiously like, he come home every
Saturday. [The] first Saturday he come home he
says, "Has thou got a black stockin', lass?"

She says, "Aye,"

"Well," he says, "come down t'cellar with me,"
he says. "Put t'money in there [i.e. in the stock-
ing]."

(He) started savin' his money, like; put it in
there. An' took a ... they were all stone (walls)
in t'cellars--it were only stones, stones ... walls,
like, you know--rough stone walls. Why, ours is
(the) same, isn't it, down here? This has been up
a hundred years (or) more, this house. And he
loosens a stone an' put this here black stockin' in
with t'money in it. He says, "Now then, I'm
goin' to put somewhat [something] in there every
Saturday when I come home," he says, "an' we'll
save it for faith, hope an' charity."

So anyway they goes down--oh, it were goin' on
for months. Every Saturday they used to go down
together. He'd pull t'stone out an' she'd put (the)
black stockin' in with t'money in. An' after months

an' months he come home one day.   She says,
"He's been!" she says.

"Who's been?"

She says, "What thou said thou was savin' that
money for."

"Why?"

"Well, an old man come to t'door.   He says,
'Have you got aught [anything] to spare, missis, for
faith, hope an' charity?'   So," she said, "I knew it
were him so I gen [gave] it him!"

Of many typical stories about fools, the following example from Filey is given a setting on the Yorkshire Wolds--
a respectable distance from the town.   It is characteristic
of such stories that the fools live at least some distance
away--perhaps in the next community or a neighboring area
where "foreigners" are felt to begin.   As with the tales of
the Austwick Carles and the Wise Men of Gotham, the element of blason populaire, in which one community regards
another as the place where foolish people live, adds point to
the story, especially for those familiar with the areas concerned.   This type of story passes in and out of print, some
versions being more formal than other.   It is probably the
case that many such tales, and indeed a number of other
tales in the present corpus, may have been derived from
printed sources and then passed into oral tradition.   The
story now to be quoted is given a setting sometime in the
past, and yet it could be very easily applied to virtually any
community, with some slight variation of the setting and the
protagonists.

At the beginning of this century there was two
village teams on t'Wolds thought they'd have a
football match.   So they arranged to meet and they
thought they'd have a good go at 'em.   So they
sets off an' when they gat to where they were goin'
to they found out they were ya [one] fellow short.
So t'captain o' t'team says to t'others, "Why," he
says, "we mun [must] have somebody if we can get
him."

Well, there was only two spectators, an' that
was a shepherd an' his lad.   So he goes across to

this lad an' he says, "Can thou layk [play] football?"

"No," (the) shepherd lad says. "I can't layk."

"Why," he says, "will thou be in goal for us?"

So t'shepherd lad says, "What? Where that net
is?"

He says, "Aye."

"Why," he says, "alright, I can go in there."

So he went in t'goal an' (in the) first twenty
minutes he'd letten four goals go through. So
t'captain went to him. He says, "What for doesn't
thou try to stop 'em?"

"Why," he says, "(the) net bihont [behind] me's
doin' that!"

It sometimes happens that a collector is fortunate
enough to find a story which is not only elaborate but also of
traditional structure. Such a story was told by a raconteur
at Filey who thoroughly enjoys storytelling. He often inter-
rupts his tales briefly to add explanations of particular points,
and some of these explanations are little anecdotes in themselves. He then returns to his original tale with renewed
enthusiasm, having satisfied himself that his audience is fully
aware of all the relevant background to the tale. The final
story, in summary form only, was his particular favorite,
and he had a high regard for it. It has a precise local setting, and he assures us that "every word on it's true," so
that we have the clear statement that it is to be categorized
as a legend. It tells how a fisherman puts some money collected for a chapel fund into some china dog ornaments on
his mantelpiece for safekeeping until he can bank it after the
weekend holiday. When he comes to get the money on the
Monday morning, it is gone. He tells his wife of this and
asks if she has touched it. When he confirms the fact that
she has not moved it, he tells her that only four people know
about the theft. When asked who the four are, he tells her
that they are herself, himself, the Lord, and the person who
has stolen the money. The rest of the tale hinges on the
fact that the fisherman decides to put some of his own money
into the chapel fund and that only those four people will ever

know this fact--that he put some of his own money into the
account because the original money had been stolen. The
years pass, and the fisherman works hard and earns enough
money to buy his own boat. When hiring some men to help
him on the boat, he comes across a man who asks him if
he ever found out who stole the money from him. As only
four people know of the theft, the questioner must himself be
the thief, and, thus, give himself away.

Tales such as this have both the structural and the-
matic elements which typify traditional narrative and are of
sufficient length and interest to illustrate, even in summary
form, the persistence of such narrative in contemporary
northern England. This same persistence is, of course, to
be found anywhere and everywhere in the British Isles in
many different forms with countless variants. Yet few of
these tales are known to the general public except, perhaps,
in a form heard casually on a single occasion. A considerable effort will be necessary if these tales are to be collected
and studied, and we have much to learn about their content,
structure, and distribution.

Although the telling of full-length folktales (i. e. Märchen) as an entertainment for adults has virtually disappeared
in England, especially in many urban centers, traditional narratives live on in the form of legends, anecdotes, and jokes;
and they continue to play a significant role in our social relationships. Many of them are rooted in the past but may be
modified in oral transmission so that they remain fresh and
typical. Newer tales may be adapted from printed versions
which in turn may have been based on a preceding oral narrative. They may also be borrowed and reborrowed by all
the mass media and take on the life of oral narratives, re-
flecting traditional themes and structures. There is an ur-
gent need to collect and record all such narratives to which
we have access, so that some of the older and often more
elaborate versions, as well as their newer recensions, may
not be allowed to slip irrevocably away.

Bibliography

1. Orton, H. and others, eds. The Survey of English Dia-
    lects. Leeds: Arnold, 1962-1965.

2. Opie, I. and P. Opie, eds. The Oxford Dictionary of
    Nursery Rhymes. Oxford: Clarendon, 1959.

3. Hole, C. English Custom and Usage, 1941-1942, and Witchcraft in England, 1945. London: Batsford.

4. Bonser, W. A Bibliography of Folklore. London: Folk-Lore Society, 1961.

5. Briggs, K. M. A Dictionary of British Folktales in the English Language, Incorporating the F. J. Norton Collection. London: Routledge, 1970.
Briggs, K. M. and R. L. Tongue, eds. Folktales of England. London: Routledge, 1965.

6. Dorson, R. M. American Folklore. Chicago: University of Chicago, 1959, pp. 244-276.

7. Aarne, A. and S. Thompson. The Types of the Folktale (Second revision). Helsinki: Academia Scientiarum Fennica, 1964, pp. 114-116.

Sherwood Forest (courtesy British Tourist Authority)

IAN SERRAILLIER AND THE GOLDEN WORLD

Brian W. Alderson

> OLIVER.   Where will the old Duke
>   live?
>
> CHARLES.   They say he is already in
>   the Forest of Arden and a
>   many merry men with him;
>   and there they live like the
>   Old Robin Hood of England:
>   they say many young Gen-
>   tlemen flock to him every
>   day, and fleet the time
>   carelessly as they did in
>   the golden world.

Without doubt the strongest impact which the mass media made upon my early years was the cinematic version of The Adventures of Robin Hood. I can still remember the pride and awe that I felt when the monkish Coeur-de-Lion pulled back the habit at his breast to reveal the leopards of England in glorious Californian technicolor, while wicked, wicked Errol Flynn humbled himself with romantic grace.

Each generation gets the Robin Hood that it deserves, and I am quite prepared to accept that this one was every bit as trite as the dull, predictable adventure series served up on television today, where the Sheriff's accent suggests the Lone Star State rather than Nottingham Castle. It is not so much the quality of these versions that matters but the

———————————
© Brian Alderson 1977. This article was first published in Children's Book Review 3.1 (Jan-Feb 1968). Mr. Alderson is currently children's book editor for the Times (London). He is an author, critic, translator, and avid reader of children's books.

mere fact of their existence and the inexhaustible variations
that can be played on the basic theme. For, from the start
of his career, Robin Hood has been the folk hero par excellence, and his exploits in the Merry Greenwood always had
a more widespread and popular appeal than, say, the stories
of King Arthur with their courtly background and literary traditions.

It is easy to see where Robin Hood's popularity lies
and why he is such an attractive figure to children. Richmal
Crompton did not need genius to make her own folk hero the
leader of the outlaws, and it comes as little surprise that re-
tellings of Robin Hood are to be bought today in Prague and
Tokyo, or that in 1876 Tom Sawyer and Joe Harper swore
that they would "rather be outlaws a year in Sherwood Forest
than President of the United States for ever." Obviously the
chance to identify themselves with the outlaw life is immediately attractive to children, for whom society still reserves
a set of rules and conventions quite foreign to what the little
ones regard as the "free" world of the adult. But there is
also a whole cluster of sensations in the Robin Hood story to
which children are completely sympathetic. There are the
external trappings: the life in the woods, roasting venison
over a homemade fire, shooting with bows and arrows (still
so much more attractive than with machine guns or mortars).
There is the delicious sense of hide-and-seek security, of
total comfort achieved beyond the range of the orderly help
of society. And there is finally the profoundly satisfying in-
volvement in guerrilla warfare against the forces of injus-
tice--the have-nots winning for once against the arrogance of
the haves. Undoubtedly the moral overtones implicit in this,
the profoundest aspect of Robin Hood, are susceptible to a
political interpretation (as was attempted by Geoffrey Trease
in his Bows Against the Barons [Meredith]), but the tussle is
really legal rather than social. What matters is that the villains have got control of the law and, for children, there can
be nothing more searing than injustice, whoever the victim.

In their attitude to the Robin Hood story, children are
behaving in complete conformity with a popular reaction that
has lasted for half a dozen centuries. The real origins of
the great outlaw have defied the most determined and the most
partisan scholarship, and there is a poetic rightness about
accepting his existence now simply as a hero and not as the
much more sordid bandit that history would serve up to us if
it could. His true life was not in Barnsdale or Sherwood and
his true monuments are not the wells and stones and graves

that scatter his name around the countryside. If you want to
find the only true record of his activities, you have to turn
not to what actually exists but to what people wanted to exist;
you have to deal with popular imagination and not with historical experience. This means that you have to turn to the
story as it was manifested in the poetry of the ballads rather
than in the account books of kings or the records of the
courts. For the ballads provided the people with their own
history of their hero and formed the basis for his subsequent
exploits, which have multiplied by the thousand in chapbooks,
broadsides, magazines, and hack stories right down to the
present day. Much of this ballad source material attests a
popularity which goes back well before the introduction of
printing. Although few early manuscript versions have come
down to us, the constant complaints of churchmen that their
flock were being distracted by these profane ballads show that
their enjoyment was widespread, while the early appearance
of Robin Hood in print shows that there was a ready market
for his stories among readers as well as among hearers.
Nevertheless, here and in the later ballads (which lasted with
declining vitality down to the nineteenth century) one is dealing with a predominantly oral culture, and what appeared in
print was only a solidification of what was meant to be told
or sung.

For this last reason, it is not surprising to find Mr.
Ian Serraillier turning to an adaptation of the ballads in his
latest children's book, Robin in the Greenwood: Ballads of
Robin Hood (Walck). It has been a characteristic of Mr.
Serraillier's own poetry and of his previous adaptations that
the words sound better off the tongue than they look on the
page. Both Beowulf the Warrior (Walck) and The Challenge
of the Green Knight (Walck) make splendid reading aloud,
and the Robin Hood ballads would seem to offer an even
richer fund of material, much of it (unlike the earlier books)
in need of only the slightest adaptation or "translation."

In making his version Mr. Serraillier has relied
heavily upon that marvelous source book of ballad literature,
the Child collection;[1] and by a cunning selection of ballads
and incidents from ballads he has achieved a reconstruction
of the life and adventures of the "popular" Robin Hood, which
has a beginning, plenty of middle, and an end. Although he
has avoided the narrative complexities of the most famous
ballad, the "Lytell Geste," which is long enough to make a
book of its own, he has managed to use a number of ballads
of like antiquity, where the oral strength is greatest. These

are also the tales which seem to give the most natural account of Robin as a character, accepting him seriously and
not clogging his story up with the bar-parlor jokes and the
Maidmarianry of later versions.

Insofar as the twelve ballads which Mr. Serraillier
has chosen are separate episodes, it may be argued that the
book does not really hang together as a story; but this is a
price which any adapter of the ballads must pay.   Much more
to the point is the unity of feeling which the author has attempted to give them by sifting them through his own sensi-
bility.   In manner of writing, his originals range from fairly
easily comprehended, almost doggerel, verse ("Robin Hood
and Little John") to the near Middle English of "Robin Hood
and the Monk" and the Northern dialect of "Robin Hood and
the Beggar," while a number also have verses missing at
vital points in their development.   Consequently, in comparing
these originals with Mr. Serraillier's reconstitutions, we find
many verses altered slightly to give a smoother flow to the
reading, many more rewritten in a style which is clearly
more personal to Mister Serraillier than to his unknown original author, and a few here and there which he has entirely
made up himself.

Some of these changes are felicitous.   For instance,
after the Curtal Friar has told Robin that he can blow his
horn till both his eyes fall out (in both versions), Robin grants
him permission to whistle through his fingers, and we find
Serraillier taking the opportunity to install a little matching
wit of his own which the ballad does not have:

Ballad:

"That will I do," said Robin Hood.
    "Or else I were to blame;
Three whutes in a friers fist
    would make me glad and fain."

Serraillier:

"I grant it gladly," Robin replied,
    "You can blow till your hair is grey.
Three whistles in a friar's fist——
    May they blast your teeth away!"

On the other hand, some of the ruggedness of the old
ballad rhythms has been smoothed out with a consequent loss

of the feeling that someone is speaking, and this is not made
up for by the inclusion of some very characteristic Serraillier
enjambments.   These give a most un-balladlike jerkiness in a
number of verses:

> "You talk like a coward, " the stranger said.
>   "See, like a coward you stand
> With your bow and arrow, while I have only
>   A quarterstaff in my hand. "

In places, too, an attempt at the traditional directness
of statement has resulted in a triteness which (given the me-
ter) bears a disconcerting resemblance to the satirical ballads
of C. S. Calverley:

> They picked him up, their master dear--
>   O melancholy task!
> What Fiendish rogue had laid him low?
>   There wasn't a soul to ask.

On the whole, however, the evenness of tone with
which Mr. Serraillier has recounted the ballads gives the
book a unity which would certainly not be present in a literal
reproduction of the texts themselves.   We are, of course,
spared some of the medieval crudities such as the murder
of the "litual page" in "Robin Hood and the Monk" and the
extra injunction to the monks in "Robin Hood's Golden Prize":

> "The second oath that you here must take
>   All the days of your lives
> You never shall tempt maids to sin
>   Nor lye with other men's wives. "

And with these has gone the untranslatable beauty of:

> In somer, when the shawes be sheyne,
>   And leves be large and long,
> Hit is full mery in feyre foreste
>   To here the foulys song:
>
> To see the dere draw to the dale,
>   And leve the hilles hee,
> And shadow hem in the levës green,
>   Under the grne-wode tre.

While there is much that is enjoyable in Mr. Serraillier's version of these ballads, the question remains as to

how far children will find it so. To them the ballad form is
likely to appear an unnatural way to treat a theme which has
all the components of a picaresque novel. If they have
thought about Robin Hood in literary terms at all, it is surely
as the hero of stories, not songs.

There are, of course, a host of volumes in print
which recount tales of Robin Hood which have some foundation
in the original sources, but few of these make any effort to
follow the traditional stories closely. Some indeed, like
Geoffrey Trease's Bows Against the Barons or Donald Sudda-
by's Fresh News from Sherwood (Barnes), break away entirely from the standard tales for purposes of their own. But
three volumes in particular--Carola Oman's Robin Hood (Dutton), Rosemary Sutcliff's The Chronicles of Robin Hood (Oxford), and Roger Lancelyn Green's Robin Hood (Penguin)--
have been written by authors fully conscious of the original
ballads. In adapting them to story form, however, each has
run into a similar set of difficulties.

The most obvious problem is simply that of giving co-
herent order to a mass of material which never had any to
start with. Each of these adapters has therefore given a
central place to the "Lytell Geste"--the longest and most
complex of the ballads--and has attempted to fit in other incidents around it. Each has also imported the late tales of
Maid Marian (called by Child a "foolish ditty") to help with
the continuity, while Roger Lancelyn Green has turned to a
veritable hodgepodge of previous versions (Scott, Peacock,
Tennyson, and Noyes included) in an attempt to represent
every previous treatment of the legend.

A second problem is that of detail. By their nature
ballads have little concern for background information or for
developing consistent plots or clearly differentiated characters. Robin Hero one minute may become Robin Buffoon the
next, and a story starting one day in Sherwood may within
twenty-four hours have moved nearly a hundred miles to
Barnsdale. Such shifts again demand that adapters seek a
logical solution where none may exist, and an uneasy balance
may have to be struck between given facts and invented situations. Miss Oman, for instance, has tried to fill out her
version with details of everyday life in the England of Edward
II, coupled with close attention to geographical settings.
This means that a number of incidents are accompanied by
descriptions which have a guidebook or school textbook flavor
quite alien to the traditions of the story.

There is also the perpetual problem of vocabulary and
the falsities of tone that result from attempts to impose
medieval-sounding dialogues where they don't fit. Although
the Chronicles was Rosemary Sutcliff's first book, her control over the dialogue has much of the sensitivity that has
characterized her later work, and it compares very well with
some of the awkward inversions and medievalisms of Carola
Oman's book. Roger Lancelyn Green appears to be quite be-
mused by the variety of texts at his demand and vacillates
between direct quotations and attempted reconstructions in a
modern tone. Thus, telling of Robin's birth, where Serraillier transcribes fairly directly from "Willie and Earl Richard's Daughter":

> He took the bonny boy in his arms
>   And kissed him tenderly.
> "I'd see your father hanged," he cried,
>   "But your mother's dear to me."
>
> "Dear to me is my grandson too,"
>   And he kissed him once, and again:
> "Robin Hood in the good greenwood,
>   O that shall be your name."

Roger Lancelyn Green elaborates a scene of almost Victorian
melodrama: "By God, I'd like to hang your father--but your
mother's dear to me still, in spite of everything. Well,
well, you're my grandson sure enough, and it would be little
kindness on my part to begin by killing your father. Joanna,
where is this villain?"--and so on for eleven more lines.

Of the three adaptations, Rosemary Sutcliff's is much
the most natural, and she has achieved this by working within
the spirit rather than within the close form of her sources.
For the ballads do not really have much to offer directly to
the writer of stories, who had much better rely on his own
abilities. They are part of a different world, with different
conventions, and it is perhaps the chief reason for welcoming
Mr. Serraillier's book that it offers a signpost to that world
and to the riches of our ballad literature. It is only fair to
point out that the signpost has been up all the time in the
nine Robin Hood ballads in Ruth Manning-Sander's A Bundle
of Ballads (Lippincott), but the freer treatment of the material in the present volume, coupled with Victor Ambrus's vigorous and atmospheric illustrations, may well prove a new incentive to children to come to grips with this unfamiliar
treatment of the "true tales" of Robin Hood.

In the final analysis there is a quality of imagination
and a sense of contact with history which is far more rewarding here than in all the modern re-enactments.   The
golden world may not have been as inviting as it sounds, and
fleeting one's time in it was probably a pretty chilly business.
But we are not so opulent today that we can afford to reject
the enjoyment that past generations had from hearing about it.
If you go to Sherwood now, you will find suburban bungalows;
and merry Barnsdale is dominated by the cooling towers of
Ferrybridge and the slag heaps of Upton Main.   Even the
rough-and-ready justice of the outlaw himself has become redundant among the impartial filing drawers of the government's Ombudsman.   It's the ballads now, or nothing.

1977 POSTSCRIPT

Ten years is a short time in the life of Robin Hood,
many a past decade having done nothing to affect the standing
of his legend.   Nevertheless, in the ten years since the above
article was published an exceptionally able contribution has
been made to "Robin Hood studies": <u>Rymes of Robyn Hood;</u>
<u>an Introduction to the English Outlaw</u> (London: Heinemann,
1976).

The core of this volume is a reprinting, with editorial
apparatus, of the chief Robin Hood ballads, including alter-
native versions where important differences are to be found.
In addition to this key textual material, however, the editors
have included popular re-workings, like the poems by Keats
and Noyes, and even related legends--not just predictable
pieces like "Adam Bell," but also surprises like "The Death
of Jesse James" from Carl Sandburg's <u>American Songbag</u>.

Supporting these texts there is a lengthy Introduction
and a group of Appendixes which do much to clarify where
truth and fiction begin and end in the long-standing debates
about the legendary outlaw.   In their careful sifting of the
evidence about who he may have been and where his territory
lay the editors admirably summarize the present state of
knowledge about Robin Hood--but, whatever the pleasure of
going as far as historical fact will take us (especially for one
like myself, schooled on the edge of "Bernysdale"), Messrs.
Dobson and Taylor are chiefly to be thanked for re-empha-
sizing the popular appeal of the hero through literature rather
than through history.

If there is anything to be regretted about Rymes of Robyn Hood it is the editors' neglect of the place of the outlaw story in children's books.   They list several well-known versions for children in their Select Bibliography, but have little to say about their relationship to sources or the possible influence of these on the public image of Robin Hood.   (In this respect it is interesting to note corroboration for Robin's place as "hero of the imagination" in Russell Hoban's essay, "Thoughts on a Shirtless Cyclist, Robin Hood, Johann Sebastian Bach, and One or Two Other Things," printed in Children's Literature in Education (4 March, 1971).

One children's book surprisingly omitted from Rymes is the very volume by Ian Serraillier under review here--surprising, because of the author's obvious desire to sustain the ballads as a living force for today's children.   It is therefore perhaps also worth noting now that two years after the publication of this volume, Mr. Serraillier went on to compile his own version of the "Lytel Geste" in a companion volume entitled Robin and His Merry Men, also illustrated by Victor Ambrus (Oxford University Press, 1969).   This re-working attracts the same plaudits and the same reservations as Robin in the Greenwood and is at its best, as I observed in a review in Children's Book News (Vol. 5, No. 1, Jan/Feb. 1970), "when it allows the spirit of the original ballad to show through the modern exterior."

Note

1.   Francis James Child, The English and Scottish Popular Ballads.   5 vols.   Boston 1882-98 (repr. New York, 1965).   Child's fully annotated texts of the Robin Hood ballads are mostly to be found in Volume 3.

King
Alfred.

Drawn by C. Walter Hodges for "The Marsh King" (Coward)

ON WRITING ABOUT KING ALFRED

C. Walter Hodges

Even the most quiet, gentle, and civilized of people (like myself for example) are apt to reserve some small corner in their hearts as a sort of Wild Life Sanctuary for their imaginations. Here flourish, harmlessly we hope, the predators and their prey, preening their gorgeous plumage and grooming their manes between kills. For some people it is the Wild West, for others the Life of Crime, for others again the hurly-burly of spies and counterspies, operating their deadly techniques in luxurious but wicked hotels. But for me, the favorite Game Reserve has always been the Dark Ages. Here the hairy Huns invade, Siegfried slays dragons in the misty wood, Viking ships menace Constantinople, and the world comes tumbling down. It is a taste I find hard to justify, liking my comfort as I do, and harder still to offer as a fit subject for children's reading. Still, some years ago I took a fancy to write a story about the Emperor Charlemagne. Saracens and Paladins thronged my fancy. But on a fairly brief study it soon appeared that Charlemagne's merits were not all they are sometimes cracked up to be, and his great empire was at his death torn apart by his children who had been, to put it mildly, very badly brought up. I do not subscribe to a belief that children's literature should be necessarily moralistic in tone; but I do believe that children ought to be encouraged, especially in historical fiction, by truthful examples of success. If Charlemagne did not measure up to this test, who, then, in the Dark Ages, ever did? Groping around in the dark, I bumped up against King Alfred.

Reprinted by permission from The Horn Book Magazine 43 (April 1967), 179-182. Copyright©1967 by The Horn Book, Inc. This English artist-author has contributed two excellent books on the folk hero, King Alfred.

He was not a character for whom I had ever felt much warmth. Victorian muscular Christianity had for me made a mere whiskery worthy out of him, and so I was not looking in his direction. But when I did look, I knew at once that the Victorians had been right. King Alfred, the only English king to have been called Great, did well and truly deserve that title. Where King Canute had made his popular reputation by demonstrating that even he, a king, could do nothing against the incoming tide, King Alfred did exactly the opposite. With the tide everywhere against him, he held it back until it turned. Where there was defeat, he averted it. Where there was barbarism, he planted culture. Where there was physical weakness he opposed it with strength of will. Thus, before he died he had by his personal effort and example altered the course of history away from the Dark Ages and toward the light.

I chose Alfred, therefore, without further hesitation. But then followed the difficulties. First, the names. Anglo-Saxon is not a pleasing language to the modern ear or eye, and young readers cannot be expected to take very kindly at first to names like Aethelheah and Tunbeorht. Still, beyond a little simplification in the spelling, there was nothing to be done about this, except to hope such ill-named characters would eventually justify themselves by their deeds; so I accepted them, weorts and all.

Next came the problem of all the fighting. The long story is thick with battles, each one very like the next in so far as the chopping and killing was concerned. Like most people, I dislike violence and do not wish to seem to commend it. How, then, was I to give to all this violent business the high character of heroic legend which surely belongs to it, and yet not hide what is to my mind an essential truth, that heroism in battle, admire it as we may, is really a tragic misuse of noble qualities. I have tried to solve this problem partly by writing in a candid way about the fighting, by certainly not making it out to be pleasant, and partly by side-stepping. Thus I have not described many of the battles fully or directly, except for the last great contest between Alfred and Guthorm at Ethandune, at the end of The Marsh King (Coward). It may be noticed that of the other great battle at Ashdown, in The Namesake (Coward), I did not actually give many details; but, having three times brought three separate characters to the battlefield, I lured the reader away, before the fighting actually occurred. One other important fight remained to be described, the battle of Kynwit; and this I contrived to treat as if it were an Anglo-Saxon poem, thus putting it a little outside the ordinary course of the narrative.   The reader may skip it without loss (though, of course, I should be sorry if he does!).

Another problem concerned the famous story of the burned cakes.   Did the disguised King Alfred really burn them?   Learned people have pointed out reasons why the story may not be true.   My own view is based on a belief that such ancient popular folk legends are usually based upon something that really happened.   I have therefore used it, combining it with another problem for which historians have never been able to find a satisfactory answer: why, in the winter of 878, when Guthorm and his Danes attacked Wessex, did they then achieve such a devastating effect?   The usual explanation is that the Saxons were taken by surprise because the Danes fell upon them in the middle of winter, when presumably no properly conducted barbarian army was expected to be out of its winter quarters.   But this was not the first time the Danes had attacked in midwinter.   They had done just the same thing before the battle of Ashdown, at which Alfred himself was present.   One may be allowed to suppose therefore that there was some other special reasons why the people of Wessex were thrown into such confusion that winter. The explanation I have offered in The Marsh King is that a treacherous attack was made upon the person of King Alfred himself.   It is a fiction, certainly, but it is one for which history can give many examples of truth.   In Anglo-Saxon times just such an attack was made upon a certain King Cynewulf, who met his death by it.   And in our own day, what attacks have we not seen upon the persons of great men, and the course of history changed by them?   In my story the attack upon Alfred at the Dragon Hall may therefore be not far away from the truth; and it is in such a context that I see an explanation for the favorite story of the burning of the cakes. Such tales are often found to have had their origins in lost but true historical events, which have left nothing behind them but a shadowy trace upon the memory of local folk, many generations after.

But, as I worked out all these things, the book I had in mind grew longer and longer; and when I began to write it and had arrived no further than the battle of Ashdown, I saw that the whole thing was going to be much too long for its purpose.   Also, I foresaw that there was going to be an awkward division in the middle which I did not know how to bridge.   Discouraged by these things I put it aside, where it remained for a long time (indeed, for several years) while I waited for a solution.

Now solutions and problems are very often the selfsame thing, only differently expressed. What is necessary is to state the problem correctly (which we do not always do) and the solution will then emerge simultaneously, by itself. In my case what emerged was that I had in hand not one story but two, and when this was seen, and the two stories had, as it were, released each other, I could again begin to work. So in my first story, The Namesake, I told how King Alfred first took charge of the beleaguered Kingdom of Wessex and saved it and its Christian culture from destruction. In that book the narrator, the young crippled boy, could himself be regarded partly as a symbol of the historical situation. But the second story is really quite different. In The Marsh King my purpose really is to show how the Danes were finally beaten by King Alfred, not simply upon the battlefield, but in regard to their whole predatory way of life. Thus the story is about the contest between the civilized man, King Alfred, and the barbarous war lords--not only the Danes, but the Saxon chieftains also--for whom fighting seemed the only proper and noble solution to the problems of life. For this purpose my narrator is a man whose parents as young people belonged to opposing sides, and were later married when, after King Alfred's treaty, Saxons and Danes settled down to a peaceful (and fruitful) coexistence. My story is thus supposed to be told from inside knowledge of both camps, which the narrator's mother and father, Hildis and Skafti, had handed on to him.

It is written in history how King Alfred obliged Saxons and Danes to make and keep the peace. Perhaps it is part of the value of my two King Alfred books that they may have helped to tame that old Dark Ages Wild Life Reserve in my own imagination.

LEGENDS OF THE GRAIL

Gwendolyn Bowers

"How long did it take you to write <u>Brother to Gala-</u><u>had</u>?"

The reviewer's question sent this writer on a long backward journey to find the answer: "I think I've been working on it since the fourth grade."

It must have begun on the day that the teacher gave out new reading books and a small girl in the third row first read about the sword in the stone. The first-time wonder never wore off; and when the last chapter was finished, the tale ending with the heartbreaking Battle of Camlan, the child could go back to the beginning again and start all over with the sword in the stone.

Other years brought other books--the fragile, roman- tic <u>Idylls</u> of Tennyson, the knights' adventurings through the dream landscapes of Malory's <u>Le Morte d'Arthur</u>, the strange wild tales of Lady Guest's <u>Mabinogion</u>. Then came college years, and Edwin Arlington Robinson's <u>Tristam and Launce-</u><u>lot</u>, and frequent visits to the Boston Public Library, where we waited for books under Edwin Abbey's gold and crimson murals showing Galahad as he rode on his Quest again, with the shadowy presence of Joseph of Arimathea in the back- ground. When the year came for writing a master's thesis, it was time to delve for an older, deeper strand of the Grail legend. Many books and years later, there was a visit to Glastonbury, where the two strands of legend seem to meet; and the discovery of Geoffrey Ashe's <u>King Arthur's Avalon</u> and <u>From Caesar to Arthur</u> and John Whitehead's <u>Guardian</u> <u>of the Grail</u>.

Reprinted by permission from <u>The Horn Book Maga-</u><u>zine</u> 42 (February 1966), 37-42. Copyright © 1966 by The Horn Book, Inc.

King Arthur's Round Table, Winchester, Hampshire. (courtesy, British Tourist Authority)

It came to this reader-writer that there must have been many unknown and forgotten figures who played small parts in the Great Adventure. One of them could have been young Hugh of Alleyn, who lived on the coast of Wales in a castle like the one at Harlech and went to Camelot in <u>Brother to Galahad.</u>

The following pages are gleanings from many sources; they will attempt to trace the development of the Grail Cycle from early warrior tales to the didactic Latin writings of medieval churchmen and the metrical romances of the troubadors; they will try to show that in the fabric of the tales Christian tradition mingles with pagan relics of some remote past.

In that early time Bran the Blessed wandered about Ireland with his magic Cauldron that was never empty. If food for one were put into it, food for a hundred might be taken out; and each man would have the food he liked best. The Cauldron had healing properties also: if a slain man were cast into it, he would then be as well as ever he was, except for the loss of his speech. Bran blessed the fifty fishless rivers of Ireland and caused them to abound in fish. The Salmon of Wisdom swam in the River Boyne. Although it was forbidden as food, if a man caught and ate it, he would become wiser than all other men. Bran was the son of Llyr, god of the waters, but legend has confused his wanderings with the missionary journeyings of Saint Brandan of Ireland.

In that country, too, was the terrible Luin of Celtchar, the spear that so thirsted for battle that it would burst into flame and could only be quenched in a cauldron of blood. And Finn Lug possessed the Sword of Light. All these deities had the power of changing shape and becoming invisible, and their possessions were described as white or shining. In an old tale King Arthur was given a cloak that made him invisible, and the cloak was called Gwenn, which was the word for white. All these wonders lay in the Celtic Otherworld, whose entrance was guarded by the Fortress of Glass.

In the land of Logres, also called White Britain, there was a mysterious island formed by a marshy plain that lay below a dark frowning tor. Glassy streams surrounded it and wound through the plain. Some called it Avalon, perhaps because wild apples (aval) grew there, or because it was the abode of Avalach, Prince of the Evening and ruler of the dead

and the shades.   But the Britons named it Ynys-witrin, the
Isle of Glass, or Glaestring, or Glaston.   At Glastonbury,
men say, the Adventure of the Grail began.

In 53 B. C. Julius Caesar sent his legions to Britain.
They built roads and baths and villas and the Roman Wall
against the wild Cymri of the North.   The Romans occupied
Britain for four hundred years while the old water-gods bided
their time.   Their legends lived on outside the Wall, among
the Celts who never submitted to Roman ways.

According to tradition, Joseph of Arimathea and twelve
followers journeyed to Glaston in A. D. 63, bringing the Cup
of the Last Supper, which was the Holy Grail.   King Arvira-
gus received the strangers kindly and gave them leave to
dwell at Glaston.   They built a chapel of rushes, round like
a beehive, and circled it with twelve huts.   From this circle
of huts grew the abbey-cathedral of Glastonbury.   At Glastonbury men tell of the Spring that bubbled blood-red from the
ground where Joseph set down the Grail.   By the ruined ar-
ches grows the offshoot of the Holy Thorn that sprang from
his staff and that bears its flowers in winter.   On the greens-
ward below, men point out King Arthur's burial mound.   At
Glastonbury, they say, was discovered a massive oak-log cof-
fin beneath a stone slab with a leaded cross embedded, and
the inscription:

> Hic Jacet Sepultus Inclytus Rex Arturus in Insula
> Avallonia ("Here lies buried the renowned King
> Arthur in the Island of Avalon").

Christianity brought other legends to Britain, among
them the tale of Longinus, the blind centurion at the Cruci-
fixion, who recovered his sight when he brushed his eyes with
a hand wet with the Blood that ran down his lance; and there
were stories of the life and miracles of Joseph of Arimathea.
From the miracles attributed to Joseph and the Grail came
that part of the Grail Cycle known as the Early History.

The tradition of Joseph's arrival in Britain could have
been based on fact; it would have been possible for him to
reach Glastonbury with some holy relic, to preach and build
a chapel, but the marvelous adventures accorded him in the
Early History are clearly fabulous.   When William of Malmesbury wrote on "The Antiquity of the Church of Glastonbury"
in 1125, he thoughtfully separated the possible from the fabulous.   In the last revision of his work, he and the Brotherhood

of Glastonbury accepted Joseph as their founder, but under-
standably they were silent on the miracles of the Grail.

In legend the Grail became a thing of magic, with
power to strike down a sinner and to surround the presump-
tuous Moyes with flame for three hundred years.   Like
Bran's Cauldron, the Grail had healing and life-giving powers,
and like his never-empty vessel, it provided food for the
faithful, though sinners were sent empty away.   Alleyn, one
of the Keepers of the Grail, caught fish for them, and he
was called the Rich Fisher.   Long after that, the Grail appeared to Arthur's knights, and it provided each one with the
food he liked best.   In the Early History a castle, remote
and mysterious, was prepared to house the Grail, and so it
passed from men's sight.

Joseph's legendary adventures were many.   Twice he
was mysteriously wounded, once by a sword and once in the
thigh by an angel's lance.   Before he died, he marked a
white shield with a cross in his own blood and prophesied
that it would be borne by a knight of the ninth generation of
his line--a knight perfect in charity and chastity, who would
be the last to see the wonders of the Grail.   This prophecy
at the end of the Early History is the link between the two
strata of Grail legend.   The prophecy is fulfilled in the
Queste, which waited on the coming of Arthur and his knights.

The historical Arthur lived in the tumultuous time after
the Roman legions sailed away from Britain, when wild tribes
swarmed over the Great Wall and laid the Roman towns to
waste.   Germanic tribes invaded the island too, and native
Britons fought the Saxons, and the Picts and Scots as well.
Evidence of Arthur as a historical figure rests on three fragments of Welsh bardic literature by poets who were his con-
temporaries.   His name is first mentioned by the warrior-
poet Llywarch Hen in an elegy on the death of this patron
Geraint, who died at the Battle of Llongborth in the early
sixth century.

> At Llongborth were slain to Arthur
> Valiant men, who hewed down with steel,
> He was the emperor, and conductor
>   of the toil of war.

The term emperor might be read here in its old meaning--
commander in chief.

In the ninth century, Nennius made the first historical mention of Arthur in the Historia Britonum.

> The magnanimous Arthur, with all the kings and military force of Britain, fought against the Saxons, and although *there were many more noble than himself*, yet he was *twelve times chosen their commander*, and was as often the conqueror. [The italics are mine.]

The italicized passage suggests that Arthur was more likely a great warrior chieftain than a wide-ruling king.   If we turn from the bardic literature that belonged to the upper classes to the popular story form, we may read four primitive tales of Arthur from the Red Book of Hergest, translated from the Welsh by Lady Guest, under the title Mabinogion.   In one of the tales, "Peredur, son of Evrawc," Arthur presents a sorry picture of knighthood, tamely enduring an insult to his Queen at his own table.   It took hundreds of years for the development of the kingly Arthur of the later romances.

Geoffrey of Monmouth in the twelfth century was the first to give Arthur the high place that writers of courtly tales have accorded him ever since.   In Geoffrey's Latin Historia Arthur has become a knightly king with the right to thirty crowns.   The account of his coronation established the theme of chivalric manners so highly developed in the Anglo-Norman romances.

Geoffrey's history was translated into French by Wace and into semi-Saxon by Layamon about 1200.   Layamon gives us the first mention of the Round Table, and in later romances one hundred and fifty knights sit down at that table together.

By the twelfth century metrical romances appeared on both sides of the Channel, and troubadors carried them through France, Germany, and Italy.   Walter Map, Archdeacon of Oxford, recast the tales of the Early History to give them deep spiritual significance; and in his Queste, Arthur's knights are the descendants of Joseph of Arimathea, and the Round Table is the table of the Last Supper.   Map created Galahad as the Grail Knight.   In Malory's Le Morte d'Arthur Galahad is also the Grail Knight, and his companion is Percivale of Wales.   Galahad goes armed with the shield of Joseph of Arimathea and the sword of his ancestor, King

David. The knightly Percivale is the Peredur, son of Evrawc, who appeared in the <u>Red Book of Hergest</u>.

In France, at about the same time, Chrestien de
Troyes wrote of Percivale's quest for the Grail. In Wolf-
ram's German version, Parzival and Gawain share the Grail
adventure.

In the many versions, details differ with the tellers;
but as each hero comes to the great and final adventure, he
moves in a recurring pattern. He must find the remote
Grail Castle; he must witness the procession of the Talis-
mans; finally--and most important--he must ask the Question.

The knight often discovers the castle at nightfall. He
may see it suddenly, where no castle was before, and, like
the possessions of the old water-gods, it may be invisible by
morning. It is usually surrounded by water, and two men
are often seen fishing from a boat. The only bridge to it is
narrow and perilous; it may be only the blade of the sword.
The lord of the castle is the Fisher King, or the Maimed
King, who suffers from a lance wound in the thigh, as did
Joseph of Arimathea; and, like Joseph, he is fed or sustained
by the Grail. His kingdom is the Wasteland, made barren by
reason of a sword stroke whereby someone has died. For
three hundred years the Fisher King has waited for the Grail
Knight.

As the knight sits at table a procession issues from
the Grail chamber carrying the Talismans--the Grail, a shining sword, and a bleeding lance. The lance is described as
white and shining, like the magic belongings of the water-
gods. Some versions clearly state that blood runs down the
shaft of the lance to the hand of the bearer, and we remember the lance of the blind centurion. When the lance appears
in the procession, the company breaks into loud lamentation.
At that point the knight is supposed to ask the Question:
"Whom does the Grail serve?"

Sometimes the knight, through pride or shyness, does
not ask it; sometimes he asks and does not wait for an answer. Peredur failed because his teacher in chivalry told him
not to ask questions. Parzival failed because of pride. Not
until he had learned humility could he return and try again.

When the Question is asked, the lamentation turns to
joy, the Fisher King is healed, and his Wasteland becomes

fertile.   The knight becomes a participant in some mystic
Grail ritual, or becomes successor to the Fisher King.

Even in those romances most heavily colored with
Christian language and symbol, the pagan origins show
through.   The Grail Castle, with its association with water
and fishing, could be the Celtic Otherworld.   We have already likened the Grail to the Cauldron of Bran.   Could the
shining sword of the Grail procession have been the Sword
of Light of Finn Lugg?   Was the lance that of the centurion
or of the war-loving Luin of Celtchar?

Much research has been done on the mystery of the
Grail, and many books have been written; but perhaps the
most satisfactory conclusion is still the one reached five
hundred years ago by a translator who "Englisht" the Early
History:

>   Ful plein this
>   Storye putteth in Mynde
>   That Al the Certeinte of the Graal
>   is hard to fynde.

OUR FAIRY GODMOTHER: MARIE L. SHEDLOCK

Anne Carroll Moore

Marie Shedlock was born at Boulogne on May 5, 1854. The first six years of her life were spent under the light of French skies. The French language was in her ears and on her tongue. French manners and the French countryside were before her eyes.

Although her parents were English, Marie Shedlock spoke French before she learned English and absorbed quite unconsciously those vivid impressions which have given to her work as an artist its rare quality of spiritual clairvoyance. She still exemplifies the old Irish proverb, "As wise as a child four years old."

The Shedlocks returned to England to live when Marie was six. Her father, an engineer under Brunel during the period of the laying of the first railroads in England and on the Continent, became in later life an eloquent preacher whose educational views must have been far in advance of his day.

At the age of about fourteen Marie was sent with one of her sisters to a school at Versailles where she remained for three years. Later on she studied in Germany, taking her diploma there.

Marie Shedlock was barely twenty-one when she became a teacher in a well-known English public day school for girls --Notting Hill. She continued to teach there for nearly twenty-five years. Her colleagues were a brilliant set and many of her pupils were no less brilliant.

Reprinted by permission from The Horn Book Magazine 10 (May 1934), 137-143. Copyright © 1934, 1961 by The Horn Book, Inc.

The last quarter of the 19th century is a significant period in the history of education, especially in relation to the advancement of women and children, and Marie Shedlock was as keenly alive to fresh thought and new ideas as she was thoroughly informed and rooted in the classic tradition of the teaching profession. When she dicided in 1900 to give up active teaching and go to America to give French monologues and recitals in English from the fairy tales of Hans Christian Andersen, she was not making so marked a departure as it might seem. She was fully aware of world thought. She had made her debut as an artist carrying on as a teacher. She had done amateur acting all her life, had recited and sung at evening parties in French and in English, and had made a serious study of the fairy tales of Hans Christian Andersen.

"I first met Marie at Hindhead, Haslemere, where we were both staying at an interesting Bohemian bording house about 1899," writes Mary Meldrum Dobie, a distinguished interpreter of Elizabethan drama, "and quickly fell under her spell. I remember one never-to-be-forgotten evening when at a party in our house in London, Marie Shedloc recited French, Beatrice Herford American sketches, and Isabel Hearne sang."

On such an evening, no doubt it was, that Earl Barnes listened to the story from Daudet of which he speaks, and in his turn fell under the spell of an artist he saw as a man of the world and a new century. And so Earl Barnes wrote to Mrs. Osgood Mason in New York on behalf of Marie Shedlock, and Mrs. Mason not only fell under the spell of a genuine artist among "elocutionists," but realized the practical necessity of combining lectures with stories in the United States of 1900.

Mrs. Mason knew the educational world as well as the social world of the New York of the time. Moreover, she knew at first hand and respected the aspirations of youth in a new century, and rightly rejected the sentimentalism of prevailing methods in kindergarten and primary school training and practice, resulting in emasculation of literature and artificiality in the presentation of it to children. It took courage to tell the truth in those days, but Mrs. Mason had both courage and vision. The matinées she arranged for Marie Shedlock at Sherry's were far-reaching.

To one of these matinées came Mary Wright Plummer, poet, librarian, and educator, to listen to a program of

French stories. So impressed was she with the dramatic skill of the artist that she sought an interview and invited her to come to Pratt Institute in Brooklyn and give a program of English stories before the teachers, students and parents of that great pioneer educational institution. This matinée was given early in the year 1902. I listened enthralled but unsatisfied. "Oh, but we must have a real story hour for the children in their own room in the Library!" I said. To this Miss Plummer readily agreed.

Clear the picture rises of that Saturday morning story hour, January 31, 1903, the Children's Room flooded with sunshine, tulips and primroses blooming on the broad window sills; outside, the snowy terraced playground called by the children "the country"; inside, lovely old Japanese prints upon the walls, fairy tales and legends in bright publishers' covers upon the book shelves, and Miss Plummer seated where she could see the children's faces--a roomful of children of all races--listening with them, as eager as any one of them to see stories come alive: "Pandora" (from "The Wonder Book"), "The Constant Tin Soldier, " "The Swineherd, " "The Princess on the Pea, " a Devonshire legend of the old woman who planted tulips, the Japanese "Rip Van Winkle" (told in honor of a Japanese gentleman in the audience who acknowledged it as he would in his own country by bowing to the floor), "The Brahman, The Jackal and The Tiger. "

The room seemed flooded with magic. "Is she a Fairy, Miss Moore, or just a lady?" The little blue-eyed Scotch girl who asked the question has been echoed by many another, and so Marie Shedlock became our Fairy Godmother in very truth before she assumed the costume.

In April of that same year she crossed over the Allegheny Mountains to Pittsburgh where stories in libraries had already been told and the time was fully ripe for the visit which Mr. and Mrs. Anderson describe in their letters. From an earlier visit to Boston Miss Lucy Wheelock gives back a tribute for the kindergartners of the whole country. John Dewey, the philosopher, speaks for the children and teachers of Chicago University and the adults of any community, and Emma L. Johnston for the training colleges for teachers.

There are many missing links in the long chain reaching from the Atlantic to the Pacific Coast between 1900 and 1907, for Marie Shedlock planted not only the love of stories

as told by herself but a lasting respect for the art of storytelling.   Her California days of 1906 are vividly brought to
mind by Marian Greene, a kindergartner turned librarian.
Often during her early American tour, Marie Shedlock returned to New York and she always came back to Pratt Institute.   It was in 1905 that Anna Cogswell Tyler, a student
in the Pratt Institute School of Library Science, heard her
tell Andersen's "The Nightingale," and woke to her own brilliant future as a story-teller.   Wide-eyed as the little Scotch
girl she came to me in the Children's Room of the Pratt
Institute Free Library.   "I believe I could tell stories," she
said.   "Why not?" I replied.   "What story would you like
to tell on May Day in the Children's Room?"

Miss Tyler chose a tale from Howard Pyle's "Merry
Adventures of Robin Hood," and she told also a story of her
own childhood.   Then and there was the story hour as organized and carried on in the New York Public Library of
today born and bred.   For twelve years Miss Tyler upheld
the tradition established by Marie Shedlock and extended its
influence by her own rare natural gifts and experience in
dramatic art.   Designated by her, one of her students, Mary
Gould Davis, continues to uphold this tradition in the New
York Public Library, and also as a lecturer on story-telling.

In 1907 Marie Shedlock was recalled by the London
County Council to take back to the teachers of England the
inspiration of her varied experience in lecturing and telling
stories in the United States and Canada.

Directors of education and training colleges in Man-
chester, Birmingham, Liverpool, Durham, York, Edinburgh,
were as eager as London for stories.

Marie Shedlock had traveled north, south, east and
west in her own country for five years when I paid her a
memorable visit at Tunbridge Wells.

It was a lovely day in early April, 1912.   Miss Shedlock came to meet me at the train and carried me off for
luncheon to the old Pantiles where Fashion once paraded, as
at Bath.   Afterward we walked up over the Common, golden
with gorse, past the great Toad Rocks, to the twin cottages,
in one of which she was then living.

There was everything and more to talk about.   Storytelling had taken on form and color and growing pains in

children's libraries. Anna Tyler was doing highly original
and constructive work in the New York Public Library, setting high standards for a wide range of stories and sound
training of the use of the speaking voice. The Playground
Association of America had published an illuminating and constructive report of what was being done over the country.

Miss Shedlock in her turn had been telling stories at
the Boys' Schools--Rugby, Winchester, King Alfred's School--
and had thoroughly enjoyed close association with the boys.
Her lectures for teachers, she said, were about over and
she was putting everything worth saving out of them into a
book on story-telling. She had already published her first
selection of the Buddha stories, Eastern Stories and Legends,
with high praise from Rhys Davids, who wrote the introduction. (While in America she revised and expanded this not-
able contribution to ethical stories and a new edition was
published in 1920.)

After tea I longed for a story but dared not ask.
"Would you care to hear a new story I've only just learned?
I'd like to try it out."

The story she told was "The Water Nixie." Listening
there in that little room, her voice grown even lovelier than
my memory of it; clearly as I could see the little Nixie herself, I saw the East Side children of New York listening to
that exquisite story of freedom, the love of country shining
in their eyes.

Persistently did the little Nixie's struggle for freedom
haunt my imagination on my travels through Norway, over
Sweden, across Denmark and back to England again. I saw
the Fairy Godmother once more before I sailed home. This
time her friend, Mary Dobie, who lived in the other twin
cottage, was with her.

To Miss Dobie I confided my dream of a return visit
of the Fairy Godmother to America. "Marie Shedlock's art
has deepened and broadened," she said. "She is a better
story-teller now that she has ever been. It is only a question
of her physical strength. She dreads the ocean crossing and
the long railway journeys, but I will do all I can to help
bring it about."

Two years went by and The Art of the Story-Teller
was ready for publication in England. (The American edition

was published in 1915.) But still Marie Shedlock refused to
cross the Atlantic.   Then like a thunderbolt the War came
and with it our great opportunity.

"A Fairy Godmother cannot be heard amid the clash of
arms. I'll risk it, " wrote Marie Shedlock at last, and while
submarines harried the Lancashire Coast she sailed alone
from Liverpool in February, 1915, recalled to America by a
group of fifty storytellers she had herself brought into the
field, reinforced by a committee of representative women in
New York who had faith in her art and in the power of good
stories to transform life at any age.   Marie Shedlock came
for a six-months' visit and stayed five years.

She even shouldered her musket like the Tin Soldier
and traveled--to Boston, St. Louis, Omaha, Chicago, Min-
neapolis, Detroit, Pittsburgh, Toronto and Montreal.   The
odyssey of those five years and of her visits to France in
1922-23 would fill several numbers of The Horn Book....

For every one who came under the Fairy Godmother's
spell she created pictures, brought music, poetry, gaiety and
calm, even in war time.   My own memory holds from the
wonderful evenings at the Cosmopolitan Club, the MacDowell
Gallery and Greenwich House.   But most vivid and dramatic
of all is that of an assembly of delegates from the Reading
Clubs of the New York Public Library.   Marshaled under
their colorful banners they streamed through the marble halls
of the great Library, 300 strong, to pay tribute to the great
English storyteller on Shakespeare's birthday.

To each of the truly eloquent tributes from boys and
girls of many races Miss Shedlock listened as if to an am-
bassador.   It was thrilling to watch her, sitting like a very
gracious queen upon a lowly throne.   And then she spoke a
few words from Shakespeare himself and told "The Nightingale, " the story to which Anna Tyler had listened ten years
before.

"I look upon you as my God-daughter, " the Fairy Godmother wrote to Anna Tyler after this celebration which had
stirred her profoundly by its genuineness, its dignity, and
its promise for the future.   "I believe your work will last.
What more can one artist say to another?"

It has ever been a generous word Marie Shedlock has
spoken by the way.   "I feel as much for one nation as for

another," she wrote when War began. She has proved beyond all shadow of doubt that a Fairy Godmother who is also a great artist can be heard amid the clash of arms. On the eve of America's entrance into the War she gave, what seemed to those who listened at the MacDowell Gallery, an inspired recital of fairy tales she had chosen from Hans Christian Andersen to build a program in key with the world of the time. Here was no propaganda for peace or war. Great stories brought to life by a great artist, like great music, belong to the whole world.

Editor's Note:

     Marie L. Shedlock (1854-1935), English teacher and master storyteller, is revered by all librarians who enjoy storytelling. Her Art of Storytelling (Dover) is still in print. The first edition in the United States was published in 1915. Bertha E. Mahony, editor of Horn Book, tells us Miss Shedlock was a genuine artist in "voice, diction, perception and dramatic power...."

MEMORIES OF MY FATHER, JOSEPH JACOBS

May Bradshaw Hays

Until I was nearly eight, I thought that all fathers wrote fairy tales to earn a living for their families. As a matter of course every morning I would watch my father, Joseph Jacobs, take his bowler hat from the hall-stand, place the crook of his umbrella over his left arm, and start out for the British Museum "to find more stories to put in the fairy books."

With the end of each week, came the fun. We three children would go into Father's library, where the red damask curtains would be drawn to shut out the heavy, greenish London fog which pressed against the windows, and a cheerful fire glowed behind the bars of the high English gate. Father sat in his scuffed and worn old black leather chair, I was perched on his lap, and Sydney and Philip were curled up on the floor on either side. Impatiently we would watch while Father filled his pipe, tamped the tobacco down with his little finger, lit it with a match, blew out a couple of puffs, and then, in his hearty voice with an undercurrent of laughter in it, he would begin: "Once upon a time, though it wasn't in my time or in your time, or in anybody else's time"---and the room was filled with magic for the three of us. We didn't know, of course, that he was "trying it on the dog"; that he was using us as a trio of child critics. If we sat entranced during the telling of a tale, that particular story would be included in the current volume of fairy tales he was planning to publish--English Fairy Tales, More English, Celtic, More Celtic, or Indian Fairy Tales. If we fidgeted, or if our attention wandered during the telling, that story was not used. We had rejected it, unknowingly, and he accepted our judgment.

Reprinted by permission from The Horn Book Magazine 28 (December 1952), 385-392. Copyright © 1952 by The Horn Book, Inc.

Sometimes, when he was tired from a hard week of research and writing, he would try to play a trick on us. He would suddenly say, "And the little prince, who was very tired, went into a nearby wood, lay down, closed his eyes and went to sleep like this...." He would shut his eyes but at once we would be on him, tickling, biting and punching, with cries of "No, you don't! You stop that! It isn't fair!" and then, thoroughly awake from the tussle, and with a shout of laughter, Father would continue, "but the little prince found a big bear in the wood, and he came running out and went on his way...." and we would settle down again, satisfied that we were going to have the whole story, then and there.

One of the delights of his homecoming each day was his pockets. In them, we were allowed to rummage, and there was always something for us--generally sweets, bull's-eyes in the winter, lemon drops in the summer. I imagine he had been calmly munching some of them out of a paper bag in the sacred confines of the Library of the British Museum and under the outraged eyes of the attendants, but Father never worried about what other people thought of him. Sometimes, on cold winter evenings, he would buy two hot baked potatoes or some baked chestnuts from the old man on the corner near the Museum, and use them to warm his hands in his pockets on the way home. We children would then open and eat them on the clean, scrubbed kitchen table, while the cook grumbled that she was trying to get the dinner; but we had our treat, and loved Father for having such enchanting ideas.

My father came from a very new country, Australia, in 1872, after he had received a degree from the University of Sydney. He planned to go on with his education at St. John's College, Cambridge, to become a lawyer, and then return to his native land to practice. But literature was in the air at Cambridge and after matriculating, he decided to go to London and become a writer. There he met Miss Georgia Horne and married her, and as we children came along and the needs of his family grew, he had to turn his pen toward any source of income which offered. He told me once, with a rueful smile, that his first published book was a piece of ghost-writing he did for a dentist, titled Dental Bridges and Crowns; but in a few years his book reviews--which always presented a fresh and ingenious point of view--began to make literary London aware of him. It was his enthusiastic review of George Eliot's Daniel Deronda which

brought him an invitation to one of her Sunday afternoon receptions at The Priory, 21 North Bank, Regent's Park.   The
delighted young reviewer was presented to the great novelist
by her "life's companion," George Lewes.   Blushing hard,
Joseph Jacobs said he hoped she liked his review of her new
book, but was met with the quiet parry, "I never read criti-
cisms of my own work." He had a very expressive face, and
his confusion and disappointment must have been apparent to
George Eliot, because she was very kind to him on his subsequent visits, and made an especial effort to introduce him
to many of the great writers and artists who became his
friends.

These men were rebels and innovators--Edward Burne-
Jones, who rebelled against the smug complacency of Victorian
art as shown by the Royal Academy, Dante Gabriel Rossetti,
William Morris and the others who formed the Pre-Raphaelite
Brotherhood.   In such a group as this, my father felt much
at home.   Proudly he hung reproductions of Burne-Jones
paintings on our walls, and bought William Morris wall-papers
for our rooms.   Although this was the era of embossed vel-
vet on walls, and elaborate and puffy Victorian furniture, our
house was furnished in the manner of which Morris approved--
the lines of our furniture were simple, the walls were light
and the woodwork white.

Another innovator whom my father admired greatly was
Dr. J. F. Furnivall, acknowledged authority on Chaucer and
Shakespeare--and firm believer in Woman's Rights.   He was
the man who founded the first Rowing Club for Working Girls,
and who hounded the owners of the ABC tea-shops until they
provided chairs for the waitresses to sit down on when they
were not working.   Rowing was his relaxation and greatest
source of enjoyment.   Every Sunday he would arrange trips
up the Thames for parties of his friends.   Many a time we
rowed from Hammersmith to Richmond, where we disem-
barked on a little island and, having eaten the invariable
lunch of cold roast lamb, tea, bread and butter, bottled
gooseberries and custard, we children would play hide-and-
seek round the island while the grownups discussed art and
literature, speaking with the quiet authority to which their
reputations entitled them.

Dear Dr. Furnivall--I can see him now, gallantly doing
his share of rowing, although he was seventy-seven.   I remember his blowing white beard and hair; his gray flannels
and the tie made of pink ribbon which he always wore.   I

remember, too, the string bag of oranges which he always brought for us children and which he insisted on our eating on the train--much to our embarrassment. It was this mixture of learning and simplicity that my father shared with all these great Mid-Victorians and he had the same lack of self-conciousness. Father used to take us regularly to museums and art galleries, and afterwards we would go to a pastry-shop where we had a choice of either cream-puffs or chocolate eclairs. These we would eat in the shop, then lick our fingers and wipe them on Father's large white silk handkerchief. We felt it wasn't quite the right thing to do but, looking back, I know it was the knowledge of the treat-to-come which took my dragging feet from picture to picture in the Tate Gallery. How well my father knew the heart of a child!

Joseph Jacobs could make friends with any child at once. He never used the trite questions, "How old are you?" or "Where do you go to school?" but began an absurd little quarrel with the child, on any subject which popped into his head. Then, when they were both stamping their feet at each other he would suddenly say, "What's this in my pocket; have a look, will you?" and there was always some little present which made the child his friend for always. When he went out to dinner, the children in the family were waiting for him on the stairs, with cries, through the banisters, of "Tell us about Tom Tit Tot, Uncle Joe!" or "We want to hear 'The King o' the Cats,' Mr. Jacobs!" In his white tie and tails, Father would sit among their little nightgowned figures until the tale was told, and then he would go and make apologies to his hostess for his lateness. He was always a Pied Piper. One look into his brilliant hazel eyes, and a child was his forever. He loved the nonsensical words which delight children--we had many in the family vocabulary, which would be sheer gibberish to an outsider. I think he would have been perfectly delighted if he knew that Mary Gould Davis, superb storyteller, had included his "Master of all Masters" (from English Fairy Tales) in her collection of humorous stories to tell children, With Cap and Bells.

Among my most vivid memories are the Sunday afternoons when Father would take me to Burne-Jones' studio, where pictures of great figures of angels and of beautiful drooping women in blue robes lined the walls. I would sit on William Morris' lap while he held his great handleless bowl of tea in one hand and stroked my pale-gold hair with the other. I didn't enjoy having my head patted, but was con-

soled by the knowledge that I had on my new green silk Kate
Greenaway dress with the yellow smocking at the yoke.
Scraps of the conversation going on around me penetrated my
childish preoccupation with myself, however, and I remember
particularly well one stormy argument between Joseph Jacobs
and Andrew Lang. Mr. Lang said, "You folklore people
(Father was president of the Folk Lore Society at the time)
would refuse to print any stories for children which haven't
been handed down from granny to granny, and if you can't
trace them right back to their beginnings among the rustic
folk of every country." To which my father mildly replied,
"Now, Andrew, do me justice, old man. In collecting the
stories for my fairy-tale books I have had a cause at heart
as sacred as our science of folklore--the filling of our children's imaginations with bright trains of images. If a story
will advance that cause I have always used it whether I knew
its derivation or not. I simply want to make children feel
that reading is the greatest fun in the world; so that they will
want to get to books for themselves at the earliest possible
moment." There spoke the young innovator from Australia,
rebelling against folklore traditions!

Then there was that other Sunday, when Rudyard Kipling (who was Lady Burne-Jones' nephew) tramped up and
down the studio inveighing against the way in which history
was taught in the schools. He declared that history could be
told in a way which would make it as interesting as any fairy
tale, and then children would never forget it. I like to think
that this was the hour in which he conceived the idea of writing those superb historical tales in Puck of Pook's Hill and
Rewards and Fairies.

At the end of each of his fairy books, Dr. Jacobs always appended the sources and parallels for the stories, and
his illustrator, John D. Batten, would draw a final picture
warning little children not to read these notes "or they would
fall asleep a hundred years." In these appendices, or in his
prefaces, the author explained that he "called them all fairy
tales, although few of them speak of fairies ... the words
'fairy tales' must accordingly be taken to include tales in
which occurs something 'fairy,' something extraordinary--
fairies, giants, dwarfs, speaking animals.... Every collection of fairy tales is made up of folk tales proper, of legends,
droll or comic anecdotes, cumulative stories, beast tales, or
merely ingenious nonsense tales put together in such a form
as to amuse children ... and generally speaking it has been
my ambition to write as a good old nurse will speak when she
tells fairy tales."

Years spent in tracing the exact derivations of fairy
tales convinced my father that many of the European folk
tales have their source in India. He never felt, as other
folklorists did, that the tales were brought to Europe by the
Crusaders, but rather that they traveled in the most natural
way, from father to son. In his notes appended to Indian
Fairy Tales he tells how he has "edited an English version
of an Italian adaptation, of a Spanish translation of a Latin
version, of a Hebrew translation of an Arabic translation of
the Indian original!" He calculated that the original Indian
tales have been translated into 38 languages, in 112 different
versions. In one of the Jatakas, or Birth Stories of Buddha,
he was of the opinion that he had traced in the story called
"The Demon with the Matted Hair" (Indian Fairy Tales, p.
194) the source of the Tar-Baby incident in Uncle Remus!

It was in 1896 that Dr. Jacobs was invited to come to
America to deliver a series of lectures on "English Style and
Composition" at Johns Hopkins University. On his return he
told us, "I've found the country I want you children to grow
up in." And so, his library of 12,000 books was packed into strong wooden boxes and swung into the hold of a Cunarder
and, at the turn of the century, we began life in a new country. Father put down strong roots at his second transplant-
ing, and always loved the United States "next to Australia."
He had a booklined library overlooking the Hudson in his
house in Yonkers in which he would contentedly play innumer-
able games of chess with my husband, David Hays. He never
needed to look at the chessboard but would play "blindfold,"
as they call it, sitting on the other side of the room with not
even a glance at the chessmen. Dave always said, "He could
beat me with both eyes tied behind his back."

Father fully intended to collect and re-tell the rich
treasure-trove of the folk tales of New England, but this was
a dream which never came true. However, when his granddaughter, Margaret Hays, was born, he said, "Peggy must
have a book of her own, just as you children have," and so
he set to work and gathered together the sixth and last vo-
lumes--Europa's Fairy Tales. In his amazing, scholarly
fashion he found and noted on the dedication page all the
variants of the name Margaret, over twenty of them!

People grow old in different ways. Some begin with
a hardening at the heart which spreads outward until no trace
of childhood is left. Others, the lucky ones, age only on the
surface and keep the sensitive core of childhood within. In
such a happy company did Joseph Jacobs belong.

After his death, letters and tributes came to us from
all over the world.   Best of all, we liked the editorial which
was headed, "That fountain of fun frozen--impossible!"
Those words described him exactly.   My father was a fountain of fun which sparkled for all who knew him--young or
old.

Editor's Note:

Joseph Jacobs, the master adapter of folktales, was
born in Australia, lived his last years in Yonkers, USA.
He made English folktales famous around the world.

A VISIT WITH ENYS TREGARTHEN

Harriet S. Wright

In the summer of 1923, my sister and I were traveling through the West Country discovering the difference between Devonshire and Cornish cream and much else besides. We gathered lore of Devon smugglers and wreckers and traced the footprints of saints and sinners along the rugged coast of Cornwall.

From New York City, I brought with me a desire to visit the village of Padstow to learn, if possible, something about the person who wrote North Cornwall Fairies and Legends. These stories had cast a spell over some children I knew in Greenwich Village. One story in particular, "Reefy, Reefy Rum," told of a little Cornish girl who dared to taunt the ancient stone animals on a church wall, calling out to them:

> Reefy, reefy rum
> Without teeth or tongue;
> If you'll have me,
> Now I am a-come!

Greenwich Village children have kinship with other children the world over who like to call saucy names and then take to their heels just as Nancy Parnell once did way off in Padstow, England. They thought Nancy herself might like to play games with them "between the lights" in their alleys or even late into the night on city streets. Then in the broad daylight they could take her uptown to see certain huge stone lions they knew. These haughty animals were awe-inspiring, too, their feet planted firm and immovable at a Fifth Avenue address.

Newquay gave the first clue to the whereabouts of
Enys Tregarthen. "Yes, Tregarthen is Cornish, " said the
local book dealer, quoting: "By Tre, Pol, and Pen you can
know the Cornish men. " He didn't think Tregarthen was her
own name but knew she lived either in Wadebridge or Padstow.

Padstow, quaint and hoary, was rewarding from the
minute we saw it. In the local post office we asked for information. A young girl on duty there had never heard of
Enys Tregarthen, but a gentleman getting his mail said to
her: "That is not her real name. She is Miss Sloggett. "
When he learned the reason for our inquiry, he said: "Miss
Nellie Sloggett is my wife's best friend. She is, however,
an invalid living in her cousin's home. " Then he invited us
to come in the afternoon to call on his wife, Mrs. Rae, who
would gladly tell us more about Enys Tregarthen.

Before our lunch at the Hotel Metropole, we explored
Padstow, making for the church first of all. The church's
square-turreted tower had settled and bulged considerably
since its early English flowers peeped out from the crevices.
The "little figures carved in stone on the buttresses of the
south wall" were there as the story said: "A lion with its
mouth wide open, a unicorn with a crown encircling its neck,
and a young knight, standing between them, holding a shield. "

Mrs. Rae, over the teacups, told us of her friend and
their close association for many years since she herself came
from East Africa to make her home in Padstow. She gave
us an invitation from Enys Tregarthen's cousin to come that
very afternoon, for Miss Sloggett wished to meet the American ladies.

No rarer good fortune could have been ours when we
finally entered an upper room and were introduced to Enys
Tregarthen's keen eyes. Her frail body was made as comfortable as possible in a reclining position on her bed, which
was placed between windows so that she could have clear vision of the far stretches of Padstow's storied land and water.

"However did you happen to seek me out in Padstow?"

"Reefy, reefy rum, " was the answer.

"Have you really seen the little stone figures on the
old church already?" She was as pleased to hear that as she

was to know about American children who read her stories. Those figures had been her special delight since early childhood when she could walk along the church lane, then through the penthouse gate into the hallowed precincts of the churchyard.

Of her own books The Piskey Purse was Enys Tregarthen's favorite. She said her experience had been that some publishers can use only a few fairy tales.

She asked about American books. Hawthorne she was very familiar with and she had enjoyed Father Tabb's verses. She longed to know about new writing, especially poetry. She herself had written some verse. Her prose is full of poetry, as the fresh discoveries show.

Speaking of Hawthorne, the theme of Reefy, Reefy Rum --a child's mingled feelings of awe and impudence--might almost have come out of one of Hawthorne's own notebooks.

PART III

IRELAND

Giant's Causeway, Aird Shout, Antrim (Courtesy the British Tourist Authority)

FOLKLORE, PRESERVING THE PEOPLE'S PAST

Séamas Ó Catháin

The Department of Irish Folklore at University College Dublin came into being on April 1, 1971, when the Irish Government decided that as from that date the work carried on by the Irish Folklore Commission (1935-1971) would be taken over by University College. Accommodation for the new Department was allotted by the College and the accumulated folklore collections of the Irish Folklore Commission and its library were transferred to the new quarters in the summer of 1971.

On the retirement of Professor James H. Delargy from the Chair of Irish folklore at the College and from the honorary directorship of the Irish Folklore Commission, Professor Bo Almqvist, formerly of the University of Iceland, Reykjavik, and of the University of Uppsala, Sweden, succeeded him as Professor and became head of the new Department. The staff of the Commission, both indoor and outdoor, were transferred from the Department of Education, under which the Commission had operated, and the work of the Commission continued as before.

The Irish Folklore Commission (Coimisium Béaloideasa Éireann) had been established by the Irish Government in April 1935 to undertake the collection, preservation, classification, study and exposition of all aspects of Irish folk tradition. The breadth of the field of inquiry may be judged from the main headings used in the system of classification of the material collected: Settlement and Dwelling; Livelihood and

Reprinted by permission from Ireland Today, Number 877, December 16, 1975, Bulletin of the Department of Foreign Affairs, Dublin. Dr. Ó Catháin is the Archivist in the Department of Irish Folklore at University College, Dublin.

Household Support; Communications and Trade; The Community; Human Life; Nature; Folk Medicine; Time; Principles and Rules of Popular Belief and Practice; Mythological Tradition; Historical Tradition; Religious Tradition; Popular Oral Literature; Sports and Pastimes.

These headings and a myriad of sub-headings also appear in Seán Ó Súilleabháin's monumental work A Handbook of Irish Folklore (first published in 1942).[1] This book was intended as a practical guide for field workers, full-time and part-time collectors of Irish oral tradition, and it was based upon the detailed scheme of classification of folklore material already in operation in folklore archives in Sweden, especially in Uppsala. Seán Ó Súilleabháin had studied the Swedish system in Uppsala and found that although everyday life in Sweden and also the customs and belief of its people differed from the Irish experience, nevertheless, the fundamental soundness and elasticity of the Swedish system made it possible to adapt it for use in Ireland. His book is dedicated to "the Swedish people whose scholars evolved the scheme for folklore classification outlined in these pages...."[2] Accordingly, all the cataloged material in the Irish archives follows the main headings of the Swedish system. Some minor changes were introduced here and there, and the sub-headings have, for the most part, been based on the card-index system which has been built up as the work of classification of the Irish material progressed. By far the greater part of this work of cataloging and indexing has been done by Seán Ó Súilleabháin himself and he has in the process acquired a unique knowledge of the contents of the manuscript material which has been pouring into the archives over the years. His many articles on folklore subjects and a worldwide correspondence with folklore scholars from every corner of the globe bear eloquent testimony to his acknowledged skill and expertise in his chosen field.

Some indication of the exhaustive nature of the various lines of inquiry followed by the full-time folklore collectors may be obtained from the following examples of sub-headings taken from Seán Ó Súilleabháin's book:

SETTLEMENT AND DWELLING: Local Settlers and Inhabitants: What accounts are available about the earliest settlers in the district? Who were they? From where did they come? When? By what route? Why did they leave their former district? How did they live? Did they follow any particular trade or occupation? Did they bring goods or

livestock with them? Where did they settle? What kind of
houses had they? Have the sites of local villages been
changed at any time? Why? What accounts have the local
people of their own first settlement in the district? Which
families have been settled there longest? etc. etc.[3]

TIME: Christmas Day: Give a description of Christmas Day as it was observed in Ireland in olden times; the
early Masses, Christmas greetings, meals during the day,
how the day was spent, and so on. Was it customary for
men (or women) to play games on Christmas Day? What
kind of game was played? Who took part in it? Where was
it played? In maritime areas was it played on the strand?
Were inter-parish games played on that day? Please give
full details of this custom. Did any family ceremony take
place at the Christmas Day dinner? What was it? Describe
how it was carried out. Were candles lighted that night?[4]

MYTHOLOGICAL TRADITION: Identity, Origin and
Fate of the Fairies: What exactly did people mean when
they spoke of the fairies? Did they regard the fairies as
spirits, as human beings, as deceased persons, or as a composite body of all three? Try to get explicit information on
this difficult point. What was the origin of the fairies according to popular tradition? Were they believed to be some
of the angels who rebelled with Lucifer and were cast out of
heaven? Were curative herbs cast out of heaven along with
them? Details. Are some of the fairies said to hover in
the air, some live on the earth, and some in the water?
Collect traditions and beliefs about this, etc. etc.[5]

It may be seen from a perusal of the Handbook,[6] as
it has come to be known, that the work of collecting the
folklore of Ireland extended to all forms of human thought
and endeavor in so far as these were reflected in popular
tradition. The task of organizing and administering was for
the instigator of the whole program--Professor James H.
Delargy--quite enormous. It was, as the famous American
folklore scholar, Richard M. Dorson, remarked, his "visionary dream,"[7] and for all intents and purposes it is a dream
come true.

The Irish Folklore Commission was a State institute
which had grown out of the Irish Folklore Institute. It in
turn had been inspired by the establishment of the Folklore
of Ireland Society in 1926, whose journal Bealoideas was
edited by Professor Delargy from 1927 until 1973.

Ernest Blythe as Minister of Finance gave the first grant in 1930 which enabled the Irish Folklore Institute to be founded, and five years later, in 1935, Eamon de Valera enabled the work of the Institute to be greatly enlarged and its work to be expanded by setting up the Irish Folklore Commission. The initial Government grant to the Irish Folklore Commission awarded it one hundred pounds for each of the thirty-two counties of Ireland.

The staff of the Irish Folklore Commission were State officials and consisted partly of field collectors and partly of archive and office workers. In later years they were to become fully-fledged civil servants and there can be few other countries in the world which can have numbered full-time collectors of folklore among the ranks of their civil servants. Numbers of occasional, part-time collectors were employed by the Irish Folklore Commission from time to time as circumstances allowed, and much valuable work was done by them.

During the period July 1937 to December 1938, the senior children in the primary schools in twenty-six counties helped, as part of their schoolwork, in collection and about a half-million pages of written folklore were acquired. Some 130 questionnaires on special topics were also sent out and in this way a very valuable documentation was made. Among the many questionnaire titles were such subjects as: Lake and River Monsters; The Feast of St. Brigid; The Famine; The Tinkers; The Spanish Armada; Emigration; Matchmaking; Wellerisms; Beverages and Local Songs.

The last named was one of the most recent and one of the most successful of the questionnaires sent out to hundreds of correspondents scattered all over Ireland. Here is a sample of the kind of information that is sought (and found) by this method of enquiry.

A LOCAL SONG

We are anxious to find out if the custom of composing songs still exists in your locality. If so, please give us a version of one (or more) song with the following details:

(a) Name of the composer, if known;
(b) Date of composition;
(c) Local name of the song;

    (d) Reason for its composition;

    (e) Was the song written down by its composer and copied by others or did it circulate orally?

    (f) Was it sung on certain occasions? Is it still sung?

This questionnaire drew a handsome response and hundreds of songs, many of them hitherto unknown and but newly turned, were added to our collection.

      The Department of Irish Folklore is greatly encouraged in its work by the wide measure of support which it receives from its informants, collectors and correspondents and the public in general; over the years a number of gifts of collections of traditional material has been received. The main bulk of the information amassed by the Irish Folklore Institute and the Irish Folklore Commission and now in the Department of Irish Folklore consists of manuscripts or typescript copies of traditions which had previously been preserved by memory and transmitted orally from one generation to another. This material was written down for the first time from the recital of mainly middle-aged or elderly informants. Ediphone recording machines were used by the full-time collectors in the early days, just as modern tape-recorders are used nowadays, so that the transcriptions of the material thus recorded are accurate both from the point of view of the information itself and of the language used.

      One historic expedition was made to the Isle of Man to record the very last of the native speakers of the Manx language before they died. It is plain that this Irish Folklore Commission did not confine its activities solely to this island, for it numbered many Scots among its part-time collectors in the Gaelic-speaking parts of Scotland and an Irish-speaking and Gaelic-speaking Scot--Calum Mac Lean--was, for many years, one of its full-time collectors.

      In all, the sound-record collection would occupy, in terms of the normal 12-inch 78 rpm discs, about ten thousand such discs. Many hundreds of tape-recordings made in the field by the full-time collectors and indoor staff are also preserved in the Department. About four-fifths of all recorded material is speech; the remainder consists of music and song. The Irish Folklore Commission employed two full-time collectors of Irish folk music and song for several years and the staff of the Department had recently been augmented by the arrival of Breandán Breathnach, a well-known expert in this field.

Full-time field workers are now salaried members of the staff of University College, Dublin. Part-time collectors are paid on results. The full-time field workers transcribe from recordings which they have collected, and send in to the Department of Irish Folklore both the recordings and the transcriptions. The material received is bound in leather-backed, numbered and paginated volumes. When the Irish Folklore Commission was taken over by the Department of Irish Folklore (April 1971) its main manuscript collection comprised 1,735 bound volumes (about 900,000 pages). This does not include the Schools' Collection. Today there are 1,832 bound manuscript volumes and the flow of information and material as well as the work of collection continues as ever.

Side by side with the foregoing activities, the ethnographical section of the archive has assembled over 25,000 photographs, plans, sketches, diagrams and other pictorial representations of the visible aspects of Irish tradition. Dr. Kevin Danaher, well-known for his many works on Irish folklore, is responsible for having ammassed a great deal of this material and is also the Department's specialist on material folk culture.

The library which the Department of Irish Folklore inherited from the Irish Folklore Commission holds more than 20,000 items of books, periodicals and papers, and is a specialist library for students and research workers. Its contents fall into three main categories: works dealing with Irish oral tradition and related subjects; works on the folklore and ethnography of other countries, especially those of western Europe; and journals and periodicals of institutions and learned societies engaged in similar work, mainly in Europe and North and South America.

Two volumes have been published under the aegis of the Irish Folklore Commission: Studies in Irish and Scandinavian Folktales (1959) by Professor Reidar Th. Christiansen of Oslo, and The Festival of Lunasa (1962) by Maire MacNeill. This latter book, drawing on materials in the Irish Folklore Commission's archive, links up in unique fashion the custom and ritual of Irish country people in recent times with the records of native pagan or pre-Christian beliefs going back to before St. Patrick.

Exchange of information with research workers in similar institutions in other countries and the servicing of international scholarship in general, activities formerly associated with the Irish Folklore Commission, are being carried on by the Department of Irish Folklore. The large preponderance of material in the Irish language is due to the main concentration of collection work in the Gaeltacht (Irish-speaking) areas, where the lore was richest and in greatest danger of being lost.

Undergraduate courses in Irish Folklore were introduced for the first time at University College, Dublin, in the academic year 1973-74. It is intended that the Department of Irish Folklore shall continue collection and field-work, carry out research on the collected material, embark on extensive publication and provide degree-level courses in Irish and comparative folklore and ethnology.

Notes

1. A Handbook of Irish Folklore by Seán Ó Súilleabháin (Dublin 1942, xxi--669; reprinted by Folklore Associates, Hatboro, Pennsylvania, 1963, and by the Singing Tree Publishing Co., Detroit, 1970).
2. Op. cit., p. 1.
3. Op. cit., p. 352.
4. Op. cit., p. 451.
5. Op. cit., p. xv.
6. Op. cit.
7. Folktales of Ireland, edited and translated by Sean O'Sullivan. Foreword by Richard Mr. Dorson, p. xxvii.

IRISH FOLK TRADITION:

A bibliography prepared by
Dr. Séamas Ó Catháin and staff

Bruford, Alan. Gaelic Folk-Tales and Medieval Romances. Dublin: Folklore of Ireland Society (Béaloideas XXXIV) 1969.

Christiansen, Reidar Thoraif. Studies in Irish and Scandinavian Folktales. Copenhagen: Rosenkilde for Irish Folklore Commission, 1959.

Evans, E. E. Irish Folkways. 5th edition. London: Rout-
    ledge and Kegan Paul, 1972.

Gailey, A. Irish Folk Drama. Cork: Mercier Press, 1969.

Logan, P. Making the Cure: Look at Irish Medicine. Dub-
    lin: Talbot Press, 1972.

Mahon, Bríd Irish Dress. Dublin: Folens, 1976.

_____. Irish Food. Dublin: Folens, 1977.

Murphy, M. J. At Slieve Gullion's Foot. Dundalk: Dundal-
    gan Press, 1940.

_____. Mountain Crack. Belfast: Blackstaff Press, 1976.

_____. Mountain Year. Dublin: Dolmen Press, 1964.

_____. Now You're Talking. Belfast: Blackstaff Press,
    1975. (Folk narrative.)

O Danachair, Caoímhin (Kevin Danaher). Folktales of the
    Irish Countryside. Cork: Mercier Press, 1965.

_____. Folktales of the Irish Countryside. New York:
    White, 1970.

_____. Ireland's Vernacular Architecture. Cork: Mer-
    cier Press for the Cultural Relations Committee of
    Ireland, 1975.

_____. The Pleasant Land of Ireland. Cork: Mercier
    Press, 1970.

_____. The Year in Ireland: Irish Calendar Custom.
    Cork: Mercier Press, 1972.

Ó Súilleabháin, S. A Handbook of Irish Folklore. Dublin:
    Educational Company of Ireland Lts. for the Folklore
    of Ireland Society, 1942; reprint eds., Dublin: Folk-
    lore Associates, 1963; Dublin: Jenkins, 1970; Dublin:
    Burns and MacEachern, 1970.

_____. A Handbook of Irish Folklore. Detroit: Singing
    Tree Press, 1970.

Ó Súilleabháin, S.   (S. O'Sullivan).   The Folklore of Ireland.
     London: Batsford, 1974.

_____.   Folktales of Ireland.   London: Routledge and
     Kegan Paul, 1969.

_____.   Folktales of Ireland.   Chicago: University of
     Chicago Press, 1966.

_____.   Irish Folk Custom and Belief.   Dublin: The
     Three Candles Ltd. for the Cultural Relations Com-
     mittee of Ireland, 1967.

_____.   Irish Wake Amusements.   Cork: Mercier Press,
     1967.

Ó Súilleabháin, S. and Reidar Thoraif Christiansen.   The
     Types of the Irish Folktale.   Helsinki: Finnish Aca-
     demy of Science & Letters, 1963.

STORIES AND STORYTELLING IN IRELAND[1]

Kevin Danaher

Storytelling is an art. It is a very ancient art, for there is no doubt that it emerged soon after man had developed articulate speech. The men who painted the caves at Altamira (Spain) and Lascaux (France) fifty thousand years ago sat around their fires at night listening to their story-tellers; the first men to set foot on the soil of Ireland 8,000 years ago heard tales, already ancient, retold during their long boat voyages and at their campfires on the strange shore.

In ancient Ireland, storytelling ranked with poetry as a recognized literary art, proficiency in which entitled its exponents to privilege and reward, to sit at table with kings and noblemen, and to enjoy lands, cattle, rich raiment, and other wealth in payment for the exercise of their skill.

These were trained men, graduates of schools of literature in which the courses of study lasted up to 12 years in duration. It must be admitted that the chief task of these court poets and historians was to flatter their noble patrons by reciting their own and their ancestors' exploits and glories. But they were also expected to entertain the company at feast and assembly with stirring tales of adventure, including, as ancient chronicles inform us, battles, voyages, tragedies, cattle-raids, military expeditions, courtships, elopements, pursuits, sieges, slaughters, exiles, banishments, and visions.[2]

In some parts of the world the new Christian teaching

Kevin Danaher, distinguished author, professor of Irish Folklore, Department of Irish Folklore at University College, Dublin, is known in Europe by his Irish name C. O'Danachair.

was opposed to the ancient learning. Not so in Ireland--here
they blended fruitfully. We are told that Saint Patrick listened with pleasure to the tales of aged survivors of the warrior Fianna and that he commanded his clerics to take pen
and vellum, and write down the old men's stories lest they
be forgotten. Thus in early Christian Ireland the art of the
poet and the storyteller flourished, with monk and bishop
listening as eagerly as noble or soldier.

The poet and the storyteller passed freely through the
country, even in time of war. When the Norsemen occupied
strategic points on the sea coast and built fortified towns
there at Dublin, Wicklow, Wexford, Waterford, Cork, and
Limerick, Irish poets visited them to entertain with song and
story and to collect reward, often princely--as that of Ru-
mann MacColmain, who demanded as payment for his art
"one silver penny from every bad Norseman and two silver
pennies from every good Norseman" in the Kingdom of Dublin. They paid up to a man, two silver pence each.

The Normans who settled in Ireland were quickly absorbed. From noble lord to simple bowman they adopted
Irish culture and the Irish language, and enriched both with
Norman-French elements. Soon, throughout the Norman half
of Ireland, there was little difference between Irish seanchaí
and Norman troubadour. Tales and poems from continental
Europe came into Ireland, while Irish tales and themes
passed overseas to enrich the literature of Europe.

During all this time, the ancient art of storytelling
flourished. The storyteller stood up before the assembled
company and told his tale, with every trick of voice and gesture. The clumsy, the hesitant, the stumbling were hushed
to silence and only the expert commanded an audience.

The prose tales were fashioned and formed for oral
recitation, and where they were recorded on parchment or
on paper they were written down as an aid to memory, not
merely to be read. The reciter embellished the tale in the
retelling--this ornamentation and elaboration was part of the
art.

With the downfall, in the early 17th century, of the
old Gaelic order, all the rich tradition of storytelling lost
its noble patrons and survived among the ordinary people.
The tales which had delighted king and chieftain, cleric and
abbot, Viking raider and Norman baron, were now to be

heard only around the hearths of farmers and fishermen, and
the art of storytelling sank into obscurity until it was redis-
covered by 19th- and early 20th-century scholarship.

Imagine the astonishment and delight of men like William Butler Yeats, Douglas Hyde, and John Millington Synge,
when they found old men and women in remote farms and villages who still practiced the storyteller's art in its full vigor
and beauty, with every trick of rhetoric, voice, and gesture.[3]
They soon discovered, too, when they began to write down
the tales, that here the written word was but a poor substitute for the oral recitation.   They found, indeed, that many
of the conventions of the oral tale--such as alliteration and
repetition--which sounded splendid in the telling, looked trite
or banal on paper.

Here is a description of a storyteller in action, written
in the early 1930s by Tadhg O Murchadha, an enthusiastic collector of the tales of south-west County Kerry:

> He sat on the hob beside the fire to tell the story,
> his eyes fixed upon me like two awls.   His body
> was swaying and his limbs trembling with the in-
> tensity of the telling.   He raised his voice now and
> lowered it again, as would an actor on the stage.
> You might think that he belonged no more to this
> present world of ours, but had gone back to the
> ancient world of the heroes and was trying to make
> that world live in his story.   All the characters in
> the tale were living people to him.   Listening to
> him one realized how great was the old-world art
> of the storytellers.
>
> He told me, too, that if I had come to him five
> years earlier he could have told me an heroic tale
> for every day in the year but that he had now for-
> gotten most of them.

This last claim is no exaggeration, for many storytellers had truly amazing repertories.   There have been recorded of several individual storytellers from one hundred to
350 tales, many of these very long and reaching 20,000 or,
in some stories, even to 40,000 words in length.

As to the subject matter of the tales, all the elements
of high romance were there.   Heroes set forth to seek their
fortune, slaying monsters, overcoming giants, setting at

naught the spells of witch and wizard.   Virtue, though sorely
beset, always triumphs in the end.   Tyrants are humbled,
oppression defeated, pride and presumptuousness chastised.
There are fantastic journeys, dangers by sea and land, impossible tasks and perilous quests, but always the hero or
the heroine wins through.   The weak little man, by his
wiles, defeats powerful and cruel enemies.   The widow's son
gains fame and fortune and the hand of a king's daughter.
The poor, forsaken maiden wins her handsome prince.   Love
and adventure, mystery and wonder are all there, and always
the right prevails, always the wicked are punished and the
good live happily ever after.

Many of the tales are international; that is to say,
they are told in many countries and languages.   Some have
spread into every country and every language from Ireland
and Iceland across Europe and Asia to India.   Where individual tales originated and how they spread is a matter of
investigation for scholars, and the material gathered in Ireland is contributing to this.

In 1963, two eminent scholars, Seán Ó Súilleabháin
and Reidar Christiansen, published a list of the international
tales told in Ireland, The Types of the Irish Folktale, which
gives the location of each written record of a tale. 4   The
sheer abundance of these is astonishing; the book lists nearly
43,000 tellings of over 900 international tales known in Ireland.

Of these international tales, the most popular type
among Irish storytellers is the wonder tale, such as "The
World Underground, " "The Bird of the Golden Land, " or
"Cinderella, " and most storytellers revelled in the wonders
and the terrors.   Another favorite class of tales is that
known as the romantic tale, in which there is plenty of both
romance and adventure, but no magical element.   Tales like
"The Pound of Flesh" and "The Taming of the Shrew" belong
to this class.   Both these themes were used by William
Shakespeare, but the stories were widely known centuries before his time and were told around firesides where his name
was never known.

Animal tales which told, for instance, how the wren
became King of the Birds, or how the clever fox stole the
peddler's fish, were also popular in Ireland, as were humorous anecdotes like that of Sean na Scuab, the simpleton
seller of brooms who, by chance, became Mayor of Limerick

and surprised even himself with the wisdom of his pronounce-
ments.

Popular and widespread as these international tales
were in Ireland, they were still outnumbered and outclassed
by the great body of stories native to Ireland.[5] Foremost
of these and among the best traditional tales of the whole
world are the Fenian Tales or Hero Tales which recount the
deeds and adventures of Fionn Mac Cumhaill and his warrior
band and of other ancient heroes. Some of these, such as
"The Pursuit of Diarmaid and Grainne" and "Deirdre of the
Sorrows," have passed into modern literature, while others
like "Conal Gulban" and "The Palace of the Quicken Trees"
are hardly known outside the circle of the folktale enthu-
siasts. There are also great numbers of Irish wonder tales
and romantic tales. There are tales of saints and hermits,
of rogues and simpletons, of hapless lovers, henpecked hus-
bands and patient wives, of animals, ghosts, and fairies, of
sea monsters, sunken cities, and hidden treasures.

Local tales abound and are always worth inquiry.
There is scarcely a hill, a rock, or river pool, a ruined
castle or abbey which has not its own story. Why this road
bends to avoid an ancient earthenwork, why that house is
haunted, why the tree stands bare but its shadow on the moon-
lit road shows a body swinging by a rope--all these are part
of the oral currency of the countryside.

We must remember that all these tales were intended
for the entertainment of adult audiences, although children,
too, listened to them with pleasure. Before the penetration
of modern media of entertainment into the countryside, the
folktale took the place now filled by the glossy magazine, the
novel, the radio and television, not forgetting, of course, the
theatre and the cinema. With the coming into the countryside
of all of these, the storyteller has lost most of his audience
to the newer forms of entertainment. There still are storytellers, but now they must be sought out and coaxed to tell their
tales, where formerly they held court night after night--es-
pecially in the long winter nights.

The art of storytelling has been carefully cultivated
and perfected over the ages and offered to listeners who were
critical as well as interested. A poor storyteller soon lost
his audience and, moreover, earned scorn and contempt as
one who had set himself above his station as expert in an art
beyond his talents.

With the passing of the interested and critical audience, the storyteller has lost the incentive to display his art and skill. He knows, too, that he is the last of his race and that nobody will learn how to tell his tales and pass them on to the future generations. If, then, in your travels through Ireland, you have the good fortune to meet a storyteller of the old style, listen with respect to his narration, for he is the end of a line which stretches back into a past so distant that we can only guess at its remoteness.

As regards written versions of folk tales we must remember that the writing down of an oral narrative involves a drastic change of medium--as many a lecturer has discovered to his cost in these days of the tape-recorder.

A tale formed by oral delivery seldom lies comfortably on the printed page.

Some of the characteristics of the orally delivered tale, such as tone, cadence, emphasis of voice, mimicry, and gesture are entirely lost; others, such as alliteration and repetition, may seem turgid or redundant. In Irish storytelling a further change-factor may be present because the best of the tales are told in the Irish language, which, although expressive, sensitive, vivid and vigorous, and thus eminently suited to oral narrative, is known only to comparatively few of the inhabitants of this planet. Most people must be content with translation which removes the tales a long step further from their original form. Again, some editing is usually necessary to fit the circumstances of publication.

In this way we may have, between the teller of the tale and its recipient, a transcriber, a translator, and an editor, any of whom may--and all of whom usually do-- leave an idiosyncratic imprint on language, on style, or on content.

To connoisseurs of the folk tale the written version is never an adequate substitute for the original oral delivery. But such are the privileged few, and ordinary mortals who must be content with the written word may be consoled by the thought that more and more of this torrent of sounding words becomes available in printed form year by year.

Notes

1. The greater part of this paper is reprinted from the Illustrated Road Book of Ireland, by kind permission of the Automobile Association.

2. See, for instance, Joyce, P. W., Old Celtic Romances, London & New York, 1894 and subsequent editions; Cross, T. P. and Slover, C. H., Ancient Irish Tales, London, 1935.

3. See Dorson, R., Foreword to O'Sullivan, Folktales of Ireland, Chicago and London, 1966; and, passim, The British Folklorist, London, 1968.

4. Christiansen, R. Th. and O Súilleabháin, S., The Types of the Irish Folktale, Helsinki, 1963.

5. Resumés of many of these tales may be found in Chapter XIII of Ó Súilleabháin, S., A Handbook of Irish Folktale, Dublin, 1942; reprinted Hatboro, Pa., 1963; Detroit, 1970.

BIBLIOGRAPHY

Danaher, Kevin.* Bibliography of Irish Ethnology and Folk Tradition. Cork: Mercier Press, 1977.

_____. Folktales of the Irish Countryside. Illus. New York: David White, 1970.

_____. In Ireland Long Ago. Cork: Mercier Press, 1962.

_____. Irish Country People. Cork: Mercier Press, 1966.

_____. The Pleasant Land of Ireland. Cork: Mercier Press, 1970.

_____. The Year in Ireland: Irish Calendar Custom. Cork: Mercier Press, 1972.

_____

*Dr. Danaher's (C. Ó Danachair) many articles and essays on Irish Folklore can be located in his new book, Bibliography of Irish Ethnology and Folk Tradition.

Ó Danachair, Caoímhin. Folk and Farm; Essays in Honour
        of A. T. Lucas. Dublin: -- , 1976.

_____. Ireland's Vernacular Architecture. Cork: Mer-
        cier Press, 1975.

STORY-TELLING IN IRELAND

Padraic Colum

Taking stock of the stories and fragments of stories that are in my memory, I recognize that the earliest strata were laid down by an elderly relative of mine. She told very vividly fragments of folklore that were unusually poetical. I remember her telling me that when the hens murmured to themselves on the roost they were telling each other where the Danes had hidden their treasures after their defeat by an Irish king--it being the Danes who had brought the hens to Ireland. I remember her telling the well-known story about the secret of the heather-ale, making the Danes the possessors of that secret. A story she told me I afterwards--long afterwards--made into a ballad: it was about a man who finds a strange woman riding on the pillion behind him as he comes home on horseback at night; she tries in every way to get him to tell a dream he has had, and as she parts from him she says in discontented admiration, "As wise as the man who never told his dream."

And I remember another story which made a great impression when I heard it from her and which I have since discovered to belong to a well-known type. It is about a family who find their corn ground for them overnight, and who make a window looking into the barn from their kitchen and who, watching, see a woman seated at the quern and grinding the corn. She is naked. The man of the house goes to the town and buys a gown of silk and leaves it beside the quern. She puts it on before she begins to grind and looking on the fine dress she has on says, "Silks to my

Reprinted by permission from The Horn Book Magazine 10 (May 1934), 190-194. Copyright © 1934, 1961 by The Horn Book, Inc. Irish by birth, Padraic Colum has introduced American children of several generations to traditional Celtic material from the British Isles.

elbow and I grinding at a quern, " and does no more for the
family, disappearing from the place.

Somehow, I always felt that this particular happening
was in the house I lived in then; I also thought that the man
who found the mysterious lady riding with him was one of my
granduncles, and I thought that the Danes' treasure was hidden somewhere around an old stronghold that I often looked
at.   I heard these stories told before I could read.   The elderly relative had listened to the shanachies or professional
story-tellers, and she had something of their way of relating
a story.   But what she mainly had from them, I suppose,
was the sense that a story was worth listening to and could
be told without any apology.   Time passed slowly at night by
the fire on the hearth where spinning wheels used to be
placed a generation before; my relative would tell how they
entertained each other with stories in the nights when the
girls would come into this neighbor's house or that, and do
the spinning of the household, turning their flax-wheels while
some one in the chimney-nook kept them entertained.

An old man, who was a survival from the time when
the mahil or working-party gathered by the hearth, used to
come to the house and sit in the chimney-nook some evenings.
He remembered when there were rushlights--the pitch of the
rush steeped in rosin--instead of candlelight or lamplight in
the houses.   He was a real shanachie, and told the longer
and more elaborate stories that are in my mind now as patterns of storytelling.   He told them with simple but very
memorable gestures.

... These first impressions of mine incline me to believe that the ideal place for the telling of a story is a room
which holds no more than a score of people, so that the story-teller's voice need not be raised unduly to reach the listener furthest from him.   The best time is night, and the
best light is the one which leaves some shadows around.   I
favor a candle, or a candle helped out by the light of a fire
on the hearth--of peat, preferably, and with some timber in
it that gives an occasional blaze.   I favor the scene, in
short, in which I heard my first stories told--the fireside of
an Irish cottage.

Are there still places in Ireland where one can even
now hear a story told according to the ancient pattern of the
shanachies?   Happily there still are--many such places.
Along the west coast, from Galway city through Connemara

for about a hundred miles, in thatched cottages smelling of
peat-smoke and noisy with crickets on the hearth and crickets
in the thatch.   The spinning-wheel and the loom are part of
the scanty furniture of the living-room.   The horse may be
given the hospitality of the house and may, shown by the fire-
light, be resting by the room-wall as the story is being told.

Generally the story-teller is a man over sixty, although
now and again a middle-aged man or woman gives the entertainment.   The shanachie is seated by the hearth; he makes
few gestures; he raises the staff he holds in his hand at some
impressive moment; he beats his hands together when he
comes to a "run"--a conventionalized description of a house,
or a ship, or a battle; the audience know what is coming and
so they let their minds rest while the story-teller, too, takes
a rest as he repeats very quickly the "run" in a kind of free
verse.   Many of these story-tellers whose language is Irish
are famous, known not only to their neighbors but to the
lovers and students of folklore even in countries outside of
Ireland.   And as we listen to the man who is in full posses-
sion of the art of the shanachie we realize that the story told
is different from the story read, so different that the story
read can never take the place of it.   The story read is not
addressed to any particular person; every one who listens
sympathetically to the story told feels that it is addressed to
him or her.   Hence it can be made part of one's history no
matter how fantastic its happenings may be.   The voice ad-
dressing us gives the story a memorable quality.   The quality
of memorableness is not in what we read silently.

It seems to me that a great deal of what goes to make
this quality of memorableness is lost in translations: when
we read Grimm in English, or Hans Andersen, or most of
the translations of the "Arabian Nights," we lose the rhythms
that a story-teller who speaks to an audience must of necessity give his communication.   These are not metrical as in
poetry, though metrical structures used occasionally are helpful and are often given in the story told.   I speak of rhythms
which consist in matching character with character, incident
with incident, word with word.   "Once upon a time, and a
very good time it was"--that is a rhythmical introduction and
is different from the introduction to a story written to be
read.   "Once" and "was" match, "time" and "time," and we
are immediately brought into a world where rhythm is more
important than individualized types.   "He set off, and there
was blackening on his soles and holing in his shoes; the little
birds were taking their rests at the butts of bushes and the

tops of trees, but if they were, he was not." It is more
important that the bushes have butts and trees have tops than
that they have colors and shapes that can be brought to the
eye.   These rhythms, varied and diffuse as they are compared with the rhythms of poetry, do what the rhythms of
poetry do: carry over to us feelings that belong to a deep
part of our natures.

Ireland has delayed long in the recording of her folk
stories, and by this time much of the treasure has been irretrievably lost.   We have had a great folklorist in Dr.
Douglas Hyde, whose various collections of stories (not to
speak of the beautiful poetry he has recovered for us) give
us the characteristic art of the shanachie.   A Folklore Society of Ireland has been established, and through this Society
the collecting of stories has been well organized.   The Society publishes a journal, Béaloideas, in which the traditional
stories in Irish and English are given.   The president of the
Folklore Society and the editor of the Journal is Dr. Delargy,
an enthusiastic and well-instructed folklorist.

The story-teller's art, which deals with the most ancient things in national history, has received aid from the
most modern and international of institutions--the Rockefeller
Foundation has given the Folklore Society of Ireland a small
grant which has helped in the gathering in of uncollected stories.   A good harvest is due to this timely aid.   The grant
provides ediphones by the help of which the collector can get
the voice and intonation of the shanachie.   Records of actual
story-tellings have been made, and these records bring over
to us the words that come from the lips of the old man
seated by the fire of peat in a lonely cottage.

ELLA YOUNG--HOW SHE CAME TO KNOW THE FAIRIES

Jane Verne Terrill

Where but in Ireland could a woman graduate from
her University with honors in political economy, history and
jurisprudence, and yet keep in lively touch with the fairies?
Ella Young has done this and we think of her achievement as
peculiarly Irish; yet forty years ago this was not so. Forty
years ago even in Ireland, except in the remotest places,
the voices of the little folk in the grasses were still and the
seabeat on the cliffs of County Kerry was like the roar of
the sea anywhere, for the fairy water chariots were gone.

All this happened because education had come to Ireland; not that education isn't a fine thing for most purposes,
but it isn't always wise in the matter of the fairies or of the
splendid old legends which have grown up without the help of
book-learning. Little Irish children learned many modern
things, but they forgot the Celtic language which their ancestors had guarded jealously in the face of foreign invasion.
Not one of them would admit that he knew a ghost or had
seen a pookah at his tricks. When their mothers and fathers
repeated stories that were like an Irish Iliad, handed down
from story-teller to story-teller, word for word for perhaps
a thousand years, the children would laugh and call it superstition. So the remnant of ancient Celtic culture lay only
with an aging people, neglected by the young. And it was
well on the way to die.

Such was the state of affairs when Ella Young was
born. Perhaps things might have happened differently had

Reprinted by permission from The Horn Book Magazine 3 (May 1927), 3-5. Copyright © 1927, 1954 by The Horn
Book, Inc. Miss Young, born 1867, lived in the Celtic Re-
naissance. Her Irish tradition collections are still basic to
all children's libraries.

Miss Young not been born a hero-worshipper.   Brave deeds
and gallant heroes were for her the flower of life.   But in
County Antrim where she grew up, her teachers knew nothing
of such things, or of such happenings in Ireland.   Not a word
could they tell her of the Gubbaun Saor and his Son, or of
Dagda Mor the World Maker, or of the little Sun God Lugh.
And the little girl, reading of William Tell, William Wallace
and Robert the Bruce, felt a shame for Ireland which had
produced no heroes.

What, then, would such a girl do when she grew up,
but search for the forgotten heroes of her country's past?

One should never go to cities to learn about heroes and
legends.   In cities the bravest deeds are soon forgotten.   It
is in the country, about the firesides of the long evenings,
that legends are cherished.   Ella Young was wise in this: she
went to the out-reaches of Ireland.   She learned to speak
Celtic; she lived in the little thatched huts on the hillsides;
she sailed in archaic Irish fishing rigs and listened to the
yarns of the fishermen; she drove through the isolated country
behind primitive ox teams.   She made the life of the Irish
peasant her own, and her reward is that she has caught the
secret of the peasant spirit.

Around the peat fires of Irish huts they told her stories of pookahs, the mischievous elves who play tricks on
people, of the lake horses ridden by fairy horsemen, of
fairies playing at favorites and dropping pennies in the path
of such as please them.   Sometimes the story-teller of the
clan would be there, and that would be an occasion worth
recording, for he would recite in rhyme--often for so long
as three evenings without break--a saga of Ireland in uncor-
rupted Celtic as ancient as the English of Beowulf!

So Miss Young collected her treasure of legend, and
from it pieced the complete cycles.   The Wonder-Smith and
His Son, which has been published by Longmans, Green &
Co., is the result of twenty years of such research.

Perhaps the strangest thing--to us--about it all is
this: none of the stories of supernatural heroes, of fairies
and the forces that are abroad at night, are foreign to Miss
Young's own experience.   She herself has heard the ring of
the fairy bells in the ocean; she has seen the pookahs at
their mischief; she has herself been enchanted on a fairy hill.
Even here in America she has heard orchestral music in the

grasses of Connecticut--music of instruments such as we all
know, and of some which have never been heard by those who
cannot hear the fairies.   And so she knows that the things
of which she writes are as true as anything is true in a
doubtful world.

But soon in Ireland--even as in America--there will
be no one to hear such things.   The priceless sagas will die
because none will stop to listen.   Another fifty years and the
Celtic strongholds will have disappeared.   Fortunately, a
few--William Butler Yeats, Lady Gregory, Dr. Douglas Hyde,
James Stephens, Ella Young--have set themselves the task of
recording, before it is too late, a dying world of genii, pookahs and of magic.

PART IV

SCOTLAND

The memorial to Robert the Bruce at Bannockbum.   (Courtesy the British Tourist Authority)

FOLKLORE--ONE WRITER'S VIEW

Mollie Hunter

For some time past now, people have been asking me questions about my use of folklore in books for young readers. They are intrigued to know how these are composed so that they seem to speak with the authentic voice of the folktale, but there is no one-sentence answer to this. Folklore has been a lifelong interest with me; and so, to explain anything of its use in these books would call first for at least some indication of what has always been my approach to it.

To give just one illustration of this through the medium of a popular folktale--that of "Cinderella"--I do not subscribe to any theory analyzing this in the Freudian terms which would perhaps show it as a tale of sexual jealousy among three women, two of whom are prepared to go as far as mutilating their feet in order to "make the glass slipper fit"-- i. e. to win the man who is the subject of competition. This, in my view, is an interpretation that necessarily regards the symbolism of the story as the projection of a single imagination; and although there are various types of folktales which do answer to this description--notably those originating in that gray area which is half history, half legend--a different source must be sought for those in the fantastic aspect of the genre. For some explanation here, it seems to me, one must reach back toward that far past which is common to all mankind and in which, therefore, the taproot of all folklore lies deeply buried. For a more penetrating analysis of the stories which have grown from that root to flower among different peoples, one must look first at the conditions of growth--in effect, at the cultural climate in which both story and people have developed.

In "Cinderella," then, the various elements appear to point towards two cultures largely coeval with one another-- that of the Celtic tribes of north-western Europe, and also that of the Picts who ruled strongly in North Britain from the 5th to the 8th century, and whose racial make-up contained a large infusion of Celtic blood. In Celtic culture, a convention traceable as far back as the 7th century B.C. demanded that a king-elect had to be an unblemished male, and the ritual shoeing of this male was an essential part of recognizing his accession to power. In the same culture, a king-elect became de jure only after mating with a female creature--either animal or human--recognized as representing the principle of sovereignty; and in the Pictish culture, which was dominated by the principle of matrilinear succession, a male could become king only through marriage to the woman through whom the royal line was traced.

Situations such as this may seem remote, but they are not so in terms of the oral tradition which has preserved the folktale into modern times. In the long, slow working of folk-memory, we have the thread which binds the experience of one generation to that of another; in the storyteller's imagination, the impulse to embroider that thread into patterns of fantasy. Memory blurs as it becomes overlaid with the effect of changing social patterns. Imagination conforms to expectations bred from these patterns, yet still flares in unexpected ways. These are complementary processes which reach their composite expression in the storyteller's "Once upon a time..."--that classic opening which immediately evokes timeless time, and thus serves as the best possible reminder that the story which follows has been a growth, rather than an invention.

Bearing also in mind, then, that--like many others of its kind--some version or other of "Cinderella" had wide currency outside its supposed country of origin and had existed long before the time of its compilation, it would not be unreasonable to infer it as having grown from folk-memory of various kingship rituals in the very distant past. Cinderella herself, in this view, becomes either the female representing the principle of sovereignty or the sought-after daughter of the royal female line--her ugly stepsisters being merely her father's daughters through another marriage. Prince Charming--the very name speaks the idea!--becomes the unblemished male who will achieve true kingship through mating with her. The glass slippers are the symbol of power; and the only arguable point of the interpretation is whether the transference

of the shoeing process from male to female has resulted from
natural confusion of detail in ancient memory, or from the
storytelling twist demanded by much later conventions of chivalry and romantic love.

It could be argued at this point, of course, that the
research needed before one can project such a reasoning process is not a necessary part of writing for children, but this
argument would ignore vital elements of the case. In a world
of adults too sophisticated to appreciate the folktale, it is
childhood's loyalty to the genre which has kept it alive as a
source of entertainment; yet any modern attempt to create
within the framework it provides can be only a rehash of
what has gone before unless one has insight on the motiva-
tions and beliefs which have shaped the classic body of such
tales. One must understand the material one uses, and it is
the academic capacity to penetrate the sources of a folktale
which allows a modern writer to give depth and dimension to
a story in similar vein--always providing, of course, that
this writer can also utilize something more basic than cere-
bral effort; a primal something which is sensed rather than
understood, but which is still nevertheless essential to creat-
ing the work concerned.

From the very depths at which the taproot of folklore
lies buried, the word itself has to be defined as something
cumulative in the blood of a people--a feeling, a current,
that has to do with the shape and climate of their land, the
life-styles they owe to environment, the encompassing web
of belief, custom, and saying, that all these weave for them.
The quality of their personal relationships is also part of
this web, as are the rhythms and cadences of their speech.
They are swaddled in the web at birth, shrouded in it at
death. Throughout life, they wear it like an invisible gar-
ment.

Throughout life, also, the individual among a people
becomes aware of the unconscious mind as having some kind
of reactor which infallibly indicates the essential rightness of
a word, a phrase, an incident in the familiar folklore; and
however good an outsider's academic knowledge of this may
be, it will still lack that essential endowment. To the native
senses, therefore, there may often be something subtly wrong
in the deployment of outside knowledge; and, in creative
terms, this means that the writer's background is all important in the composition of a story which seems to be
authentically in the style of a folktale.

The conclusion to be drawn from all this, of course, is that I hold no brief for the use of folklore in anything but its purest form. The fairies of folklore, for instance, are not tiny, airy sprites, but lordly creatures who might well be mistaken for humans if they were not both so beautiful in form and so apparently terrible in their powers. In my view, therefore, to write otherwise of them would be to lose all the sense of fear they anciently inspired; and it is when one can relate this sense of fear to some situation within the reader's understanding that a story which may appeal to him begins naturally to evolve.

To give an actual example of this from my own work, The Haunted Mountain is a story based on the old superstition which made farmers set aside a small portion of their land for the use of the fairies. The story's hero, McAllister, needs every inch of his land. He is too stubborn to yield to this practice, and thus he creates a situation which involves not only himself but also his wife and young son in running conflict with all the forces of magic traditionally ascribed to the fairies of folklore.

If these forces were not dangerous to humans, if the fairies were not presented as the powerful and terrible creatures they were thought to be, there could be no tension in such a story. If it did not begin with the very human situation of a man too stubborn to let himself be robbed by something which seems to be no more than a superstition, there could be no reader-identification with either that man or his situation. These, in my view, are the two complementary story-elements projecting the reader into the atmosphere of the folktale where one accepts fantastic circumstance through acceptance of the characters involved. And the more truly once can delineate folklore concepts of the sources of fear in these circumstances, the more powerful and tense the story will be.

The over-riding need to set these concepts within the framework of their origin, however, is the point which must bring me briefly again to the matter of the writer's background--in my own case, that of Scotland. When McAllister of The Haunted Mountain has to spend a stormy winter's night in conflict with the supernaturals of a gloomy mountain pass, his sense of human smallness among the mountains' wild and looming grandeur is an essential part of conveying the terror of his experience to the reader. And to have been nurtured in a land of mountains and winter storms is to

feel in one's very bones this same frightening sense of contrast.   Similarly, as in The Kelpie's Pearls where I have
given the creature called the kelpie its traditional form of a
great, powerful horse rising from the depth of a rock-pool,
imagination has worked through an equally atavistic influence.
The rivers of the Highlands run fast and gather deep; and to
live in sight of such rivers is occasionally to have the odd
feeling that one may have actually glimpsed the kelpie's mane
in their tossing foam, or sensed his lurking presence in the
darkness of a pool.

"...the shape and climate of their land..."

        But Scotland is really two lands--the Highlands and
the Lowlands, each with its different traditions and life-styles,
and it was those of a Lowland village that shaped my early
years.   On many a day there I lingered at the door of the
village smithy, watched the rituals of ploughing match and
harvest home, or brought the quick eye of childhood to the
observance of superstition and time-honored custom.   The
result of this, long afterwards, was Thomas and the War-
lock--a book where I made a blacksmith the hero and could
thus take for my theme the folklore that tells of the magical
powers of metals.   And for the setting, of course, I had a
Lowland village; that sharply-remembered one of those early
and formative years.

"...the life-styles they owe to environment..."

        Scotland is also its many islands, with aspects of its
total folklore peculiar to their different groups; and it is in
the Shetland Islands--the great breeding-ground of the grey
or Atlantic seal--that one finds the main body of seal legends.
Ancient belief in the seal's supernatural ability to take human
form is the basis of all these legends; A Stranger Came
Ashore was the book which gave me the chance to use the
research I had done on their origins, and to explore in fiction the long-time fascination they had held for me.   And
yet, as always, before it was possible to write a story giving
some new dimension to old legends, the terror and enchantment these formerly inspired had to be comprehended in
terms of native feeling for the mysterious blend of land, sea,
and sky, which is the surrounding horizon of Shetland.   That
feeling had to be related to an equally strong sense of the
way in which Shetland life in past times had been deeply per-
vaded by so many other forms of superstition.

"...the encompassing web of beliefs, customs, sayings..."

In this book, too, I have shown the story's characters as a family which includes a young boy and his grandfather, with these latter two enjoying the strong bond which often builds up between such disparate age-groups. And, as in all my other books of this nature, the tension needed to grip the reader's imagination is climaxed at some final point of confrontation between the real world and that of the supernatural. In all these other books also, therefore, the human characters answer to one or both of the same descriptions--a family group held together by mutual affection, a child and elderly person who have developed a special bond. And always at the time of confrontation, this affection, this bond, is tested to the ultimate. Yet always also, it triumphs in the end, because this is the thread running through all that aspect of folklore which records belief in encounters of the real world with that of the supernatural--the power of human love to defeat the soul-less and therefore loveless powers of that Otherworld.

"...the quality of their personal relationships..."

More mundane than this, yet still essential to consider within the theme of characterization, is the technical advantage the writer gains in filtering both dialogue and narrative of a story through such mutually dependent relationships. Questions asked by the young people in it are those the young reader himself would ask. The answers the story's older characters give are those the reader must have if he is to acquire the background of folk wisdom that will allow him to grasp the significance of events. The technique in question, indeed, is a chief means by which the true significances of folklore need never be watered down or distorted for the young reader--a contention most charmingly illustrated in some Gaelic tales where a child's question has been so frequently asked that tradition now has both the question and its answer embodied in the tale itself. My own experience, however, is that no part of this is achieved without some living and scar-free graft between the language of present times and that of folklore; and here, consequently, there are two related points to be made.

When a folktale is received in an oral rendering delivered from a long chain of memory, its language is idiomatic, with turns of phrase which may create a poetic im-

agery denied to the standard form of a language.   Thus, in
one of the Gaelic tales mentioned above, there is a passage
in which a young man declares his intent to arm himself for
the long and dangerous journey needed to free him from a
spell.

"Let the smith make a good strong sword," he says,
"and I will go to the end of fortune."

Nothing could improve on this last phrase.   All the
journey's physical potential for good or ill is in it, together
with the implication of that journey's symbolic nature; and
its poetry, of course, derives wholly from the speaker's native mode of expression.

"...the rhythms and cadences of their speech..."

A further outstanding characteristic in the oral rendering of a folktale is the use of those word patterns that flow
smoothly off the tongue; and for a modern writer to achieve
this fluency means first of all testing every word used, in
terms of its surrounding context.   Say aloud, for instance,
"The horse which drew the cart," and follow this with "The
horse that drew the cart."   In the first version there is a
change of position for lips, teeth, and tongue, in saying
"which" after the word "horse."   No such changes are required in the second version, and so this must be the one
preferred.

This matter of choice, however, extends to the still
wider dimension created by the fact that an oral rendering
of the best among genuine folktales has more to commend it
than either fluency or native rhythms of speech can achieve.
The style of this is spare and smooth as polished bone.
One could suppose it as an evolution from centuries of repetition by storytellers who had to hold successively in mind a
whole body of such tales--a circumstance which would inevitably mean a paring-away of all excess verbiage.   But
whatever the operative factors here, the work of the modern
writer must still somehow match that strong and simple
beauty of style.

The problem thus presented is, of course, immense,
a simple style calling axiomatically for simple words, yet
"simple" in this context by no means equating with "easy."
On the contrary, every word used must be deployed with the

greatest subtlety, in order to extract its ultimate meaning
both within the broad patterns of phrasing and in terms of its
immediate context. It must have the color which will light
that context, the sound which will make it musically ring, and
it must also pass the general test of fluency. Only when it
passes all such tests can it be accepted as answering to the
traditional style of the folktale. And finally, the exercise
will be completed only when all this can be made to melt har-
moniously with the reader's own knowledge and uses of language; this harmony being the very factor needed to give that
reader the sense of enjoying a story that seems relevant to
himself and his own times, even while it projects for him
the atmosphere of folklore.

The degree of professional satisfaction this offers the
writer may be easily imagined--but one is writing for children, and it could be asked whether children care enough about
language for the required effort to be worth while. The letters I receive from young readers are very revealing in this
respect. Very often these letters are clearly not the work
of highly literate children; and yet in nearly every case they
tell of being impressed by the language encountered in my
books--to the point, sometimes, where some of these young
readers have felt impelled to create a poem based on a particular phrase which has taken their fancy. I think of these
letters, I am touched by the aspirations they unwittingly
show, and I have my own answer to whether or not children
care about language.

Children care about other aspects of their reading,
too, of course. They demand--and quite rightly--that a story
should not only move, but move fast. They enjoy a feeling
of terror, provided that the story which offers this, offers
also a safe ground of retreat from terror; and all of these
requirements may be admirably satisfied by one which takes
the style of the folktale. But children also have a keen sense
of justice, and this can be their further satisfaction, since
the folktale is always explicitly moral. The good triumph,
the bad receive their just deserts. And so always also, the
modern writer in this genre must be concerned with some
aspects of the eternal conflict between good and evil. To ex-
ploit this concern a theme must be developed, and explored
at two levels--a superficial one of incident to engross the
reader's attention, a deeper one to convey some underlying
symbolism. And with every book of this kind I write, the
more I am convinced that only the strong yet subtle uses of
language above described can provide the key giving simul-
taneous entry to both these levels.

To try re-creating the feeling of folktale, then, is to attempt some total alliance of one's literary skills with the results of research and with one's personal sense of that tap-root in which the common experience of mankind lies, and from which the genuine folktale has flowered. Successfully to project a story from such an attempt is to identify in a very deep way with one's readers. Such has always been my aim in combining my interest in folklore with my desire to write for children. And if that has indeed allowed them to hear the authentic voice of the folktale in my work, I can truly say that they are no more enriched by the sound than I have been in the process of re-creating it for them.

Bibliography of Mollie Hunter's Works

The Bodach. London: Blackie and Son, 1970.

The Ferlie. London: Blackie and Son; New York: Funk, 1968.

The Ghosts of Glencoe. London: Evans, 1966; New York: Funk, 1969.

The Haunted Mountain. New York: Harper and Row, 1972.

The Kelpie's Pearls. London: Blackie and Son, 1964.

The Kelpie's Pearls. New Edition. New York: Harper and Row, 1976.

The Lothian Run. New York: Funk, 1970; London: Hamilton, 1971.

Patrick Kentigern Keenan. London: Blackie and Son, 1963. Issued in the United States as The Smartest Man in Ireland. New York: Funk, 1965.

A Pistol in Greenyards. New York: Funk, 1968; London: Hamilton, 1975.

A Sound of Chariots. New York: Harper and Row, 1972.

The Spanish Letters. London: Evans, 1964; New York: Funk, 1967.

A Stranger Came Ashore. New York: Harper and Row, 1975.

The Stronghold. New York: Harper and Row, 1974.

Talent Is Not Enough. New York: Harper and Row, 1976.

The Thirteenth Member. New York: Harper and Row, 1971.

Thomas and the Warlock. London: Blackie and Son; New
        York: Funk, 1967.

The Walking Stones. New York: Harper and Row, 1970.

A SASSENACH IN THE HIGHLANDS

Edith Ballinger Price

> Gray land of Lews that welcomed me,
> A stranger, to its sod;
> Bleak land of heather, turf, and sea,
> And men who toil for God;
>
> The sheiling on the lonely moor,
> The surf upon the rock;
> The silent house, the low-pent door,
> So still you dare not knock.
>
> And yet within--the peat-fire flame,
> Kind speech and kind old face;
> Tears at the memory of a name
> Still treasured in that place.
>
> And simply, with your tea and bread,
> In many a Gaelic phrase,
> God's blessing called upon your head
> In words of Columb's days.
>
> Proud Isle of Lews--by wind and rain,
> By heather, hill, and sea,
> I swear that I will come again--
> For you were good to me.

The treasured name still loved and spoken in many a black-house on the Long Isle of Lewis, was that of Rory Ban Macleod--and I had the good fortune to be traveling with his granddaughter. That was why these proud, shy people of the Hebrides swung wide their doors to me--a Sassenach and a

Reprinted by permission from The Horn Book Magazine 5 (November 1929), 3-8. Copyright © 1929, 1956 by The Horn Book, Inc.

stranger--and why it was that about the peat-fire burning in
the hollowed floor, I too might share the bread and blessings
of old folk who remembered Fair Roderick. A fearless, god-
ly man, of rare eloquence in his native Gaelic, he had fought
for the sorely oppressed farmers of the Lewis during their
bitterest struggles, fifty-odd years ago, and had done much
to further the passing of the Crofters' Act of 1886. Now his
granddaughter came from America to visit for the first time
the lone and misty island where her father was born. She
found there a welcome so great that its warmth could over-
flow to include a stranger as well. A brave sight--old Mhor
in her spotless mutch, patting my friend's shoulder and
squeezing her hand with the repeated pressures of a Highland
handshake. "And it is a blessed day that brings you here.
Oh, that, is it so! Blessed shall be my threshold, that the
granddaughter of Rory Ban will be stepping upon it!" Thus
our hostess quickly translated for us from the old woman's
tear-choked Gaelic.

And the old gardener at Stornoway Castle nodded his
grizzled head as he stared into the past. "Och, ay, I remember Rory Ban. A fine Christyan man--and ech, the
beauties of his speaking in the Gaelic! The English has no
such words. "

It was from the deep, undying loyalty of these people
that I learned the Highland fealty which, in my book, The
Luck of Glenlorn, keeps poor mad Lady Macmorair's clan
so leal to her. There in the northernmost wilds of Scotland,
the love and loyalty the people extend to their own folk is only equalled by their shyness and doubt of strangers. It is
not exaggerated, the picture I have drawn in the book, where
"Andrew" finds every door in Benntach suddenly shut to him.
To us, on the Lews, every door in Garrabost or Sheshadir
was shut, and you might have thought all life was extinct--
till the news ran somehow that it was the granddaughter of
Rory Ban who approached down the bare gray road, or among
the peat-cuttings. Then every low door swung open, and
every kettle was on the boil for tea.

Supreme generosity, with nothing to give; we, with so
much, cannot conceive of the open-handedness of these folk
who have so little. But the episode in The Luck of Glenlorn
is not overdrawn; the bit where "Andrew" nearly has to accept as an offering a live hen in a bag. Rory Ban's granddaughter did have to accept one! Wresting the most meager
living from the cold sea and the barren soil--and praising

God for it; so live the people of the Hebrides. In primitive
black-houses where the byre opens into the single room with
a peat-fire raising its constant column of reek in the middle;
in lonely sheilings--little turf huts on the vast and windy
moorland--they live and toil, those that are left. Mostly old
people, they are, with a daughter, perhaps, staying to care
for them, and sons in every outpost of Empire, finding bigger work to do and doing it well. The Hebrides, barren
and desolate, robbed of their fishing by prowling steam
trawlers, are slowly becoming less and less populous, as
the younger folk leave to find a kindlier foster-land.

        For the purposes of my tale, The Luck of Glenlorn
could not be laid in the Lewis. The history of Stornoway
Castle--its only Seat--is too recent and well known to brook
of fanciful plotting, and the scenery of the Lews--even of
the wilder Harris at its southern end--is not rugged and
enormous enough to fit the plan of my purely invented romance. Last year another trip--this time by motor--through
the northern Highlands, corroborated my idea that the county
of Sutherland would be the most fitting place for my young
Laird's adventures.

        I drove the motor; it was my own Ford, and had
faithfully borne my mother and myself all the way from
Naples. And now here we were heading out of Inverness with
all the signboards saying merely, "To the North," with a
charming simplicity that somehow made us tingle with a
sense of exploration. All up the coast to remote Wick, the
road grew narrower and wilder, with great rolling moorland
to left of us, and far below at our right hand the northern
sea crying at the foot of sloping, green-crested cliffs. John
o' Groats, shut off by a wall of clammy fog, seemed a place
apart, uninhabited. We were far ahead of the tourist season,
and now, when we had run on beyond Thurso, and Bettyhill
on its white-sanded bay, we were even beyond the tourist
region. No railway runs through western Sutherlandshire.
Only one small road cuts down through its lonely length--a
road just wide enough for the car, stony and steep, with
treacherous bogland on either side. There startled sheep
sprang up from before the strange noise of the engine that
stirred the silences; there quiet-stepping deer fled away, re-
turning to their fastnesses in the unbroken forests far on
some mountain side. There Ben Loyal, Ben Hope, and Ben
Hee, lifted their noble heads, amethyst with changing cloud
shadows, above the silver sheet of a high-held loch. Beside
a wild tarn in the heart of loneliness, we stopped, and the

ceasing of the engine was like the closing of a door whereby
all sound might be stilled. There was nothing but enormous
silence and complete solitude--and the lifting shapes of those
great bens that seemed to defy the possibility of any change
coming to the Highlands. We tried to sketch, feeling infini-
tesimal now that we were on our own small feet, cut off even
from the friendly confines of the car. The paint-water had
been forgotten, and I let some wetness seep into the jar from
the bog edge--not daring to venture far, for tales of people
vanishing into bogs are by no means mythical. Nor, I judge,
as I think of that wild and darkling landscape, are tales of
Kelpies and Banshees.

All that day we saw no human life--not even in the
few tiny whitewashed houses of turf black-huts we passed.
Here the road would life over the brow of a pass between
two bare-shouldered blue hills, there it would drop swiftly
to run beside a rushing stream like the "Ruich-Vuina" of my
tale. We had always with us a curious and not altogether
comfortable feeling of being utterly alone, yet watched. Not
by human eyes--there were none--but by the hills themselves,
vigilant and immovable. To a person used to the sea, as I
am, I think a mountain country has always this quality; the
austere regard of hills is not so easily met as the many and
impersonal moods of the sea, busy with its own rush and
flow. Here in this wild heart of Sutherland, the feeling was
intensified by the vastness and silence (strange that such little
hills, as measured by feet and inches, should weave so potent
a spell of grandeur and magnitude!); intensified, too, by the
fact that we were two lone women in a Ford, and that we
really didn't know exactly where we were to stay that night.

I wish I could relate that we stumbled into Castle
Glenlorn--but though I felt quite sure it might well enough
exist in any fold of these shrouding hills, we actually brought
up in Lairg, the rail stop for Torroboll, where "Andrew"
lost touch with civilization and plunged into Sutherland by mo-
tor and afoot on his adventure. Here is the westernmost bend
of the railway, coming inland for a bit on its way from Inverness to Wick. Where we had been adventuring, no railway
is known, so that although Lairg is a very tiny and most
charming hamlet on a loch of sufficient beauty to commend it
highly, we felt that we had reached civilization and that the
peak of our exploration lay behind us in the almost inacces-
sible region of the northwest.

My tale about the young Laird of Glenlorn is, I admit,

improbable--but not impossible.   Far in the deep glens between those hills, and on the edge of in-reaching emerald
sea-lochs, old castles are hidden--some in ruins, a few
tenanted by great gentry whose deer feed on a hundred hills
and whose clan rights extend over thousands of acres.   It is
by no means impossible to imagine a boy like the young Glenlorn, who, surrounded by the influences of race and environment, shut off in a country difficult of access, and beset by
the peculiar sequences of my plot, might very well react as
I have set forth in the story.   All of the scenery, and much
of the behavior and temperament of the people, I actually saw.
For the invented dramatics of the plot, I crave the lenience
of the reader.   And at that, dear reader--if you have driven
at dusk over the Devil's Elbow in Harris with Loch Erisort
five hundred shuddering feet below, and seen the dark moorland gleam with eyes in the midnight silence, and sat in the
peat-reek to hear a Gaelic blessing and dipped your paint
brush into bog water far above sea level while the stillness
listened, and seen the deer tread the snow-white sands of a
jade-green sea-loch, and harkened to the descending roar of
a white stream in spate dropping straight down from the
mists that hide a mountain's streaming head--if you have done
it all, dear reader, and left your heart in the North, you will
believe--as I do--that Calum Macmorair even now pipes the
Cumach na Cloinne in the dark hall of Castle Glenlorn, somewhere in Sutherlandshire, and that everything happened just
as I have set it down in The Luck of Glenlorn.

SCOTTISH HISTORY TALES

Sorche Nic Leodhas

For every collection of Scottish history tales that finds its way into print there are at least ten books of Scottish folk tales offered by publishers for the pleasure of their reading public. This is an amazing circumstance when one considers that of all the stories that have been handed down by oral tradition in Scotland the history tales far outnumber those of any other genre and are still favorites with storytellers in those remote places where stories still are told.

I have a feeling of sadness that so few of them have found their way into books. Folk tales have had their meed of well deserved attention and are well on their way to being preserved for future generations, but the history stories have been given so little consideration that, if the present disregard of them continues, it is very likely that they will soon sink into oblivion.

The fault is not in the stories, for with few exceptions they possess the qualities that good stories need. Each one can boast a spirited style, a well-formed plot with excitement in its incidents, and the vivacity and homely humor that is typical of the old orally told tale. Yet in spite of these eminently good qualities, collectors of old stories have passed them by. Even Mr. James Campbell,* an able and avid col-

Reprinted by permission from The Horn Book Magazine 43 (June 1967), 323-327. Copyright © 1967 by The Horn Book, Inc. LeClaire Gowans Alger died in 1969. She leaves many books of Scottish tradition stories for our children's collections yet most of us did not know she worked as a librarian in Carnegie Library, Pittsburgh also.

*John Francis Campbell. Popular Tales of the West Highlands. 4 vols., 1860-1862 (editor's note).

lector of Gaelic stories, who traveled about in the Highlands
from 1850 to 1860 searching for old tales that had been
handed down by word of mouth, specified that he wanted to
hear any old tales except "true stories," by which he meant
tales based upon historical events.   Later story collectors
have followed in his footsteps, spurning tales of things that
really happened, almost to a man.   The reasons they have
given are various.   Mr. Campbell himself said that although
true stories were abundant and had a great hold on the minds
of the Scottish people, he considered them to be local rather
than national in origin and thus out of his range of interest,
and anyway they could be left for the historian to preserve
if he had a mind to do so.   The trouble with that recom-
mendation is that historians do not tell stories.   They are
much too concerned with historical trends, political currents,
and dates.   So the small incident that makes a very fine
story for the storyteller to tell at length is usually given no
more than a paragraph or two, or perhaps only a finely
printed note at the bottom of a page in the history book.

Many of the collectors say flatly that they are folklorists, not collectors of Scottish stories in general, and that
they do not want to divert their interests into any other channel than that of their chosen category, the folk or traditional
fairy tale.

This insistence upon the folk tale as a category has
always seemed odd to me, for it has been conceded by folklorists that the origin of the old Scottish folk tale lies in the
ancient and lost history of the people.   They have said that
it is their opinion that the giants, the fairies, the noble
heroes of the tales were once real men, who lived real lives.
They have come down to us through the mists of centuries,
having become enchanted, and enchanting, on their long course
through time.   Folklorists say that the giants no doubt were
a race of unusually large and primitive men who were conquered by the larger armies and superior intelligence of invaders of their land and who fled to the fastnesses of the
Scottish Highlands to make their last stand.   Probably these
people actually were great in stature and abnormally strong.
Bones found in old barrows by archeologists in Scotland have
done much to sustain this theory.   Probably, too, these
primitive people had the habit of cannibalism, as the giants
do in the old Gaelic tales.   But the old history became a
folk tale, and as it was handed down from one age to another,
the giants who once were men grew in the telling, bigger and
bigger, and increasingly horrible.

As for the fairy folk, it is supposed that they too were an early people of Scotland, but of less than normal size compared with their conquerors. Many of them, like the Lapps, were earth dwellers. Traces of subterranean homes have been uncovered by men hunting for relics of the past. Before the onslaught of the enemy they withdrew underground, and with the passing of time became in legend the Sidh, those fairies as tall as men, resembling men except for their slanting eyes and pointed ears. Later they grew smaller and smaller, as the stories were told and retold through the ages, and became the fairies of the fairy dun or mound.

The history, intrinsic and inherent, of the people is there within the folk tale, although the ages have obscured it with magic and supernatural elements. Old customs, old ways of living, old beliefs of the ancient race show the historical origin of the folk tale. Well, then, is not the folk tale, perhaps in a small way, a history story of a kind after all?

Another objection that the folklorists make to the purely historical tale is that it is too modern, too new. Although it must be conceded that the history stories cannot claim antiquity, as the folk tales do, still many of them possess a reasonable degree of the dignity and grace of age. Stories which were made between the tenth and the seventeenth centuries are anywhere from nine hundred to three hundred years old and, with justice, can hardly be called new. The bulk of the history stories which have been handed down from one storyteller to another were made before 1700. Actually most of them were made before 1603, when Scotland came to an end as an independent kingdom. The great heroes, the great battles, the great rogues and rascals all preceded that time. There some history stories of the oral tradition that have come down to us from the seventeenth and eighteenth centuries, most of them dealing with the fall of the House of Stuart, and the rebellions that attended it. Only the early stories belong to the storytelling tradition. The later ones were written to appear in print and lack the qualities of the tales that are told. All the stories of Jacobite times and of the Young Pretender, Charles Edward Stuart, have been worked and reworked so often for publication that there are few of them that can be considered part of the oral tradition now. Stories are still told about those times, but it is hard to distinguish what part of them was born in the mind of the storyteller and what part of them came from the printed word.

It would not be fair to attribute the predominance of
the history tale in Scottish oral tradition entirely to a pre-
dilection of the people for stories of that sort, although its
popularity is undeniable.   From the beginning of the Reforma-
tion the Scottish clergy made a determined effort to drive out
old superstitions and beliefs.   The telling of old tales of supernatural happenings, of fairies, giants, ghosts, and witches,
was not only frowned upon.   It was forbidden by the somber
ministers who shepherded Scottish souls into Heaven with un-
flagging vigor.   There were even cases in which persons who
trafficked in the old stories were cast out of the kirk.

Because of this onslaught many of the old popular
tales were lost and forgotten, but on the whole they were
too much a part of the people to be entirely destroyed.   The
tellers of folk tales, like the giants and witches, withdrew
to safer places.   In many a remote and lonely shieling far
enough away from the manse to be safe from the minister's
surveillance, the people gathered, some of them coming from
great distances in those sparsely settled regions, to listen
through the whole of a winter's night to the old sgeulachdan,
or fairy tales.

On the other hand, the history stories had an excellent
chance to survive.   Perhaps it was purely a matter of luck.
These stories were not so furiously attacked by the clergy
because they had within them the kernel of truth.   They were
about things that had really happened and about people who
had really lived and died and had done the things that were
told about in the tale.   The finger of truth could point, as
proof, to the houses they had lived in (or at least to the
ruins of them) and often to their graves.   But even the history tales were not given a wholehearted approval.   The telling of them was considered a terrible waste of time that
might be better employed.   Perhaps, above all, the history
stories were not forbidden entirely because their makers
were such stern moralists.   Particularly in the older stories
there was no intermediate degree between black and white.
Good was good and bad was bad, evil men sinned and were
punished accordingly, good men for their good deeds reaped
rewards.   Angus of Islay in "The Tale of the Wrath of God"
loses his ill-gotten treasure and his infant son because he
violates the sanctuary of the Church.   In "The Tale of the
Lady on the Rock," when Lachlan Maclean is impelled by
greed and avarice to commit a murder, he is deprived of
his home, estates, and fortune, and eventually of his life.
Justice is served and good deeds are rewarded.   In "The

Tale of the Debt Repaid" the hospitality extended by the Earl
of Sutherland to his enemy, Uilleam Dhu Aberigh, is rewarded when Uilleam Dhu saves the lives of the Earl's uncle
and his men.

Of course this insistence upon moral values is true of
all old tales, whether folk or history, but the advantage held
by the latter at the time when the folk tales were being most
savagely assailed was that there were no spells, no magic,
no fairies in them at all. Even the storm in "The Tale of
the Wrath of God" is a matter of historical record. The
ministers were not averse to having it considered a manifes-
tation of God's anger and inevitable punishment of sin.

After the folk tales had suffered years of persecution
and banishment, the disposition of the church relented and
grew more lenient. The old folk tales began to creep back
to light again. As early as the last decade of the eighteenth
century, collectors busied themselves going about the Highlands and hunting out the old supernatural stories and popular
tales. Two remarkable things about these stories have
amused and pleased me very much. The first thing is that
ever since the beginning of this revival of the popular story,
some of the most devoted and energetic collectors have been
ministers of the Scottish church who in their collecting have
often specified, as Mr. James Campbell did in the 1850s,
that they did not want "true" or history tales.

The other circumstance that has taken my fancy is
that, although oral tradition is fast dying out, the nineteenth
and the twentieth centuries have each contributed orally one
great history tale. Both of these have been told and retold
and both are widely believed. Both deal largely with supernatural occurrences although they rank as history tales.
The first is the tale of the ghostly pipers who, at the Siege
of Lucknow in 1857, foretold the relief that was soon to
come by playing "The Campbells are comin'." The other is
the account of the celestial battalion that rallied a desperate,
exhausted, and ready-to-give-up company of Scottish and
British soldiers and carried them to victory during a battle
of World War I.

Even if there are no elements of the supernatural nor
any of the denizens of a fairy world in the history tales,
they have virtues of their own which the collector should not
disregard. They have not only that ingredient of historical
truth which won them the somewhat grudging approbation of

the clergy, but they have, besides, liveliness, earnestness, and humor. The persons in them are real, and, never stereotyped, they have distinctive personalities. Someone, I cannot remember who, once said that the Celtic temperament so dominates time that a hundred years ago, or a thousand years ago or more, is remembered as if it were yesterday. This feeling of timelessness pervades the Scottish or Gaelic history story. It is what makes it come alive.

Perhaps what draws collectors to the folk tale is its emphasis upon fantasy and illusion. Perhaps in our present world there is too much hard fact, and too much of it unhappy and disturbing, so that the magic world is pleasanter to contemplate. Perhaps the fun of the chase is part of the attraction, for certainly the old folk tales are fewer and harder to find. But I should like to woo with honeyed words a few of the great gatherers of Gaelic folk tales and to persuade them that the old history stories of Scottish oral tradition have values of their own and should not be permitted to perish of neglect.

BIBLIOGRAPHY OF SCOTTISH FOLK LORE AND FOLK TALES

Alison Douglas

Folk Lore

McNeill, Florence M. Hallowe'en, Its Origins, Rites and Ceremonies in the Scottish Tradition. Edinburgh: Apbyn O., 1970.

_____. The Silver Bough, a 4-volume study of the national and local festivals of Scotland. Glasgow: Maclellan.
    v. 1. Scottish Folk-Lore and Folk-Belief. 1957.
    v. 2. A Calendar of Scottish National Festivals: Candlemass to Harvest Home. 1959.
    v. 3. A Calendar of Scottish National Festivals: Hallowe'en to Yule. 1961.
    v. 4. The Local Festivals of Scotland. 1968.

Folk Tales

Brown, George Mackay. The Two Fiddlers, Tales from Orkney. Chatto & Windus, 1974.

Douglas, Sir George, ed. Scottish Fairy and Folk Tales. Walter Scott Publishing Co., 1893.

Grierson, Elizabeth W. Children's Tales from Scottish Ballads. Black, 1906. New edition: Tales from Scottish Ballads.

Lyford-Pike, Margaret. Scottish Fairy Tales. Dent, 1974.

Macdougall, Carl. A Cuckoo's Nest, a Collection of Lesser-known Scottish Folk Tales. Glasgow: Molendinar P., 1974.

MacFarlane, Iris. The Mouth of the Night, Gaelic Stories Retold. Chatto & Windus, 1973.

MacGregor, Alasdair Alpin. The Peat-Fire Flame, Folktales and Traditions of the Highlands and Islands. Moray P., 1937.

Mackenzie, Donald A. Wonder Tales from Scottish Myth and Legend. Blackie, 1917.

Manning-Sanders, Rosmary. Scottish Folk Tales. Methuen, 1976.

_____. Stories from the English and Scottish Ballads. Bodley Head, 1975 (USA; Dutton, 1968).

Montgomerie, Norah and William. The Well at the World's End, Folk Tales of Scotland. Hogarth P., 1956.

Nic Leodhas, Sorche, pseud. Thistle and Thyme, Tales and Legends from Scotland. Bodley Head, 1965 (USA; Holt, Rinehart and Winston, 1962).

_____. Twelve Great Black Cats, and Other Eerie Scottish Tales. Bodley Head, 1972 (Dutton, 1971).

Petrie, Winifred M. Folk Tales of the Borders. Nelson, 1950.

Ratcliff, Ruth. Scottish Folk Tales. Muller, 1976.

Robertson, Ronald Macdonald. More Highland Folktales. Oliver & Boyd, 1964.

_____. Selected Highland Folk Tales. Oliver & Boyd, 1961.

Scott, Heather. True Thomas the Rhymer, and Other Tales of the Lowland Scots. O.U.P., 1971.

Smith, Gregor Ian. Folk Tales of the Highlands. Nelson, 1953.

Stories from Scotland, as told in Jackanory by James Robertson Justice. B.B.C., 1968.

Wood, Wendy. Legends of the Borders. Aberdeen: Impulse Bks., 1973.

Wyness, Fenton. <u>Legends of North-East Scotland</u>. Aberdeen; Impulse Bks., 1970.

Nursery Rhymes and Street Games

Fraser, Amy Stewart, ed. <u>Dae Ye Min' Langsyne? A Pot-Pourri of Games, Rhymes and Ploys of Scottish Childhood.</u> Routledge & Kegan Paul, 1975 (USA; Routledge & Kegan Paul, 1975).

Gullen, F. Doreen. <u>Traditional Number Rhymes and Games.</u> U. L. P. 1950.

Montgomerie, Norah and William, eds. <u>The Hogarth Book of Scottish Nursery Rhymes.</u> Hogarth P., 1964.

<u>The Singing Street.</u> Oliver & Boyd, 1964.

Fiction Based on Scottish Folk Lore

Curry, Jane Louise. <u>The Sleepers.</u> Dobson, 1968 (Harcourt, 1968).

Dickinson, William C. <u>Borrobil.</u> Cape, 1944.

_____. <u>The Eildon Tree.</u> Cape, 1947.

_____. <u>The Flag from the Isles.</u> Cape, 1951.

Finlay, Winifred. <u>Beadbonny Ash.</u> Harrap, 1973 (U. S. A; Nelson, 1975).

_____. <u>Singing Stones.</u> Harrap, 1970.

Hunter, Mollie. <u>The Bodach.</u> Blackie, 1970.

_____. <u>The Ferlie.</u> Blackie, 1968 (Funk and Wagnall, 1968).

_____. <u>The Haunted Mountain.</u> Hamilton, 1972 (Harper and Row, 1973).

_____. <u>The Kelpie's Pearls.</u> Blackie, 1964 (Funk and Wagnall, 1966).

_____. A Stranger Came Ashore. Hamilton, 1975 (Harper and Row, 1975).

_____. Thomas and the Warlock. Blackie, 1967.

Jackson, R. E. The Wheel of the Finfolk. Chatto & Windus, 1972.

Lang, Andrew. The Gold of Fairnilee, and Other Stories. Gollancz, 1967 (The Gold of Fairnilee was first published in 1888).

MacAlpine, Margaret. Anra the Storm Child. Faber, 1965.

_____. The Hand in the Bag. Faber, 1959.

_____. The Black Gull of Corrie Lochan. Faber, 1964.

Macrow, Brenda. Amazing Mr. Whisper. Blackie, 1958.

_____. The Return of Mr. Whisper. Blackie, 1959.

Mitchison, Naomi. The Big House. Cambridge, 1970.

Rundle, Anne. Tamlane. Hutchinson, 1970.

Tarn, W. W. The Treasure of the Isle of Mist. Oxford University Press, 1938.

Editor's Note:

Miss Douglas for many years served as Youth Services Librarian in the Edinburgh Central Library. She welcomed children and American visitors with open arms. A knowledgeable librarian who read her books and could talk about them, she has just retired. She will be missed.

Publishers listed in this bibliography are in the British Isles. Those in parenthesis are in the USA.

PART V

WALES

THE WELSH FOLK TALE: ITS COLLECTION AND STUDY

Robin Gwyndaf

Since the Middle Ages, which gave us the Mabinogion-- one of the finest collections of tales in European literature-- Wales has not seen professional storytellers with a large repertoire of long wonder tales, so characteristic of such countries as Ireland. Yet, up to the beginning of the 20th century, the role of the ordinary storyteller in the Welsh community was an important one. He was the active folk narrative tradition-bearer who kept the old and the new tales and traditions alive by retelling them to others. He always had a ready audience. These were the days when the community not only had to create its own culture and entertainment, but also when the magic of folklore delighted and sustained the spirit of man.

By today there has been a change. We have less need for magic and there is less belief in the supernatural. There is less leisure and much of our culture is ready-made. In areas where the Welsh language has died, a great wealth of legends and traditions have died with it. In some districts there has been a gradual breakdown of communal life and traditional channels of transmission, and in many rural areas depopulation and the disappearance of old, deeply-rooted families with strong kinship connections have greatly affected the continuity of the narrative tradition. And yet, when all is said, we still have in Wales many passive folk narrative tradition-bearers: men and women who still remember the old tales and who are prepared to tell them again if we are pre-

pared to listen with sympathy and understanding. Although
many of these people do not themselves believe in the supernatural elements, they will recite the tales with sincerity and
reverence.   Their attitude is that of the Carmarthenshire man
who confessed:

> I cannot tell how the truth may be,
> I say the tale as 'twas said to me.

These then are the people who have been recorded by
the Welsh Folk Museum since 1966. The purpose of this work
is to make as complete a survey as possible of Welsh folk
narratives from very early times to the present day, and to
record as much information as possible about the social background to the reciting of these narratives.   Today these passive tradition-bearers are decreasing rapidly and when they
die their tales and traditions die too.   They must be recorded
now, for their like will not be heard again.   The words of
the countryman, quoted in a 17th century English tract (see
George Ewart Evans, Ask the Fellows Who Cut the Hay), are
just as true now as they were then, if not more so:

> We old men are old chronicles, and when our
> tongues go they are not clocks to tell only the time
> present, but large books unclasped; and our speech-
> es, like leaves turned over and over, discover
> wonders that are long since past.

And we in Wales today could well add our own remarks to
those of the countryman: to make these silent, self-taught,
cultured people speak is our challenge; to listen to them is
our privilege; to record, study and present their tales and
traditions is our most rewarding duty.

* * *

Welsh folk narratives may be classified into three
main categories, although these categories often overlap.

1) Magic and the Belief in the Supernatural

Civilizations may disappear, man's beliefs may change,
but his inner-most desires remain the same all through the
ages, and one of his most constant desires is to avoid the
routine and certainty of this world and escape into the enchanting world of the unknown.   Man in Wales was no excep-

tion.   He too resorted to magic especially when chance and
circumstances were not fully controlled by knowledge.

The earliest known term for magic in Welsh is the
Celtic word hud, and the use of this word in the Third
Branch of the Mabinogi (one of the Mabinogion tales) clearly
conveys the atmosphere of the early Welsh prose narratives:
Y mae yma ryw ystyr hud, "there is here a magic meaning."
We could also refer to the Second Branch of the Mabinogi,
the story of Branwen, in which the swineherds of Matholwch,
King of Ireland, say: Arglwydd, y mae gennym ni chwedlau
rhyfedd, "Lord, we have wondrous news."   We could not have
a better description than this of the nature of the early tales
of magic.   They are based in a world of wonder where the
most ordinary youth has the power of a magician and where
fields and trees disappear at the twinkle of an eye.

By today few of the tales of magic--or Märchen as
they are known internationally--still exist in current Welsh
oral tradition, and even these are usually very much shortened versions.   Even so, they give us a brief glimpse of
the ever-present atmosphere of wonder which was so characteristic of the medieval world.   For example: the tale of
the magic ring which gives a poor boy anything he wishes;
the tale of the magic mill which still grinds salt at the bottom of the sea; and the tale of the monk of Maes-glas,
Flintshire, who listens to the nightingale's song, and when
he returns to his monastery it is in ruins and all his colleagues have been dead for many years--the same motif of
the supernatural passage of time which we find in the tale
of Branwen, where the Birds of Rhiannon sing a most beautiful song to the seven men at Harlech for seven years.

In the early Welsh tales the other world of magic is
a world of contradictions.   It defies definition in space and
it "transcends mundane time.   On the one hand, a very short
time in the Other World corresponds with a very long time
in this world....   On the other hand, a long time in the
Other World sometimes transpires to have been but an instant
in this world" (Celtic Heritage, pp. 343-4).   And thus, we
have the same paradox as in the Second Epistle of Saint
Peter: "One day is with the Lord as a thousand years and a
thousand years is as one day."   Under the spell of the storyteller's art, the world of magic becomes a reality and our
world less real.   "When the spell is over, the hearer 'comes
back to earth,' but the earth now is not quite so solid as it
was before" (Celt. Her. p. 342), and we are reminded of the

words of Saint Colaim Chille:

> If poets' verses be but stories,
> So be food and raiment stories;
> So is all the world a story;
> So is man of dust a story.

If there is a shortage in Wales of international long
wonder tales (Märchen), there is no shortage of brief local
legends illustrating man's belief in the supernatural (Sagen).
These local belief-legends refer to the fairies, the devil,
witches, conjurers, ghosts and apparitions (such as death
omens), giants, and mythological animals, such as dragons
and water monsters. They have developed from one or more
folk beliefs (though the same belief may also develop into a
folk custom). When a person experiences a certain belief,
folk tale scholars refer to this experience as a "memorate,"
a term first coined by the Swedish scholar Carl W. von
Sydow. A memorate describes a supra-normal experience
undergone by the narrator or, more often, an acquaintance
or ancestor. With the process of time the contents of many
of these empirical narratives have become stereotyped and
less personal. They follow a certain plot formula that can
travel easily from one district to the other. Thus the experience or memorate develops into a local belief-legend.
Because these legends are based on various folk beliefs, it
is important to remember that their content was, at one
time, at least, believed to be true, and this is one of the
main differences between a folk legend and a folk tale or
story.

2) History and Tradition

The narratives included in this group reflect the close
interrelationship which exists between history and tradition,
fact and fiction. The description of an horrific 18th-century
murder may be a fact, but what about the irremovable blood-
stain on the wall?

In the Trioedd Cerdd, "the poetic or song triads,"
we read the following words: Tri pheth a beir y gerddawr
vot yn amyl: kyvarwyddyt ystoryeau, a barddoniaeth a
hengerdd, "three things that give amplitude to a poet: knowledge of histories, the poetic art and old verse." Ystoryeau
here means, to quote Rachel Bromwich, "the national inheritance of ancient traditions." The word is a later borrowing

from the Latin "historia" and the repertoire of a number of cultured tradition-bearers in Wales today is a remarkable reminder of the eleventh century triad. This "national inheritance of ancient traditions" includes:

> (a) Local legends and traditions relating to historical and pseudo-historical characters, such as: the Saints, King Arthur, Myrddin (Merlin, the magician), Taliesing, Owain Glyndwr, Owain Lawgoch, Oliver Cromwell, and famous or remarkable men, such as poets, harpists, and preachers.

> (b) Local legends and traditions relating to historical and pseudo-historical events, such as the adventures of Gwylliaid Cochio Mawddwy, "the red bandits of Mawddwy," and the landing of the French at Abergwaun (Fishguard) in 1797.

> (c) Local legends and traditions relating to place-names and physical features, such as fields, stones, rivers, bridges, lakes and caves. Many of these narratives are onomastic; they explain the origin of a name or the location of a stone, lake or any other physical feature.

3) Humor

There has been in Wales, as in most other countries, a long tradition of reciting humorous tales, jokes and anecdotes. There are collections, for example, in the manuscripts of the 16th century, and the tradition is very much alive today. The narratives which illustrate the Welshman's humor may be divided into the following main groups:

> (a) The numerous white-lie or tall tales which reflect the great imagination and narrative gifts of certain individual characters. Many of these tales, like other tales of humor, tend to form cycles, and the same story may be told about different characters in different districts.

> (b) Humorous anecdotes relating to well-known characters.

> (c) Humorous anecdotes relating to untoward local incidents, known in Welsh as troeon trwstan. These

are lively descriptions of some unfortunate, but usually humorous incidents, which have befallen certain
members of the community. For example, a group
of young people block the door and chimney of a house
during a <u>noswaith wau</u>, "knitting evening." The narratives are characteristic of small, intimate communities, in which the person involved is well-known to
everyone and in which those who narrate the incident
may do so in a happy, leg-pulling atmosphere. Often
the incident is quickly recorded in verse by a local
poet. Indeed, in Wales, as elsewhere, the role of
the poet and the storyteller is still very similar.

(d) Humorous stories and anecdotes based mainly upon
humor of speech (wit), which reflect the interest,
work, and personality of a certain social group. For
example, the miners of South Wales or the quarrymen
of North Wales.

(e) Humorous stories and jokes which are generally
known throughout Wales and have very similar versions in other countries.

Today we have less time for the long story, so we make it
short and to the point. But sometimes a humorous story,
which appears to be modern in every sense, may be but a
shortened version of an older and longer international popular
tale. These are known as Romantic Tales (<u>Novelle</u>). Unlike
the wonder tales (<u>Märchen</u>) the Romantic Tales are about human characters in a real world. Marvels do appear, but
they call for the listener's belief. These tales are also often
witty and humorous. Here is one example.

During the nineteen forties my father used to entertain
us children at home on the farm in Llangwm, Denbighshire,
North Wales, by reciting stories, poetry, proverbs, nursery
rhymes, riddles and tongue-twisters. One story which I well
remember is the "Story of the Two Brothers: Bob and Jack."
Bob wanted to become a Parson and one day he goes to see
the Bishop of Llanelwy (St. Asaph). The Bishop asks him
three questions:

1.   "How deep is the sea?"
2.   "How much am I worth in this oak chair?"
3.   "What am I thinking?"

Bob has no answer to any of these questions, so the

Bishop tells him to return in one week's time.   Bob goes
home and tells the story to his brother Jack.   "Oh, don't
you worry, Bob bach, " says Jack, 'I'll go to see the Bishop
next week. " So Jack goes.   "First questions, " says the
Bishop, "How deep is the sea?" 'Ergyd carreg, Syr, " Jack
answers. (As far as a stone will travel).   "Very good, "
says the Bishop.   "Second question: What am I worth in this
oak chair?" "Twenty-nine pence, Sir, because Jesus Christ
was only worth thirty pence. " "Very good indeed, " says the
Bishop.   "Third question: What am I thinking?" "Well,
Sir, " says Jack, "you think that I am my brother Bob!"

        Many years later I learned that my father's humorous
story was but another shortened version of an international
popular tale which has been recorded in many countries.
According to Walter Anderson (author of Kaiser und Abt) the
tale could be of Jewish origin, dating from perhaps the 7th
century and brought over to Europe, possibly, by the Crusaders.

                            * * *

        These, then, are the three main categories of Welsh
Folk tales.   But folk tales were never intended for neat
classification and, while such classification is often essential,
the folk tale scholar must also constantly keep in mind the
storyteller himself and his community.   After saying this, I
will now mention what I consider to be four of the most important aspects in the study of Welsh folk tales.

1.   The Origin, Growth and Distribution of Welsh Folk Tales

        One should consider, for example, which tales repre-
sent Wales as once a part of the continents of Europe and
Asia; Wales as a part of the Celtic countries; Wales as a
part of Britain; and Wales as, more or less, an independent
unit.

2.   The Morphology (Structure, Form and Style), of Welsh Folk Tales and the Nature of their Oral Transmission--A Study of the Folk Tale as a Living Art

        How does a folk tale change by being transmitted oral-
ly from one person and district to the other? To what extent
is a folk tale tradition-bearer also a tradition-creator, sup-

plying his own additions and corrections to the original material? How can the recording of an informant under different conditions or after the lapse of some years teach us about the nature of a storyteller's memory? Which tales were once part of the oral tradition, were later recorded in manuscripts or printed material, but have now once more returned into the oral tradition? A study of the morphology of folk tales will show, for example, how a number of old motifs may be combined in one tale and how these old motifs may be adapted to a new environment at a later period.

3. Folk Tales in Their Living Context

Who were the storytellers? Who are the storytellers today? To whom did the storytellers recite their tales and what role was played by the audience? Was it an active or passive role? When, where, and on what special occasions were these tales recited? One should also consider how these tales were an organic part of the lives of the people and would be recited during working time as well as during leisure hours. This point is made by the poet John Davies (Taliesin Hiraethog), for example, in a Welsh essay entitled "Old Traditions," in which he refers to the period around the middle of the 19th century. This is a translation of the opening paragraph:

> Cerrigydrudion is the highest and most remote parish in Denbighshire. Its coarse-grass hills and heathery mountain pastures are full of interest to the antiquarian. Every mound and hillock, every brook and river are full of old traditions of days gone by, and its rural inhabitants on long winter nights have much delight in reciting the tales and folklore that belong to this land. When the writer was a young boy, shepherding his father's sheep along the banks of the river Alwen and Llyn Dau Ychen ('the lake of the two sources'), he and his fellow shepherds spent many a happy hour reciting these tales while sitting on a small heap of rushes to keep the sheep from wandering on early summer days.

The scholar should also consider how a study of the community will help him towards a better understanding of the tales themselves and of the role of the storyteller--to see, for example, the close connection which often exists

between folk tales and other folkloristic genres, such as:
folk songs, folk poetry, folk customs and games and amusements.

4. Use, Meaning, and Function of Folk Tales

Many folk tales are based on folk beliefs, but what
world do these beliefs represent? What was the driving
force behind the creation of these tales? How many of the
old folk beliefs are derived from the primitive mythology
connected with pre-Christian gods and heroes? How did these
folk beliefs sustain the spirit of man? Which tales were
merely retold for entertainment? Which tales were recited
for didactic purposes, and which tales express one of man's
most constant desires: "to void the routine and certainty of
this world and escape into the enchanting world of the unknown?"

* * *

If one were asked today, what is the value of collecting and studying Welsh folk tales, my answer, briefly, would
be threefold:

Firstly, they deserve our attention because of their
aesthetic qualities. Many of the stories and legends are minor works of art, great in their sincerity of purpose,
vividness of characterization and simplicity of style and
form.

Secondly, an understanding of the storyteller's role in
the community and of the function of his tales will help us to
understand the nature of the whole community.

And thirdly, the more we study these folk tales, the
closer we come to an understanding of the nature of human
culture and of life itself. We are given a glimpse, as it
were, of the development of man's mind and culture through
the centuries until the present day. The one great essential
of any folk narrative collector is a sympathetic attitude towards his subject. It is so easy for us today to regard our
forefathers' tales as merely entertainment and the old motifs
as merely superstitions. But we must always remember that
to them these tales and motifs were an intrinsic part of man's
belief. They had meaning which the people accepted with
reverence. We are reminded that the Latin word historia not

only gave us the Welsh word ystoreau, "histories," but that it also gave us the Welsh word ystyr, "meaning." We are reminded too that the early Welsh word for storyteller was y cyfarwydd, "the familiar one." His task was cyfarwyddo, "to direct." The Welsh word gweled, "to see," and the Irish word fili both derive from the same Indo-European stem. The Welsh cyfarwydd, like the Irish fili, was a poet-- a visionary, and interpreter--the one who helped his people to "see"--to visualize the invisible; to give meaning to the meaningless.

To us today, this meaning is often a magic one. But we must always remember that to our forefathers there was meaning in the magic. The folklorist's task, indeed his privilege, is to endeavor to understand this meaning. His efforts will not be in vain, because, as the Irish proverb says:

> Ys bwine port no glor ny nean,
> Ys bwine focyl no toice yntel.

> --"a tune is more lasting than the song
> of birds, and a word more lasting than
> the wealth of the world."

Selected Bibliography (in English)

1. Davies, J. Ceredig. Folk-lore of West and Mid-Wales. Printed at the "Welsh Gazette" Offices. Aberystwyth, 1911.

2. Howells, William. Cambrian Superstitions, Comprising Ghosts, Omen, Witchcraft, Traditions, etc. London: Longman, 1831.

3. Jacobs, Joseph. Celtic Fairy Tales and More Celtic Fairy. London: David Nutt, 1892-1894. Reprinted by The Bodley Head, London, 1970.

4. Jones, T. Gwynn. Welsh Folklore and Folk Custom. London: Methuen, 1930.

5. _____. Welsh Legends and Folk-Tales. London: Oxford University Press, 1955.

6. _____ and Jones, Thomas. The Mabinogion (trans.

into English).   London: J. M. Dent (Everyman),
1949.

7. Loomis, R. S. Wales and the Arthurian Legend. Cardiff: University of Wales Press, 1956.

8. Owen, Elias. Welsh Folk-lore: A Collection of the
Folk-Tales and Legends of North Wales. Oswestry
and Wrexham: Woodall and Minshall, 1896. Reprinted by E. P. Publishing Group, 1976. Also reprinted by Norwood Editions.

9. Parry-Jones, D. Welsh Legends and Fairy Lore. London: B. T. Batsford, 1958.

10. Rees, Alwyn, and Rees, Brinley. Celtic Heritage.
London: Thames and Hudson, 1961.

11. Rhys, Sir John. Celtic Folklore: Welsh and Manx.
2 vols. Oxford: The Clarendon Press, 1901.

12. Roberts, Peter. The Cambrian Popular Antiquities.
London: E. Williams, 1815.

13. Sampson, John. XXI Welsh Gypsy Folk-Tales. Newton:
Gregynog Press, 1933.

14. Sikes, Wirt. British Goblins: Welsh Folk-Lore, Fairy
Mythology, Legends and Traditions. London: Sampson
Low, 188?. Reprinted by E. P. Publishing Group,
1973.

15. Thomas, W. Jenkyn. The Welsh Fairy Book. London:
T. Fisher Unwin, 1907. (Re-issued by University of
Wales Press, 1957).

16. Trevelyan, Marie. Folk-Lore and Folk-Stories of
Wales. London: Elliot Stock, 1909. Reprinted by
E. P. Publishing Group, 1973. Also reprinted by
Norwood Editions.

Editor's Note:

One of the most interesting places in Wales to visit
is the Welsh Folk Museum in St. Fagans, a village adjoining
Cardiff, Wales. The size of the facility clearly indicates the
importance of folklore to the Welsh people.

The Folk Museum complex covers many hundreds of acres and includes a typical castle, St. Fagan, dating back to the Middle Ages. The gardens are lovely. Local workmen demonstrate crafts such as weaving and wood craft. Model homes of many types from different periods and sections of Wales can be visited by the public. They are furnished as they would have been. A "Gipsy" Caravan, tannery, cockpit, tollgate house, a "Capel" (chapel) and a barn are among the places to visit.

The Main Museum is divided into many large display rooms that feature costumes, farm machinery, furniture, cooking, and much more. The Folk Museum staff is divided into the Department of Natural Culture, Department of Oral Tradition, Department of Dialects, and Department of Buildings.

The Department of Oral Tradition's main stress at this time is on the collection and studying of various forms of folktales: jokes and anecdotes, tall tales, animal tales, religious tales, and onomastic tales connected with place names, fields, stones, rivers, etc. A study of the supernatural--in witchcraft and ghosts, in death omens and other apparitions, in mythological beings such as fairies, giants, dragons and the devil--is also being made and recorded. However, this department endeavors to carry out fieldwork, research, publishing, and lecturing.

The Museum has tape, disc, manuscript, photographic collections and an archive as well as a library, listening room, and bookstore.

For the folklore enthusiastic, a visit to the Welsh Museum is a must. Anyone interested in Wales would enjoy a visit, but do plan to devote more than a day to visit.

HIGH FANTASY AND HEROIC ROMANCE

Lloyd Alexander

The White Queen proudly told Alice she had learned to believe six impossible things before breakfast. We do much better. Science appears on the verge of discoveries that may let us live forever, at the same time perfecting ways to get rid of us altogether. We can fly to any place in the world in a matter of hours, if we can find a parking space at the airport. We have a beachhead on the moon-- for the moment free of beer cans and oil slick. We have the material benefits of labor-saving machines, along with the cultural benefits of Jacqueline Susann and her Love Machine. As time goes on, Lewis Carroll seems more of a realist than ever.

When our own world is so fantastic, I am amazed and thankful that we can still be deeply moved by worlds that never existed, and touched by the fate of people who are figments of our imagination. Perhaps our daily diet of impossibilities and incongruities is lacking some essential ingredient. Our systems of information retrieval still have not retrieved the one vital bit of information: How shall we live as human beings? The same questions that preoccupied the ancient Greeks preoccupy us today. Shakespeare is truly our contemporary. Or we, perhaps, are not as modern as we like to think we are.

The arts, surely, are not as modern as we might be-

Reprinted by permission from The Horn Book Magazine 47 (December 1971) 577-584. Copyright © 1971 by Lloyd Alexander. Mr. Alexander, noted American fantasy writer, Newbery and National Book Award winner, uses Welsh folk literature as a basis for his work.

lieve--despite Oh! Calcutta! If not quite sisters, Lysistrata and Lena of I Am Curious (Yellow) are distant cousins under the skin. However much their forms and functions have changed, the arts show a line of organic growth from a common ancestry. Poetry, dance, theatre, comedy, and tragedy have roots in the most ancient religious rituals. The first language of art was the language of magic and mythology. And decoding this language has long been a study--for poets, philosophers, philologists, and psychiatrists.

Most recently, the structural anthropologist Claude Lévi-Strauss in The Savage Mind and in The Raw and the Cooked has tried to analyze man's capacity for myth-making and the processes at work in primitive thought. Despite speculations and insights, the original meanings of a great many, perhaps most, of our earliest legends are still as shadowy as the ancient ceremonies they mirror. We glimpse the seasonal progress of sacred kings in a calendar of birth, death, and resurrection. But the substance of these mysteries is long lost, or preserved only in fragments: a fairy tale may hint at figures in forgotten dramas, or a child's game of hopscotch pattern the Minotaur's labyrinth.

While its full meaning remains tantalizingly unknown, we can still trace mythology's historical growth into an art form: through epic poetry, the chansons de geste, the Icelandic sagas, the medieval romances and works of prose in the Romance languages. Its family tree includes Beowulf, the Eddas, The Song of Roland, Amadis de Gaule, the Perceval of Chrétien de Troyes, and The Faerie Queene.

In modern literature, one form that draws most directly from the fountainhead of mythology, and does it consciously and deliberately, is the heroic romance, which is a form of high fantasy. The world of heroic romance is, as Professor Northrop Frye defines the whole world of literature in The Educated Imagination, "the world of heroes and gods and titans ... a world of powers and passions and moments of ecstasy far greater than anything we meet outside the imagination."[1]

If anyone can be credited with inventing the heroic romance as we know it today--that is, in the form of a novel using epic, saga, and chanson de geste as some of its raw materials--it must be William Morris, in such books as The Wood Beyond the World and The Water of the Wondrous Isles. Certainly Morris showed the tremendous strength and poten-

tial of the heroic romance as an artistic vehicle, which was
later to be used by Lord Dunsany, Eric Eddison, James
Branch Cabell; by C. S. Lewis and T. H. White. Of course,
heroic romance is the basis of the superb achievements of
J. R. R. Tolkien.

Writers of heroic romance, who work directly in the
tradition and within the conventions of an earlier body of
literature and legend, draw from a common source: the "Pot
of Soup," as Tolkien calls it, the "Cauldron of Story," which
has been simmering away since time immemorial. [2]

The pot holds a rich and fascinating kind of mythological minestrone. Almost everything has gone into it, and
almost anything is likely to come out of it: morsels of real
history, spiced--and spliced--with imaginary history, fact
and fancy, daydreams and nightmares. It is as inexhaustible
as those legendary vessels that could never be emptied.

Among the most nourishing bits and pieces we can
scoop out of the pot are whole assortments of characters,
events, and situations that occur again and again in one form
or another throughout much the world's mythology: heroes
and villains, fairy godmothers and wicked stepmothers, princesses and pig-keepers, prisoners and rescuers; ordeals and
temptations, the quest for the magical object, the set of
tasks to be accomplished. And a whole arsenal of congno-
minal swords, enchanted weapons; a wardrobe of cloaks of
invisibility, seven-league boots; a whole zoo of dragons,
helpful animals, birds, and fish.

But--in accordance with one of fantasy's own conven-
tions-- nothing is given for nothing. Although we are free
and welcome to ladle up whatever suits our taste, and fill
ourselves with any mixture we please, nevertheless, we have
to digest it, assimilate it as thoroughly as we assimilate the
objective experiences of real life. As conscious artists, we
have to process it on the most personal levels; let it work on
our personalities and, above all, let our personalities work
on it. Otherwise we have what the computer people delicately
call GIGO: garbage in, garbage out.

Because these conventional characters--these personae
of myth and fairy tale, though gorgeously costumed and capa-
risoned--are faceless, the writer must fill in their expressions. Colorful figures in a pantomime, the writer must give
them a voice.

Since I have been talking about the "Cauldron of Story," I am now reminded of the Crochan, the Black Cauldron that figured in one of the books of Prydain. Now, cauldrons of one sort or another are common household appliances in the realm of fantasy. Sometimes they appear, very practically, as inexhaustible sources of food, or, on a more symbolic level, as a lifegiving source or as a means of regeneration. Some cauldrons bestow wisdom on the one who tastes their brew. In Celtic mythology, there is a cauldron of poetic knowledge guarded by nine maidens, counterparts of the nine Greek muses.

There is also a cauldron to bring slain warriors back to life. The scholarly interpretation--the mythographic meaning--is a fascinating one that links together all the other meanings. Immersion in the cauldron represented initiation into certain religious mysteries involving death and rebirth. The initiates, being figuratively--and perhaps literally--steeped in the cult mysteries, emerged reborn as adepts. In legend, those who came out of the cauldron had gained new life but had lost the power of speech. Scholars interpret this loss of speech as representing an oath of secrecy.

One branch of The Mabinogion, the basic collection of Welsh mythology, and one of my own prime research sources, tells of such a cauldron of regeneration, and how it ended up in the hands of the Irish. And, in the tale of Branwen, the Welsh princess rescued from the Irish by King Bran, a great number of slain Irish warriors came back to life. Naturally, this cauldron posed an uncomfortable problem for the Welshmen, who were constantly finding themselves outnumbered; until one of the Welsh soldiers sacrificed his life by leaping into the cauldron and shattering it.

This incident gave me the external shape of the climax of The Black Cauldron (Holt). Though changed and manipulated considerably, the nub of the story is located in the myth--except for one detail of characterization: the essential internal nature of the cauldron, its inner meaning and significance beyond its being an unbeatable item of weaponry.

And so I tried to develop my own conception of the cauldron. Despite its regenerative powers, it seemed to me more sinister than otherwise. The muteness of the warriors created the horror I associated with the cauldron. Somehow, I felt that these voiceless men, already slain, revived only to fight again, deprived even of the oblivion of the grave, were less beneficiaries than victims.

As the idea grew, I began to sense the cauldron as a kind of ultimately evil device. My "Cauldron-Born," then, were not only mute but enslaved to another's will. If they had lost their power of speech, they had also lost their memory of themselves as living beings--without recollection of joy or sorrow, tears or laughter.

They had, in effect, been deprived of their humanity: a fate, in my opinion, considerably worse than death. The risk of dehumanization--of individuals being manipulated as objects instead of being valued as living people--is, unfortunately, not confined to the realm of fantasy.

Another example of the same kind of creative invention on the part of a writer has to do with the birth of a character; and in this case a most difficult delivery. Writing The Book of Three (Holt), the first of the Prydain chronicles, I was groping my way through the early chapters with that queasy sensation of desperate insecurity that comes when you do not know what is going to happen next. I knew vaguely what should happen, but I could not figure out how to get at it. The story, at this point, needed another character: whether friend or foe, minor or major, comic or sinister, I could not decide. I only knew that I needed him, and he refused to appear.

The work came to a screaming halt; the screams being those of the author. Day after day, for better than a week, I stumbled into my work room and sat there, feeling my brain turn to concrete. I had been reading a very curious book, an eighteenth-century account of the various characters in Celtic mythology. One of them stuck in my mind --a one-line description of a creature half-human, half-animal. The account was interesting, but it was not doing much to solve my problem.

I was convinced, by now, that I had suffered severe brain damage; that I would never write again; the mortgage would be foreclosed; my wife carried off to the Drexel Hill poor-farm; and I--quivering and gibbering, moaning and groaning--I did not even dare to imagine what would become of me. The would-be author of a hero-tale had begun to show his innate cowardice, and I was feeling tremendously sorry for myself.

At four o'clock one morning, I had gone to my work room for what had become a routine session of sniveling and

hand-wringing. I had decided, one way or another, to use
this hint of a half-animal, half-human creature. The eighteenth-century text had given him a name--Gurgi. It seemed
to fit, but he still refused to enter the scene. I could see
him, a little; but I could not hear him. If I could only make
him talk, half the battle would be over. But he would not
talk.

And so I sat there, expecting to pass the morning as
usual, crying and sighing. All of a sudden, for no apparent
reason whatever, I heard a voice in the back of my mind,
plaintive, whining, self-pitying. It said: "Crunchings and
munchings?" And there, right at that moment, there he
was. Part of him, certainly, came from research. The
rest of him--I have a pretty good idea where it came from.

My point, in these examples, is simply this: a writer
of fantasy, like any writer, must find the essential content of
his work within himself, in his own personality, in his own
attitude and commitment to real life. Whatever form we work
in--fantasy or realism, books for children or for adults--I
believe that the fundamental creative process is the same. In
his work, the author may be very heavily disguised, or altogether anonymous. I do not think he is ever totally absent.

On the contrary, his presence is required; not as a
stage manager who can be seen busily shifting the cardboard
scenery, but as the primary source of tonality and viewpoint.
Without this viewpoint, the work becomes more and more abstract, a play of the intellect that can move us only intellec-
tually. It may be technically brilliant, but it becomes sleight
of hand instead of true magic. If art--as Plato defined it--
is a dream for awakened minds, it should be, at the same
time, a dream that quickens the heart.

High fantasy indeed quickens the heart and reaches
levels of emotion, areas of feeling that no other form touches
in quite the same way. Some books we can enjoy, some we
can admire, and some we can love. And among those books
that we love as children, that we remember best as adults,
fantasy is by no means least. It would be interesting to cal-
culate how many of the classic works of children's literature
are works of fantasy.

The logical question is: what makes fantasy so memorable? Unfortunately, art is not always susceptible to logical
analysis, or at least not to the same patterns of logic that

apply in other areas. Instead of provable answers, we have
possibilities, hints, and suggestions. The most obvious answers are the least accurate. Fantasy can be considered an
escape from complex reality to a more simplistic world, the
yearning for a past that never existed, or a vehicle for re-
gression. Attractive as these answers may be, fantasy offers no such escapes from life. It can refresh and delight,
certainly; give us a new vision; make us weep or laugh.
None of these possibilities constitutes escape, or denial of
something most of us begin to suspect at a rather early age:
that being alive in the world is a hard piece of business.

There may be subtler forces at work. In even the
wildest flights of fantasy, there seems to be an undercurrent
of rationality. On its own terms and in its own frame of
reference, the fantasy world makes a certain kind of sense.
If there are ambiguities, they are recognizable as such.
The fantasy realm includes superb villains--utterly fiendish
and irretrievably wicked--but no neurotics. The story does
not move as the result of irrational behavior, capricious-
ness, or sudden whim. The "bad guys" have very good
reasons for perpetrating whatever villainy they have in mind.

And there is always the possibility of effective action.
The hero wants to do something, he can do something, and
he actually does do something. So much of current adult
literature offers us the anti-hero: I might say the hero as
clodpole, the hero as a crashing bore, or as an existential
loser. The fantasy hero may lose, too. But in the process,
at least, he has made some effort to cope with his environment. He may be a sacrificial figure but never a passive
victim.

The fantasy hero is not only a doer of deeds, but he
also operates within a framework of morality. His compassion is as great as his courage--greater, in fact. We might
even consider that his humane qualities, more than any others,
are what the hero is really all about. I wonder if this re-
minds us of the best parts of ourselves? A reminder, as
Lewis Mumford says, that our potential is greater than our
achievement. An ideal, if we choose to call it that; but an
ideal that may actually be within our reach. We cannot know
for sure unless we do try to reach out for it.

Or, does the vitality of fantasy come from a deeper
source: from its deliberate use of the archaic, the imagery
of our most ancient modes of thought? Jung believes it does,

and spoke eloquently about "primordial images," which at times overpower us and make us aware of what is universal, and therefore eternal. In practice, this point of view seems to have a great amount of truth in it. Whether this also implies, as Jung believed it did, a common racial memory, a collective unconscious, is open to speculation.

We are now starting to wade into some rather deep metaphysical waters. But the "Cauldron of Story," we realize, does not serve up No-Cal carbonated beverage. The brew is considerably stronger. But certainly not too strong for children. They love it and thrive on it; and I believe they need the experience of fantasy as an essential part of growing up.

Strong emotions, moments of triumph or despair, are surely familiar to children. They respond to them and identify with them because these feelings are already a part of their inner lives--lives which, as we are continually discovering, are richer and more complex than we might have imagined, on both an unconscious and conscious level. Graham Greene touches on this in his essay "The Lost Childhood," when he says: "A child ... knows most of the game.... He is quite well aware of cowardice, shame, deception, disappointment." I think these statements are true. And equally true that the child is aware of courage, pride, and honesty. Greene continues with what I think is the operative phrase: "it is only an attitude ... that he lacks."[3] And here, on this point of attitude, the goals and values of high fantasy merge with those of all literary and artistic forms. Each work of art, in its own way, suggests a possible attitude toward life: a variety of life-styles, ways of seeing ourselves and others.

George Steiner, in his book Language and Silence, says: "the critic ... must ask of it [contemporary literature] not only whether it represents a technical advance ... or plays adroitly on the nerve of the moment, but what it contributes to or detracts from the dwindled reserves of moral intelligence." High fantasy as we write it today must, of necessity, be included as contemporary literature, whether its apparent content pretends to look back to an imaginary past or ahead to a future (that may or may not be altogether imaginary). It must be able to answer the question that Steiner also raises: "What is the measure of man this work proposes?"[4]

The question is not an abstract one, of merely literary judgments, but fundamentally one of how we choose to see ourselves. Shall we measure only our present condition, which is far from a happy one? Or is there some larger scale--not only to measure man, but which man can measure up to? Fantasy imagines there is. And if we can dream, maybe we can really measure up to the dream.

Bibliography

1. Northrop Frye. The Educated Imagination. Bloomington: Indiana University Press, 1964, p. 100.

2. J. R. R. Tolkien. Tree and Leaf. Boston: Houghton Mifflin Company, 1965, p. 26.

3. Graham Greene. Collected Essays. New York: Viking Press, 1969, p. 16.

4. George Steiner. Language and Silence: Essays on Language, Literature, and the Inhuman. New York: Atheneum, 1970, p. 9.

PART VI

U. S. A.

FAVORITE FOLK TALES OF THE BRITISH ISLES IN AMERICAN CULTURE AS PERCEIVED BY CHILDREN'S LIBRARIANS

Eloise S. Norton

The growing interest of the American public in its roots and heritage has broad implications for its libraries. Library services for children need to reconsider their place in this movement. After all, the majority of the citizens of the United States have some ancestors from the British Isles.[1] The present study was conducted to determine what 100 children's librarians would perceive to be the most important folktales from the British Isles in the culture of American children.[2] These folktales are an important area of our culture to consider and represent important literature to pass on to children.

This study was structured to answer five basic questions:

(a) From a list of folktales, what are the five most important folk tales from England, from Ireland, from Scotland, from Wales, and from Cornwall, in rank order?

(b) Overall, what are the ten most important folktales, drawing from all these cultures, in U. S. culture?

(c) What culture group of stories is best known and least known to this sample?

(d) How many folktales that are listed are unknown in each culture to this group of librarians?

(e) What are the conclusions and implications for those who work with children and those who prepare these librarians to serve the children?

An attempt was made to prepare a list of important folk tales from the cultures of the British Isles. The examination of the basic or standard children's folklore collections from each culture of the British Isles was the first step in preparing the list; those duplicated were noted. The traditional chapters of several children's literature texts were examined. My twenty years of working with children's materials, as well as my experience as an American child, were drawn upon. In addition, discussions of the project were held with friends considered informed on the subject. It was decided that no comprehensive list could be prepared. Hence, some important stories from each culture were listed, and the participants were provided spaces for write-ins, to list those overlooked. The Welsh list was made in consultation with an English professor who had lived as a child in Wales and England but has been in the United States for the last 15 years. Welsh stories seemed to change titles with each editor or translator and proved to be the most difficult to handle.

The list (see appendix A) of folktales was divided into five sub-groups: England, Ireland, Wales, Cornwall, and Scotland. The respondents were asked to rank the five most important stories in each group and to check the stories that were unfamiliar to them. Then each was requested to draw from the overall list of stories and list the ten stories she or he felt were the most important.

One hundred questionnaires were mailed and 64 replies were received. The random sample was stratified by states and included 24 librarians from the West and 76 from the East. [3] Some of the replies were compiled by groups of librarians, some were by the Children's Services Coordinator, and others were completed by a staff member selected by the coordinator. One coordinator duplicated the questionnaire and sent it to all the children's librarians in her system to respond, so that the returns increased by eight.

Report of Data

ENGLAND

Of the 64 that replied, only 52 made an effort to mark the English section. Of these, seven stories were known by all 52 respondents with nine others known by 45 of them. The folk tales least known to the respondents were the "Three

Wishes of a Fox, "* not known by 22 of the respondents; and
"Travels of a Fox," second, with 14 who did not know this
story.   "Mr. Miacca" and "Mr. Vinegar" tied for third, with
eight not knowing these stories.   Of the 20 folktales, each librarian knew an average of 18.5 stories (93%).

   The result of the ranking can be seen in the following
table.   Of the 20 folktales, twelve were assigned first-place
rank of importance at least once, while five were not assigned any rank by the same person.   Fourteen added entries
were made (see appendix B).   Eleven were not English folktales in the classical sense.   "Robin Hood," Beowulf, and
"Elsie Piddlock Skips in her Sleep" (fiction) may be questionable as folk tales.   "Jack the Giant Killer," "Robin Hood,"
and "Tom Thumb" were added by two respondents.   All the
others were added once.

Most Important Folktales

(1) Three Little Pigs	22
(2) Story of the Three Bears	21
(3) Jack and the Bean Stalk	15
(4) Henny Penny	10
(5) Henny Penny	16

Most Often Receiving No. 1

Story of the Three Bears	21
Three Little Pigs	12
The Old Woman and Her Pig	4
Jack and the Bean Stalk	4
Little Red Hen	3

Most Often Heard

	H	NH
Three Little Pigs	52	0
Dick Whittington and His Cat	52	0
Story of the Three Bears	51	0
Cock Robin	50	0

---

*This was a typing mistake on the instrument and was
not discovered until all the compiling was finished.   This
should have read "Three Wishes."

	H	NH
Three Sillies	50	0
Teeny-Tiny	50	0
Jack and the Bean Stalk	50	0
Henny Penny	49	1

Most Often Not Heard	H	NH
Three Wishes of a Fox	29	22
Travels of a Fox	36	14
Mr. Miacca	43	8
Mr. Vinegar	43	8
Molly Whuppie	46	6
Hare and the Hedgehog	46	6
Master of All Masters	46	6

IRELAND

Of the 64 that replied, only 52 made an effort to mark the Irish section. Of these, none of the folktales was known by all 52 respondents. Six were known to 30 or more respondents. Eleven were known to 20 or more respondents. The folktales least known were "Children of the Salmon" (23 of the respondents), "Little Dermot and the Thirsty Stones" (22), and "Connla and the Fairy Maiden" (22). Of the twelve listed titles, each librarian knew an average of 8.24 (69%) Irish stories.

The results of the ranking can be seen in the following table. First-place ranking was assigned to 11 stories at least once. Only "Connla and the Fairy Maiden" was not assigned first once. Fourteen added entries were included. "Wee Meg Barnileg and the Fairies" was added by three respondents. All the others were added only once. "Sagas of Cuchulain" and "Finn McCool" were included, as well as several well known collections, such as Green's Leprechaun Tales, Pilkington's Shamrock and Spear, and Jacobs' Celtic Fairy Tales.

Most Important Folktales

(1) Old Hag's Long Leather Bag   7

(1) Children of Lir   7
(2) Billy Beg and the Bull   10
(3) Bee, the Harp, the Mouse,
    and the Blum Clock   7
(4) Bee, the Harp, the Mouse,
    and the Blum Clock   6
(5) Widow's Lazy Daughter   7

Most Often No. 1

Old Hag's Long Leather Bag   7
Bee, the Harp, the Mouse,
    and the Blum Clock   5
Billy Beg and the Bull   5
The Well of the World's End   4

Most Often Heard	H	NH
Widow's Lazy Daughter	36	7
Children of Lir	33	9
The Well of the World's End	32	10
Patrick O'Donnell and the Leprechaun	32	11
Billy Beg and the Bull	32	11
Bee, the Harp, the Mouse, and the Blum Clock	32	11

Most Often Not Heard	H	NH
Children of the Salmon	21	23
Little Dermot and the Thirsty Stones	22	22
Connla and the Fairy Maiden	22	22
The Old Hag's Long Leather Bag	15	28
Peddler of Ballaghhaderseen	15	28

SCOTLAND

Fifty-one of the 64 who replied made an effort to
mark the Scotland section. No one of the ten folktales was
known by all 51 respondents. Thirty or more knew "All in
the Morning Early" and "Wee Bannock." Four stories were

known by 20 or more respondents.   The least known were
"Fairy Flag of Dunnigan" and "Page Boy and the Silver Goblet."   Each respondent knew an average of 5.2 (52%) of the
ten stories listed.

The table which follows reveals the ranking results.
Of the ten folktales listed, six were assigned first place at
least once.   One added entry, "Always Room for One More,"
was given first place by a respondent.   All of the folktales
listed placed at least once in the ranking of first, second,
third, fourth, or fifth order.   Nine added entries were made.
Among these were one collection, <u>Heather and Broom</u> (Nic
Leodhas), and "Loch Ness Monster."

Most Important Folktales

(1) All in the Morning Early	13
(2) Wee Bannock	9
(3) Black Bull of Narroway	9
(4) Assipattle and the Giant Sea Serpent	7
(5) Wee Bannock	5

Most Often No. 1

All in the Morning Early	13
Wee Bannock	8
Tam Lin	5
Black Bull of Narroway	4
Whippety Stourie	2

Most Often Heard

	H	NH
All in the Morning Early	35	6
Wee Bannock	34	5
Black Bull of Narroway	29	13
Tam Lin	23	17
Assipattle and the Giant Sea Serpent	19	20
Whippety Stourie	18	21

Most Often Not Heard

	H	NH
Fairy Flag of Dunnigan	27	8

	H	NH
Page Boy and the Silver Goblet	26	9
Perrifool	23	12
The Brownie O'Ferne-Den	22	13
Whippety Stourie	21	14
Assipattle and the Giant Sea Serpent	20	15

WALES

Fifty-two of the 64 respondents made an effort to communicate with us about the Welsh section. None of the 12 stories was known by all respondents. Only four stories were known by 20 or more respondents. The least known story was "The Sigh of Gwyddn Long Shank" (38 respondents), with "Rhitta of the Beards" (37) running a close second. Each respondent knew 3.6 (30%) of the Welsh stories listed.

The results of the ranking of the 12 folktales are listed in the following table. Nine were assigned first place rank at least once. Only one was not assigned any rank, "Rhitta of the Beards." There were 10 added entries. Arthurian legends were listed twice. Two collections, Pugh's Tales from Welsh Hills and Jones' Welsh Legends and Folktales, were listed.

Most Important Folktales

(1) Where Arthur Sleeps	6
(2) The Man Who Killed His Greyhound	5
(3) Where Arthur Sleeps	5
(4) The Quest for Olwen	3
(5) The Quest for Olwen	4

Most Often No. 1

Where Arthur Sleeps	6
The Lad Who Returned from Faerye	5
Lleu and the Flower Face	3
Harp on the Water	2

Most Often Heard	H	NH
Where Arthur Sleeps	26	26
The Lad Who Returned From Faerye	24	26
The Quest for Olwen	23	28
A Harp on the Water	22	29

Most Often Not Heard	H	NH
The Sigh of Gwyddn Long Shank	38	10
Rhitta of the Beards	37	14
Lleu and the Flower Face	35	15
The Dream of Macsen Wledig	34	17
The Man Who Killed His Greyhound	33	18

CORNWALL

Of the 64, 52 respondents marked the Cornish section. Only eight folktales were listed, and "Duffy and the Devil" was known to all respondents except one. "Peter and the Piskies" and "Parson Wood and the Devil" were known to 20 or more of the respondents. Over 30 of the respondents did not know "Skerry Werry," "Skillywidden," "The Knockers," and "Lyonesse." Of the eight stories listed, the respondents knew an average of 3.8 (48%) stories.

The chart below conveys the ranking order of folktales from Cornwall. Five stories were assigned first place at least once. All stories placed somewhere in the ranking process. "Lutey and the Mermaid" and "Betty Stag's Baby" were the added entries.

Most Important Folktales |
---|---
(1) Duffy and the Devil | 31
(2) Peter and the Piskies | 15
(3) Skillywidden | 6
(3) Parson Wood and the Devil | 6
(4) Parson Wood and the Devil | 7
(5) Skerry Werry | 5

Most Often No. 1

Duffy and the Devil	31
Peter and the Piskies	10

Most Often Heard

Duffy and the Devil	43
Peter and the Piskies	30
Parson Wood and the Devil	23

Most Often Not Heard

Lyonesse	39
Skillywidden	34
The Knockers	28
Parson Wood and the Devil	26

When asked to list the ten most important stories drawing from all cultures of the British Isles, the respondents replied as follows:

Twenty Most Important Stories

1.	Story of the Three Bears	E
2.	Three Little Pigs	E
3.	Henny Penny	E
4.	Jack and the Beanstalk	E
5.	Little Red Hen	E
6.	The Old Woman and Her Pig	E
7.	Duffy and the Devil	C
8.	Tom Tit Tot	E
9.	Dick Whittington and His Cat	E
10.	All in the Morning Early	S
11.	Mollie Whuppie	E
12.	Wee Bannock	S
13.	Well of the World's End	I
14.	Teeny-Tiny	E
15.	Black Bull of Narroway	S
16.	Three Sillies	E
17.	Children of Lir	I
18.	Master of All Masters	E
19.	Old Hag's Long Leather Bag	I
20.	Mr. Miacca	E

There were 59 stories listed on the questionnaire. The average number of checks (an indication the respondent did not know the story) of all the respondents from the East was 25.4 stories. From the West it was 25.3 stories.

Four of the respondents listed only English stories in the ten most important folktales section. Seventeen respondents' lists consisted of mostly English (over 60%), while 14 listed at least 50% English stories. A very mixed-culture list was submitted by nine respondents, and no response was attempted by 13.

The computation of the ten most important stories drawn from all the cultures were all English with the exception of the seventh in rank, "Duffy and the Devil" (Cornish), and the tenth, "All in the Morning Early" (Scottish).

Duffy and the Devil (Farrar Straus, 1973), the picture book, has been rewritten by Harve Zemach with illustrations by Margot Zemach. This picture book won the Caldecott Prize in 1974. It is a variant of the German story "Rumpelstiltskin," or "Rumpelstiltskin" may be a variant of "Duffy and the Devil." Eighth on the list, "Tom Tit Tot" is the English variant of "Duffy and the Devil" or "Rumpelstiltskin." "Whippety Stourie" is the Scottish version of the same story, but it did not place in the top twenty folktales. It was known to 14 respondents.

The picture book, All in the Morning Early (Holt, Rinehart, and Winston, 1963), has been recorded by Sorche Nic Leodhas and illustrated by Evaline Ness. It is also a Scottish nursery tale told to the recorder by her grandfather. It is interesting to note that the most important Scottish folktale first recorded was in 1963 in picture book form.

All of the top ten selected have been released as picture books. Either the availability of the folktale as a picture book has had considerable influence on the respondents' choices, or the most important folktales have found their way into picture book form. Most of the commentary by the respondents reflected that they felt the picture-book format has greatly influenced how well a story like "Duffy and the Devil" is known, and therefore how important it is to our culture.

Several respondents suggested that picture books had made popular some folktales which originally lacked real

merit as stories for children.   Barbara Wolfson, Nassau Library System, cited "Mr. Miacca" as an example.   "Mr.
Miacca" placed twentieth in the most important stories section.
She stated, "This was first brought to my attention by a bor-
rower who complained.   I had several librarians child-test it
["Mr. Miacca"] on our own children ... Kindergarten to Grade
Three.   All children seemed to regard us with astonishment,
or perhaps betrayal, that we seemed to find this story fit to
tell. ...   I for one was disgusted that Bettleheim in The Uses
of Enchantment[4] pretended throughout his book that what he
had to say had universal application.   The least he could have
done was point out that he drew from highly parochial sources. "

    Several others commented that the picture book, Mr.
Miacca, an English Folktale, illustrated by Evaline Ness
(Holt, Rinehart, and Winston, 1967), has certainly made this
story popular.   Another commented, "Many of these tales
are so useful or popular in libraries because of a particularly
attractive edition, but [that] does not make the folktales themselves inherently 'important'. "

    A list of folktales was given to librarians at an in-
service meeting in Houston, Texas (Independent School District) about twenty years ago.   The introduction states that
the "list was prepared by the National Council of Teachers of English* ... and these are folk and fairy tales
that should be in the heritage of every child. "   They were
listed in rank order.   The top five were very interesting:

    1.   The Three Bears (listed first in this study)--Eng-
    lish
    2.   Little Red Riding Hood--French
    3.   Three Little Pigs (listed second in this study)--
    English
    4.   Cinderella--French
    5.   Jack and the Bean Stalk (listed fourth in this study)
    --English

    In this current study, of the top ten most important
stories, six were nursery tales.   The other four were suitable for kindergarten, first, and second grades.   One librarian commented, "the stories heard earliest have the greatest

---

*NCTE headquarters has been unable to furnish any
confirmation or information about this list.

influence.   The English stories are largely nursery tales and hardly comparable to stories for older boys and girls. "

In the second ten most important (11-20), the selection of folktales seems to be for an older group.   "Teeny-Tiny" and "Three Sillies" could be the exceptions to this.   Of the second ten, five have been released as picture books.

Five of the second ten were English stories, two were Scottish and three were Irish.   None of the top 20 selected was Welsh.   In the overall top 20, 13 were English, three were Scottish, one was Cornish, and three were Irish.

The label "important" caused the most comment from the respondents.   Eleven respondents wrote both long and short comments about their problems with this word.   The cover letter stated that the checklist was being sent out to librarians to determine the importance of various folktales from the British Isles in American culture.   This statement was left off the instrument because it was feared it might overwhelm the librarians into not responding.   This omission may be the main weakness of this study.

Nevertheless, several picked up the purpose of the study from the cover letter and indicated that they did not consider themselves as being knowledgeable enough about how these stories fit into our culture to respond confidently. Others stated the same but did respond as to their use of this literature in the children's room.

An answer based on their experience was the hopeful response.   The realm of their education, work as children's librarians, and their personal experience as children in the United States were what they had to bring to this study. Certainly, variables would enter into their decisions; most requested, best liked for storytelling, comments from conversations noted ("I'll hoof and poof and blow your house down," "the sky is falling down"), most familiar or best known, availability, meaningfulness to children.   Variables were not being considered in this study, only the perception of the librarian as to their merit or importance at this time.

One librarian conveyed her difficulty in making these judgments by stating, "I hope you are asking writers and poets and others. "

One librarian from California stated: "My opinion, for

what it is worth, is that these stories are no longer influen-
tial in American culture at large (in the South perhaps, but
I wouldn't know about that).   The stories, undoubtedly, influence writers and children who may write, also preachers
and psychologists.   Their 'importance' to most librarians
lies, in my observation, in how well they can be told or are
liked.... Children's librarians as a group are helping to
keep the stories retold to new generations, but unfortunately
many of these same children's librarians discover the stories
as adults. "

A young professor and his wife, who have lived in the
South all of their lives, were asked to respond to this comment about these British stories being unimportant in American culture today.   They agreed with this statement.   They
stated they felt it was much more important for their son in
his daily life in second grade to know "The Bionic Woman"
(a popular television program) than to know "Jack and the
Beanstalk. "   "It would help him more in play. "   This couple
is third or fourth generation American, of Slavic, Catholic
background.

The classification "important" gave others problems
because "some [stories] fit special categories and have special uses in America, scary for Halloween, Irish tales for
Saint Patrick's Day, English tales with all ages, Welsh because of their complexity, for older, smaller audiences. "

Some very interesting comments were given by respondents concerning their own personal knowledge of the
stories listed on the checklist.   Four questionnaires arrived
three months after they were sent out.   No checks (an indication they did not know the story) were included on these
lists, and each one had added choices of their own.

Some of the early comments concerning their knowledge
about the stories were:

> "I am embarrassed that so few are known to me. "

> "I am shocked at the lack of knowledge of stories
> other than Irish and English.   We will do some-
> thing about this right away. "   (Compilation of a
> group of librarians)

> "I kept a copy so I could find all these stories I've
> never heard of. "

"I am not familiar with these folktales.   In fact,
only this spring we are beginning a storyhour,
Folktales Around the World. "

"I only use stories for pre-school as I am not familiar with the others. "

"I do not feel there are five important stories in
this particular list but can think of no alterna-
tives. "   (Under Scotland and Cornwall sections)

"I am embarrassed by my lack of knowledge of the
above folktales. "

"I really don't know the stories from Wales and
Cornwall well enough to judge. "

"I'm sorry, I don't know these others well enough
to choose. "   (Wales, Scotland, Ireland, Cornwall sections)

"I'm lost here. "   (Wales)

"This is difficult.   Could I mark two sets of five?
One for primary children, say pre-school to
second grade, another, third up through sixth.
I use all these stories. "   (England)

Pre-school--Second	Third and Up
1. Story of Three Bears	1. Molly Whuppie
2. Three Little Pigs	2. Dick Whittington
3. Henny Penny	3. Jack and the Beanstalk
4. Old Woman and Her Pig	4. Three Sillies
5. Tenny-Tiny	5. Tom Tit Tot

Availability is certainly a point to consider.   What
about the availability of stories from parent to child?   Did
all the parents of Irish, Scottish, Welsh heritage tell their
children English stories?   This study would be more valuable
if there were time to check on the British folklore collections
printed in the last thirty years and to verify the availability
of the stories and collections from each culture.   This study
used the collection in the Department of Library Science labo-
ratory collection (a very old collection, 1943-1977), which has
experienced little weeding.   Many of the collections on the
shelves are out of print.   Nevertheless, the collections were
with one predominant culture:

English   10
Irish   12
Scottish   7
Cornish   0
Welsh   2

One librarian stated, "I was struck by how much of our familiarity with all these stories is influenced by the sources available. Through many years we have had the Joseph Jacobs and Padriac Colum and Seuman MacManus collections available, so those are the most familiar tales. More recently the Sorche Nic Leodhas tales from Scotland and Virginia Haviland's popular collections have influenced which stories become known."

IMPLICATIONS

This study, based on sixty-four returns from 100 questionnaires, has revealed some new and informative things about folk literature of the British Isles and American children's libraries.

The five most important English stories were no surprise. Each has been a household staple where children live for many years. The Irish stories were the second best known group. Sixty-nine per cent of the stories were known to respondents.

The Scottish stories are still little known in spite of the very fine work of Sorche Nic Leodhas and others in this area in recent years. Only 52% of these stories were known by librarians.

Welsh stories are more difficult to read and tell. Charlotte Huck states in Children's Literature in the Elementary School (Holt, Rinehart, and Winston, 3rd ed., 1977) that English stories are the first stories most children in the United States hear, because Joseph Jacobs "deliberately adapted them for small children...." Perhaps Welsh stories need a Joseph Jacobs. With the exception of Duffy and the Devil, the Cornish stories have an availability problem. Duffy and the Devil is a picture book available in almost every library in the United States.

English stories have had the most influence on our culture, a culture whose majority is derived from English, Irish, Scottish, and Welsh background.

The comments of the respondents were the most revealing and perhaps the most important part of this study. Several did not want to assume the role of determining or expressing what stories they felt were important in American culture for children. They were happy to state the stories they used for storytelling, the most requested stories, and their own favorite stories; but American children and their culture was not their concern.

The respondents were shocked at their own lack of knowledge about folktales from the British Isles. Several even expressed guilt. Others were defensive.

CONCLUSIONS

1.   Librarians who work with children should know many good stories, but one step better would be to learn good stories from Ireland, Scotland, Africa, etc.

2.   Children's librarians are the most versed group we have in children's literature, but are they well versed enough in the area of folk literature?

3.   Schools of Library Science need to review their curriculum for the librarian who works with children. It may be suffering from "old age."

4.   Continuing Education should do more research to discover what is really needed for the librarian who works with children.

Perhaps our ethnic roots and heritage are not as important to children's librarians as a good story. The two could be easily combined. Using our different cultures as a basis for children's library programming might be very rewarding for the librarian, children, and the community. In this way music, customs, costumes, food, stories and the people could certainly be coordinated. American culture is significant, and all cultures from which it is derived are significant to know about and accept.

Children's librarians may be the best informed group we have in children's literature at this time. As school library media centers require more and more diversity of activity and knowledge, most media specialists insist that they cannot begin to read children's literature to the extent that children's librarians in public libraries can or do.

Would children's librarians know more German stories or French stories? What are the important stories in the American culture from these countries? This might be of interest for future studies.

What does this study say to Schools of Library Science where it is still believed that one course in children's materials is all that is needed by a librarian who works with children? One or even two courses may no longer be enough to learn the basic materials one needs to know to be a specialist. On the job she or he will be devoted to the new material each year. The more the budget is cut, the more the children's librarian needs basic or background knowledge about children's literature in order to be selective.

Perhaps more courses should be required in children's literature for those who work with children. One could be Folk Literature for Children. The option of a proficiency test to remove this requirement might be made available to the student who has had undergraduate courses, experience working with children's books, or a good background in children's literature. A broader, basic knowledge of children's literature might be possible for the children's specialist, given this provision. Another possible option is the re-evaluation of the selections for a "Children's Literature Anthology" for the one course now required. The trend in Schools of Library Science is to move as far away from anthologies as possible. A good world anthology of folk literature for children would be a helpful resource for a student with a poor background in folk literature.

In some states, the basic course in children's literature is being split into an early childhood course (pre-school to grade three) and middle childhood (grades three to eight). New teacher certification requirements for an Early Childhood Specialist Degree lends itself to a special course in materials for these two age groups. Both courses are required for certification for the kindergarten through eighth grade elementary school teachers, but they are not required for librarians who serve in the same schools as these teachers.

The purpose of this research was not to re-design the library education program for children's librarians but to point out how outdated this program may be in many accredited library schools where most of these respondents would have earned masters degrees. It might be suitable to pass some of the guilt these librarians feel on to the trainers.

Hopefully, more librarians will have an opportunity to attend and/or sponsor continuing education activities in children's literature in specialized areas, e.g. folklore, fantasy, science fiction, so that more in-depth information can be obtained in these several areas. Very generalized sessions where librarians hear several authors discuss their latest book are stimulating, but the long-range value may be questionable.

This inquiry into the extent to which British folktales are used may change little in the area of children's library service, but the responses from the questionnaires clearly indicated that stimulation and guidance in continuing to learn about children's literature is needed.

Notes

1. Encyclopedia Americana, © 1976, Vol. 27, p. 525.

2. These librarians were selected randomly from Children's Services Division's (American Library Association) 1975 Directory of Coordinators of Children's Services and of Young Adult Services in Public Library Systems serving at least 100,000 people.

3. The State lines of Texas/Arkansas, Kansas/Missouri, Nebraska/Iowa, Dakotas/Minnesota were the East/West dividing line.

4. Knopf, 1976.

OUR BRITISH FOLK HERITAGE--
IMPLANTED OR SHELVED?

A Study of Major Texts Used in College
Courses in Children's Literature

Ada McCaa Sumrall

There is great interest in the backgrounds of the
American people as we begin our third century as a nation,
with the stimulus of historical research into the past two
centuries, with families looking for information about their
ancestors, with the impact of the novel and the motion picture Roots; the stage should be set for acceptance of the
traditional lore for most Americans, whose ancestors came
from the British Isles. [1]

Are we losing our folk heritage? How is a country's
lore transmitted? Is it important to the times? What can
be done to preserve in the minds and hearts of our people
what was once basic?

An idea lost to a generation may be a lost idea; a
gem of folk literature undiscovered by children may never be
transmitted to a future generation. The heritage of folk literature of the British Isles is basic to American culture.

The majority of United States citizens have ancestry
in the British Isles--England, Scotland, Ireland and/or Wales.
If the folk literature of this region is to be preserved, it

must be shared with each generation's offspring and trans-
mitters. Librarians, college professors, school teachers,
parents, grandparents, all share in the responsibility of
"passing on" the traditional literature which they possess.
In the training of teachers and librarians, the college professor of children's literature has a major responsibility as
a transmitter, for this influences the selection of books and
children's reading.

Are text books designed primarily for college courses
in children's literature, in an effort to meet pressing current
needs, deleting the folk heritage of the literature of the British Isles? Cultures in America whose traditional folk literature has been neglected are now being heard--Native Americans, Chicanos, Afro-Americans, Orientals--and new editions
of text books are including all types of lore from their ancestral lands. Is this crowding out the folk literature of the
British Isles?

To seek an answer to this question, a survey was
made of the folk literature of the British Isles included in
nine major text books (four of these with only three publish-
ers--Scott Foresman; Holt, Rinehart & Winston; and Macmillan) compiled, respectively, by Arbuthnot & Sutherland,
Hollowell, Huck & Young, and Meigs et al. Each of these
is in at least a second edition, and their printing dates cover
the last forty years. Is there a trend in their inclusions in
this area? These four are also compared with five single-
edition texts published within the last eight years by five different publishers (Wadsworth, Prentice-Hall, Random House,
Science Research Associates, and McGraw-Hill) and written,
respectively, by Anderson & Groff, Georgiou, Lonsdale &
Mackintosh, Sebesta & Iverson, and Smith.

Hollowell (1939), with the earliest copyright date, has
the least recent revised date, 1966; Arbuthnot (now Sutherland), the most recent, 1977. Arbuthnot might have been
considered in the four editions for which she was largely responsible, and then Sutherland considered as a new work,
though the latter still carries much of material from the early editions. For the six-year period, 1968-1975, four new
texts have appeared, with three coming out almost in successive years: 1972, 1973, 1975. In almost forty years only
four major texts, which continued to be updated, were published; in the past six years there are five texts with five
different publishers, not one included in the previous forty-
year group. Only three publishers were involved for forty

years: Holt, Rinehart, and Winston published Huck's and
Hollowell's texts; two others, Scott Foresman and Macmillan,
published Arbuthnot and Meigs.

Eighteen editions, spanning approximately forty years
(1939-1977), of nine major text books used in teaching college courses in children's literature are surveyed here in an
attempt to determine if the folk lore of the British Isles is
being omitted. If teachers, parents, librarians lose knowledge of stories, poems, legends of these folk so rich in native lore centuries old, who will transmit this to the children
of this day?

Since there are no myths from the British Isles or
fables in the truest sense of the term, though these are included in the overall coverage of folk literature in texts, they
are not treated separately in this study. Modern fantasy often
includes stories based on folk themes or plots, but since each
has a literary author rather than one who translated, edited,
or retold the story, they are not included.

Folk literature from the British Isles here includes the
four countries of England, Scotland, Ireland, and Wales, although some texts treat Wales separately from the other three.
Cornwall and the Isles of Great Britain are often treated as
sub-areas; in this study there are no geographical sub-divi-
sions. Sebesta treats the folk literature in a chapter entitled "Picture Books and Folk Literature" which includes
true folk tales along with modern fantasy and other picture
books which have no traditional base. Since some of the
works do not give any breakdown of folk literature by countries, it becomes difficult to compare the extent of inclusion.

The terms traditional and folk literature are used syno-
nymously here. The types to be studied are: "Mother
Goose"--rhymes and jingles and nursery rhymes without literary authorship; folk tales--simple stories with folk characters, sometimes called hero tales, or treated in texts under
character types such as witches, little people, animal, or
even plot patterns such as cumulative tales, epics, ballads,
legends and fairy tales.

Definitions: Folk Literature, Folk Tale, Fairy Tale
_____

Folk literature as a portion of universal literature
belongs to everyone--growing out of the oral story-

telling tradition, folk literature reflects and pre-
serves the unscientific thinking, feeling, superstitions, faith, and dreams of simple peoples the
world around. A body of tales rooted in a humanistic tradition. [2]

The folk tale is part of the oral story telling tradition of a people. Told primarily to present moral values or explanations of the environment. --An
ethic is always present in a folk tale. --The good
and the humble are always rewarded with riches or
a marriage to royalty--the irrational, the proud,
the foolish are always punished. [3]

Fairy tale--strain of folk literature which embodies
a universal truth in highly imaginative, fanciful
form. Use of extraordinary and supernatural happenings differentiate it from other tales of folklore. [4]

Definitions: Ballads, Epics, Folk Tales,
Hero Tales and Legends

To clarify and differentiate these terms as they are
used in this study definitions are necessary. Also an attempt is made to show the various groupings as the terms
are used in the texts.

Arbuthnot (1957) defines the epic as an "heroic narra-
tive--strongly national in its presentation of human character. "[5] Epics may be in prose or in verse form. Arbuthnot
(1947) defines the epic "the glorification of man, the doer,
the hero. "[6] In the latest edition (1977) the influence of society on man is identified: "tales of human heroes buffeted
violently by gods and humanity but daring greatly, suffering
uncomplainingly, and enduring staunchly to the end. Such
tales, having a human hero as the focus of the action and
embodying the ideals of a culture, are called epics, the ce-
ment of society. Legends are not a separate form. They
are any story coming down from the past particularly taken
as historical though not verifiable. "[7]

"Ballads are short narrative poems which have been
adapted for singing or give the effect of a song, usually with
refrains and a dramatic and rapidly unfolding plot especially
those recounting a legendary event. "[8]

Some difficulties which arose in making the planned comparisons of the various texts were the different viewpoints and basic thrusts of each author. For example, Meigs is an historical accounting of the entire area of children's literature. Part I, "Roots in the Past," covers the areas of folk literature in completeness and with enriching thoughts. The second edition has only editorial revision for Part I and thus does not reveal trends. This work is for scholars and those interested in an in-depth background study of the field. Perhaps Meigs should not have been included in this study; it is thus treated separately in most instances.

Hollowell, on the other hand, is an anthology-text, as almost all of the selections mentioned are, printed with full texts of the stories, poems, fables, etc. A literary analysis is given, which makes it especially suitable for courses taught in English departments. Knowledge of the selections as literary works is the chief emphasis. The latest copyright date is 1966, which makes it difficult to compare with 1976 and 1977 editions as to inclusions and omissions.

Huck's purpose is a practical combination of presenting the literature and ways of using it with children. Thus pages devoted to folk literature may be only half on the literature itself and the other half on its use. Again comparison is difficult.

Arbuthnot's love of and appreciation for folk literature permeates her texts. She gives title-by-title keen evaluation of selections and their appropriate place in a child's life.

The five new texts vary greatly in coverage, approach, and emphasis. Anderson (1972) devotes nearly half of the book to Part II, "Types and Uses of Children's Literature," and in the folklore section uses eleven pages on an in-depth examination of the plot structure of one fairy tale; another story is compared in several translations. Part III deals with "Teaching Literature to Children" and Part IV is a one-hundred page annotated bibliography. This design defies comparison with other texts. Georgiou (1969) allows four chapters, in whole or in part--History of Children's Literature; Folk Tales; Fairy Tales; Myths, Fables and Legends--to the traditional, but a limited index, which does not list titles found in bibliographies, causes overlooking of works actually discussed. Lonsdale's (1973) approach is to the child's experience with literature and gives full text of a number of selections. Again bibliographic listings, which are extensive,

are not included in the index.   Sebesta (1975) gives many
exercises, games and work-book type questionnaires in presenting selections.   The approach is somewhat akin to a pro-
grammed learning text.   Smith's (1967) viewpoint is the critical one, with no quotes and only eight pictures.

These variants limit the ease and the validity of the
study, yet trends can certainly be substantiated.   Also these
differences in emphasis, inclusions, and indexes influence the
use of folk literature in course content.

Influence of Variants in Indexing and Table of Contents

A comparative look at the extent and comprehensive-
ness of the indexes in the eighteen editions of the textbooks
reveals a very wide range of detail and inclusion.   Also some
editions have used a very small type for the indexes--Huck
(1976), for example--and thus reduce pages by one-fourth
while including more entries.   One text, Meigs, has no subject index in either edition.   Arbuthnot (1972), with the most
extensive indexing, has forty-four three-column pages, and
the 1977 edition has forty pages with reduced spacing, allowing for even more entries.   Huck had the next most comprehensive indexes.

Extensive indexing in which countries are listed and
their fairy tales, folk tales, legends and ballads are clearly
identified, encourages teachers and students of children's
literature to discover and use these selections.

Hollowell, in all editions, has a much more limited
index but offsets this with the most extensive Table of Contents.   Since Hollowell gives the full text of the selections
and lists each in the Table of Contents, this is an excellent
source to supplement the now available children's books of
folk literature.

The study is based principally on a rapid survey of
these eighteen texts, using largely the index and/or table of
contents of each.   Bibliographies at the ends of chapters on
folk literature were examined and descriptive passages noted.
Modern fantasy and fairy tales are not included, although picture books based on traditional lore are sometimes interfused
with the earlier tales and are thus included.   Trends that
seem obvious may be questioned, but they are evident to the
writer.

Mother Goose: All Mother Goose Belongs to England

The traditional Mother Goose rhymes handed down by
word of mouth are the ones included in this study. Overlap-
ping are other nursery rhymes, ABC books, counting books,
tongue twisters, riddles, days of the week verses, and
months of the year jingles; and these are, in many cases, included because separation was not possible. All Mother
Goose belongs to England although Perrault's eight stories in
his Contes de ma Mère l'Oye (Tales of Mother Goose) were
translated into English and perhaps helped launch John Newbery into publishing and proving that there was a market for
children's books. These stories--"Sleeping Beauty," "Little
Red Riding Hood," "Blue Beard," "Master Cat" or "Puss in
Boots," "Diamonds and Toads," "Cinderella" or the "Little
Glass Slipper," "Riquet with the Tuft," and "Little Thumb"--
are now more commonly classified as folk tales or fairy
tales than as traditional Mother Goose rhymes or jingles, and
will be discussed as such.

Robert Powell's puppet shows (1709-1711) exhibited in
London popularized the name of Mother Goose. The Goose-
footed Bertha of France perhaps introduced a visual concept
of Mother Goose to future artists, but the traditional dame
who came to our shores with the Pilgrims and the Puritans
is the one whose life we need to insure.

Arbuthnot devotes twenty-seven pages to Mother Goose
in 1947, only twenty in 1957, eighteen pages in both 1964 and
1972 editions, and only ten in Sutherland (1977). Hollowell
dropped from ten pages (1939 & 1950) to seven in 1966.
Huck (1961) gives historic background to Mother Goose but
opens the discussion with the idea of children in the colonies
having access to Mother Goose. She discredits historical
basis for these rhymes and doesn't claim their British origin.
Seven pages are devoted to their appeal to children and to a
discussion of editions English and American. One column is
devoted to English editions, with the inclusion of Kate Greenaway, Arthur Rackham, Leslie Brooke, and more recent editions of Kathleen Lines (1954); six columns are given to
American editions listed as the best and include Feodor Ro-
jankovsky, Blanche Fisher Wright, Tasha Tudor, Marguerite
De Angeli, Gustaf Tenggren. Huck (1969) has six pages of
Mother Goose but only added new editions and single editions
plus a section on the evaluation of the many new titles.
Among the artists added in this edition who are producing
Mother Goose books are Joan Walsh Anglund, Philip Reed,

Paul Galdone, Antonio Fransconi, Maurice Sendak, Barbara Cooney, and Juliet Kepes. Huck (1976) has much the same coverage as the earlier editions, with no emphasis on the traditional background of the verses. Barbara Cooney's Mother Goose in French and Mother Goose in Spanish are mentioned and also Robert Wyndham's Chinese Mother Goose Rhymes as new variants. Brian Wildsmith's Mother Goose contrasts the rich and the poor on opposite pages, he being "mindful of the Medieval origin of some of the Mother Goose rhymes, "9 Huck's only reflection of them as traditional works.

The five new texts by Anderson, Georgiou, Lonsdale, Sebesta, and Smith range from one to six pages devoted to discussion of these jingles, with little or no identification of selections as being Mother Goose. The term is not used as an author entry in the indexes; in some texts, only when a title begins with Mother Goose is there any entry. Criticism of these rhymes and jingles as not meeting literary standards, not being credited as traditional, or not being pertinent to a child's experiences are reasons given for their omission.

Anderson (1972), in one page of text, explains why Mother Goose appeals to young children and further states, "A qualified representative of modern Mother Goose is Brian Wildsmith's illustrated collection, though he only uses a part of each verse to leave room for his illustrations. "10 Paul Galdone is mentioned as making a "more intense use of nursery rhymes for picture books. "11 In a 107-page list of books for children, only one page is given to Mother Goose and only five compilers/illustrators are listed, with one title each except for Peter Spier whose Mother Goose Library series is included. The others are Raymond Briggs, Leslie Brooke, Marguerite De Angeli and Brian Wildsmith. There is no reference to this Mother Goose bibliography in the Index or in the Table of Contents. Mother Goose as folk literature is not presented.

Georgiou (1969), in six pages, one-half illustrations, does give excellent descriptions of the types of illustrations found in collections. Credit is given to Newbery, to Caldecott, and to Leslie Brooke and others. Only brief reference is made to the English background. "Along with some adverse criticism--poets have alluded repeatedly to the literary significance of certain Mother Goose rhymes. Walter de la Mare defined them as 'tiny masterpieces of word craftsmanship. '"12

Lonsdale (1973) devotes a little over two pages to the origin and background of Mother Goose, with mention of Perrault, of an unknown artist as having given us the image of Mother Goose, of John Newbery and Oliver Goldsmith as publishers, of Isaiah Thomas in America as a publisher, and of Iona and Peter Opie's as "most comprehensive collection of nursery and Mother Goose rhymes available today."[13]   There is no reference to England as the source of this folk literature.   The one-page bibliography of Mother Goose is not included in the single index, nor are the titles found in the chapter listings even though there are three entries--Mother Goose, Mother Goose books, and Mother Goose rhymes-- found in the index.

Sebesta (1975) does not use the term Mother Goose until the last page of the three-page index reference, and only once then to state: "Mother Goose rhymes, though reportedly written as political satire, have long been the property of children, appropriated by them along with versified riddles, game-songs and tongue twisters."[14]   No reference is made to their English origin or to English editions of Mother Goose books, or to their having been perhaps the very stimulus for Newbery's giving so much to the printing of children's books.   In the "Booklist: Mother Goose and Other Nursery Rhymes,"[15] which includes twenty-seven titles, the majority are special collections from China, Japan, Spain, France, America, on the Rio Grande, and rewritten and expanded versions such as The Space Child's Mother Goose by Frederick Winsor or Maurice Sendak's Hector Protector and I Went over the Water.

Smith's (1967) two-page index reference to Mother Goose is only to general sources such as Louis Untermeyer's The Golden Treasury of Poetry and books of games and songs. The alphabetical listing by compiler, illustrator, or title does not identify titles as traditional Mother Goose.   Included are Norah Montgomerie's A Book of Scottish Nursery Rhymes and the Opies' Oxford Nursery Rhyme Book.

This survey shows that the traditional Mother Goose rooted in the British Isles is passing out of children's literature tests.   "Children should be exposed to the rhythm and rhyme of Mother Goose.   It is a part of their literary heritage and may serve as their first introduction to the realm of literature."[16]   Children respond to, quote, delight in, and relive Mother Goose rhymes.   They enforce the passing on of these gems of our heritage, but adults could increase the

numbers of rhymes known and insure against their being lost
by having them identified and discussed in children's literature.

Cinderella's Fate

What's Cinderella's real name? That depends on from
whence she came. If France or Germany, Cinderella; if
England, Tattercoats or Catskin; if Scotland, Rushen Coatie;
if Ireland, Fair, Brown and Trembling, or The Girl Who Sat
by the Ashes.

Since Cinderella is one traditional fairy tale that almost everyone knows, this title was surveyed in all eighteen
editions of the children's literature textbooks to discover if
she is being passed on only in the French or German versions and whether the English girl, Tattercoats, perhaps the
oldest of the tales based on this folk character, will pass
from the scene. These are the findings:

Meigs in both editions (1953 and 1969) presents five
of the titles--all except the Irish story, "The Girl Who Sat
by the Ashes. "

Interestingly, Arbuthnot in her first edition (1947) does
not have an entry for "Cinderella" but includes the full text
of "Tattercoats, " though Arbuthnot has few entire selections
in any editions of her texts. Also there is an illustration
from "Tattercoats" by Arthur Rackham. In 1957 "Cinderella"
is listed in three different page references, including one of
Marcia Brown's illustrations and a description of her as being
"as French as the Perraults";[17] however, she retains Arthur
Rackham's illustrations for "Tattercoats" and the complete
text of the story. In the three later editions Arbuthnot does
not even have a reference to "Tattercoats, " although "Cinderella" has as many as eleven page references (1972). Even
"Cinderella" drops in the 1977 edition to only eight page
references. No edition includes "Catskin, " "Rushen Coatie, "
"Fair, Brown and Trembling, " or "The Girl Who Sat By the
Ashes. " If only one version, why not a Welsh, English,
Scottish, or Irish one? Perhaps the new editions of this favorite story which children do enjoy and which are market
successes are being listed.

Huck, in the three editions (1961, 1968, 1976), has
seven, fourteen and twenty-two page references, respectively,

to "Cinderella" as an exercise for children to compare and
evaluate illustrations, literary style, and plot. Could not an
excellent in-depth study of this character and book have been
made, looking at the different cultural backgrounds of Ireland,
Scotland, England and Wales, their own "roots," and a com-
parison of "Cinderella" with "Tattercoats," "Catskin,"
"Rushen Coatie," "Fair, Brown and Trembling," and "The
Girl Who Sat by the Ashes"? Such a study is possible of the
many different versions of the English "Johnny Cake," the
Norwegian "The Pancake," the Russian "The Bun," the Japanese "The Funny Little Woman," the American "Journey
Cake, Ho!" by Ruth Sawyer, and the Southern version "The
Gingerbread Boy." All of these are variants of the Scottish
"The Wee Bannock," which Arbuthnot includes in all five edi-
tions in the discussion of "Native Variants of European Tales,"
though the title is not included in the indexes of the first three
editions and could easily be overlooked. It is in the 1972 and
1977 indexes. Doesn't Cinderella need the same treatment?
The simplest and probably the oldest of them all is "Tattercoats," the English version, and also "Catskin," thoroughly
English.

In the five new single-edition texts--Anderson, Georgiou, Lonsdale, Sebesta, and Smith--only one even refers to
any one of the English, Scottish, or Irish versions of the traditional "Cinderella" story. Anderson compared The Grimms'
and Perrault's telling, but had no reference to the five versions from the British Isles. Georgiou has twelve page references to "Cinderella," no reference to any other version.
Lonsdale compares Marcia Brown's and Walter de la Mare's
versions of Perrault's stories and is the only text among the
eighteen to include "The Girl Who Sat by the Ashes," the
Irish variation. Lonsdale gives the full text of the story,
clearly identifies it as Irish, and discusses the differences
between Padriac Colum's telling and The Grimms' story. [18]
Sebesta and Smith have three to six page references to "Cinderella" but none to the other five of the traditionally Irish,
Scottish and English versions.

"Fairy tales are survivors. Authorless, timeless,
placeless, they are also flawless.... Children like fairy
tales--because they are wonderfully severe and uncondescend-
ing. They like the kind of finality that really slams the
door."[19] Children are doing their part to save fairy tales.
Are adults?

Folk lore of all kinds--Mother Goose, fairy tales,

other folk tales, legends, epics, ballads--coming from England, Ireland, Scotland, and Wales--the heritage of Americans,
must be available and passed on to succeeding generations.

Ballads, Epics, Folk Tales, Hero Tales, Legends

Huck has greatly increased her coverage of traditional
literature from twenty-two pages (1961) to ninety pages (1976),
with a thirteen-page bibliography of 406 titles in the latest
edition. Though there is no breakdown for England, Scotland,
Ireland and Wales under "Folk Tales of the World," British
folk tales appear first and a clear interpretation of their
characteristics is given through discussion of individual titles
with mention of their background--for example, the story of
"Dick Whittington and His Cat," based on the Mayor of London, Richard Whittington. Lusty broad humor, foolish behavior, an element of realism and suitability for young children
are characteristics brought out in the discussion of a number
of the tales. Comparisons are made to French, Russian,
and other European tales.

An outstanding feature of Huck's latest edition (1976)[20]
is the three pages of charts which graphically summarize a
cross-cultural and cultural study of folk tales. The cross-
cultural study includes:

> 1. Types of folk tales: the six types have four to
> five tales each, representing as many cultures. Eng-
> land is included in four of the six, and England and
> Scotland are represented in the cumulative tale.
> 2. Sample motifs: Britain is not represented.
> 3. Sample variants: England is included in three of
> four groups--with England, "Tattercoats"; Cornwall,
> "Duffy and the Devil"; and Scotland, "Whippety Stou-
> rie," all in with only four other countries.

The Cultural Study of Folk Tales includes eight cultures and British is first with six of Joseph Jacobs' typical
tales listed; their characters--Mr. Vinegar, Lazy Jack,
Giants, "wee-folk," and Dick Whittington--and their characteristics are given.

The conclusions seem evident, but let's summarize
them. We who are the balancing wheels--teachers, librarians, parents--must focus on areas of traditional folk literature of the British Isles which are being omitted from col-

lege textbooks and keep the "roots" for most Americans enriched and growing. Publishers, editors, writers, illustrators, booksellers need to be made aware of the opportunities to enrich children's book collections with the folk literature of the British Isles through promotion and production.   Teachers of children's literature should be alert to the need for their being knowledgeable of the wealth of folk lore of the British Isles.   Do colleges need to offer a full course in folk literature suitable for children?   Research may be needed to show what colleges are offering courses in this field.   To whom are the courses open?   How many adequately trained professors are there to teach such courses?

Now that children at a very young age are being taught to read critically by comparing different versions of the same story, a real opportunity is available in the folk tales of the various areas of Britain such as England, Cornwall, Ireland, Wales, Scotland, and the land of the Celts: children will be digging into the roots of their own past heritage.

National Geographic in a recent lead article features the Celts, and its vice-president states, "On the west coast of Ireland and Scotland, in Wales and Brittany and other Celtic domains there is a new pride in the ancient heritage-- the old spirit of the Celts burns again."[21]   The article continues, "robust folklore and customs harken back to prehistoric days."   Asked if there was anything Celtic in twentieth-century Ireland, he said, "A lot.   The folklore.   The fairies or good people.   Some will say 'I don't believe in them'-- but they're there!"[22]

"No type of literature has suffered such persecution as has the folk and fairy tale, nor has any other shown such indomitable and irrepressible vitality.   Considered worldly and immoral in the Puritan period, impractical and frivolous in the didactic age, it has lived from generation to generation in the memories of the common people."[23]   Encouraging is the fact that many picture books and illustrated stories, in single titles and in sequels, based on Irish, Scottish, or Welsh folklore and many more from Britain may be forthcoming.

A four-year-old heard read "The Three Little Pigs"-- no pictures to look at, no book to handle, as was the custom. Complete silence after the reading.   Thinking that this story was not the right one at that time, the reader was surprised ten days later to be greeted at her door by a wee voice, 'I've come to 'huff and puff and blow your house down!'   But

I wouldn't blow your house down and maybe I couldn't.   It's
brick. "   Then, very seriously, the question, "The wolf was
killed when he fell into the hot water, wasn't he?"   "Yes. "
"But he had eaten two little pigs before he was killed. "

     Should any child miss the opportunity to see evil
punished?   To meditate on building a sturdy house?   Traditional themes of folk literature of the British Isles are right-
ing wrong, replacing evil with good, defending the poor and
downtrodden, following the king.   All violence is for a purpose.   These principles of our founding fathers came from
their own traditional lore and must be passed on to each new
generation.   Moral education is currently being emphasized.
Isn't the use of folk literature a means?

     "The tree of Liberty grew and changed and spread,
but the seed was English. "[24]   Keeping those roots nourished,
live and growing, and that culture true in its concepts, can
be achieved in part through traditional folk literature of the
British Isles, implanted in the hearts of children of America
by their teachers, librarians, and their parents.

Notes

1.   First Federal Census, 1790:   83% population in America
     of European background, with 60% English, 14% Scotch
     or Scotch/Irish, 4% Irish, 78% British.   1775-1815--
     hiatus in immigration.... "Whole American-born gene-
     ration grew up detached from and indeed pointedly re-
     jecting their ancestors' homeland. "   The 1820-1970
     census figures on immigration show that of the approxi-
     mately forty-five million entering the U. S. A. from all
     countries of the world, nine and one-half million were
     from England, Ireland, Scotland, and Wales, almost
     one-fourth, against all the rest of the countries of the
     world.   Encyclopedia Americana, 1977, Vol. 27, page
     526.

2.   Georgiou (1960), p. 154.

3.   Ibid., p. 155.

4.   Ibid., p. 186.

5.   Arbuthnot (1957), p. 298-299.

6.   Arbuthnot (1947), p. 275.

7.   Sutherland (1977), p. 191.

8.   Huck (1961), p. 324.

9.   Huck (1976), p. 98.

10. Anderson (1972), p. 160.

11. Ibid.

12. Georgiou (1969), p. 66.

13. Lonsdale (1973), p. 186.

14. Ibid., p. 309.

15. Ibid., p. 138-139.

16. Huck (1976), p. 101.

17. Arbuthnot (1957), p. 32.

18. Lonsdale (1973), p. 312-314.

19. Sutherland & Arbuthnot (1977), "Viewpoints" by Eudora
     Welty, p. 165.

20. Huck (1976), p. 176-178.

21. National Geographic, May, 1977, p. 581.

22. Ibid., p. 617, 621.

23. Meigs (1969), p. 288.

24. Alice Duer Miller. White Cliffs. Coward-McCann,
     1940, p. 70.

Bibliography of Texts Used in Survey

*Anderson, William and Patrick Groff.   A New Look at

---

*The single editions of recent date.

<u>Children's Literature</u>. Wadsworth Publishing Company, 1972. 362 pp.

Arbuthnot, May Hill. <u>Children and Books</u>. Scott Foresman, 1947. 626 pp.

_____. _____. rev. ed. 1957. 684 pp.

_____. _____. 3rd. ed. 1964. 688 pp.

_____ and Zena Sutherland. <u>Children and Books</u>. 4th ed. 1972. 836 pp.

Sutherland, Zena and May Hill Arbuthnot. <u>Children and Books</u>. 5th ed. 1977. 699 pp.

*Georgiou, Constantine. <u>Children and Their Literature</u>. Prentice-Hall, 1969. 501 pp.

Hollowell, Lillian. <u>A Book of Children's Literature</u>. Farrar and Rinehart, 1939. 942 pp.

_____. _____. 2nd ed. 1950. XV and 697 pp.

_____. _____. 3rd ed. 1966. XI and 580 pp.

Huck, Charlotte S. and Doris A. Young. <u>Children's Literature in the Elementary School</u>. Holt, Rinehart and Winston, 1961. 522 pp.

Huck, Charlotte S. and Doris Young Kuhn. <u>Children's Literature in the Elementary School</u>. 2nd ed. 1968. 792 pp.

Huck, Charlotte S. <u>Children's Literature in the Elementary School</u>. 3rd ed. 1976. 815 pp.

*Lonsdale, Bernard J. and Helen Mackintosh. <u>Children Experience Literature</u>. Random House, 1973. 540 pp.

Meigs, Cornelia, Anne Eaton, Elizabeth Nesbitt, and Ruth Hill Viguers. <u>A Critical History of Children's Literature</u>. Macmillan, 1953. 624 pp.

_____. _____. rev. ed. 1969. 708 pp.

---

*The single editions of recent date.

*Sebesta, Sam Leaton and William J. Iverson. Literature
    for Thursday's Child. Science Research Associates,
    1975. 566 pp.

*Smith, James Steel. A Critical Approach to Children's
    Literature. McGraw-Hill, 1967. 442 pp.

---

*The single editions of recent date.

SUMMARY OF PAGES DEVOTED TO THE FOLLOWING

	Total	Index	Table of Contents	Mother Goose	Folk Literature	British Folk Literature
Arbuthnot						
1947	626	8 (2c)	6	27	76	2
1957	684	14 (2c)	7	20	37	3
1964	688	22 (2c)	5	18	37	4
1972	836	44 (3c)	5	18	47	10
1977	699	40 (3c)	4	10	44	16
Hollowell						
1939	969	13 (2c)	12	10	366*	47
1950	713	13 (2c)	9	10	192*	26
1966	591	13 (2c)	6	7	130*	14
Huck						
1961	522	23 (3c)	8	7	22	-
1968	792	41 (3c)	9	7	59	10
1976	815	30 (3c)	2	7	90	4
Meigs						
1953	624	19 (2c)	4	$5_+^\dagger$	†	†
1969	708	39 (3c)	4	$13^\dagger$	†	†
Anderson						
1972	362	10 (2c)	1	2	25^+	
Georgiou						
1973	510	20 (2c)	1	6	134	
Lonsdale						
1973	540	14 (2c)	3	3	56	
Sebesta						
1975	566	15 (3c)	1	4^x	35	
Smith						
1967	442	22 (2c)	$\frac{1}{2}$	2	10	

*Hollowell: Full text of each selection
-Huck: Index not adequate to include
†Meigs: No listings in index
+Anderson: 14 pp. of the 25 are bibliography
xSebesta: From bibliography

2c, 3c = two columns, three columns.

FAIRY TALES IN ALL THE TEXTS:

Cinderella and Variants From the British Isles

	French Cinderella	English Tattercoats	English Catskin	Scottish Rushencoatie	Irish "Fair, Brown and Trembling"	Irish "The Girl Who Sat by the Ashes"
Meigs						
1953	+	+	+	+	+	-
1969	+	+	+	+	+	-
Arbuthnot						
1947	-	+full	-	-	-	-
1957	+	+ text	-	-	-	-
1964	+	-	-	-	-	-
1972	+11p. ref.	-	-	-	-	-
1977	+ 8p. ref.	-	-	-	-	-
Hollowell						
1939	-	-	-	-	-	-
1950	-	-	-	-	-	-
1966	-	-	-	-	-	-
Huck						
1961	+ 7p.	-	-	-	-	-
1968	+14p.	-	-	-	-	-
1976	+22p.	+	-	-	-	-
Anderson						
1972	+	-	-	-	-	-
Georgiou						
1969	+12p. ref.	-	-	-	-	-
Lonsdale						
1973	+ 6 pages compared	-	-	-	-	+ full text
Sebesta						
1975	+	-	-	-	-	-
Smith						
1967	+	-	-	-	-	-

Index listings or Table of Contents as in Hollowell

+ included in text
- not included in text

BRITISH FOLK TALES INCLUDED IN THE EIGHTEEN TEXTS:
THE FOUR MULTIPLE EDITIONS

	Arbuthnot 1947, 1957, 1964, 1972, 1977	Hollowell 1939, 1950, 1966	Huck 1961, 1968, 1976	Meigs 1953, 1969
Three Little Pigs	+ - + + +	+ + +	- + +	- +
Henny Penny	- - - + +	+ + -	- - +	- -
Fox and the Little Red Hen	- - - - -	+ + -	- - -	- -
Wee Bannock	- - - + +	+ - -	- - +	- -
Tom Tit Tot	+ + - + +	+ + +	+ + +	- +
Lazy Jack	- - + + -	+ + +	- - +	- -
Three Sillies	- - - - -	+ + +	- - +	- -
Dick Whittington and His Cat	- + + + +	+ + -	+ + +	- +
Childe Rowland	- - - + +	+ + -	- - -	- -
Hudden and Dudden and Donald O'Neary	- - - + -	+ + +	- - -	- -
Jamie Freel and the Young Lady	- - - - -	+ - -	- - -	- -

+included in text
-not included in text

Note: Based on index listings except for Hollowell's Table of Contents. Meigs
index very limited: titles varied (Three Little Pigs or Story of...) See:
chart of pages in indexes and tables of contents to aid interpretation.

BRITISH FOLK TALES INCLUDED IN THE EIGHTEEN TEXTS:
FIVE SINGLE EDITIONS

	Anderson 1972	Georgiou 1969	Lonsdale 1973	Sebesta 1975	Smith 1967
Three Little Pigs	-	+	-	-	+
Henny Penny	-	-	-	-	+
Fox and the Little Red Hen	-	-	-	-	+
Wee Bannock	-	-	-	-	-
Tom Tit Tot	-	-	-	+	-
Lazy Jack	-	+	-	-	-
Three Sillies	-	+	-	-	-
Dick Whittington and His Cat	-	+	-	-	-
Childe Rowland	-	-	-	-	-
Hudden and Dudden and Donald O'Neary	-	+	-	-	+
Jamie Freel and the Young Lady	-	-	-	-	-

+included in text
-not included in text

USING TRADITIONAL FOLK STORIES
IN UNTRADITIONAL WAYS IN HELPING CHILDREN
CLARIFY THEIR VALUES AND FEELINGS

Robert J. Stahl

Traditional storytelling is an entertainment which can be a private personal experience and a group-shared experience. Modern tellers of stories also set as their goal the entertainment of their audiences. But storytelling can be much more than mere entertainment. Why shouldn't it be a learning experience of a different dimension? Why shouldn't storytelling and the stories themselves be used as stimuli to help children reflect upon their personal values and emotions? This chapter first provides background as to the skills necessary for effective storytelling and then describes how the storyteller can use questions in order to assist children in the process of clarifying their values and feelings.

Folktales, like fairytales, were meant to be told, not read. For this reason, storytelling became an art and good storytellers were recognized for their unique and particular skills in "telling" tales. In addition, because the content, message, and characters of these tales were valued in their own right by the people of a particular culture, stories were more effective when they were told rather than read. Skillful storytellers took advantage of the relationship between a tale and its cultural content. They built up characters, dramatized minor incidents, and enlarged upon the feats and qualities of the heroes in accordance with the needs and background of the audience. To survive, these tales and their tellers had to have special meaning to their respective cultures. Storytellers were allowed some freedom to improvise upon the basic story, but were not expected to change the message of the story itself. This is why so many different versions of the myths, folktales, fairytales, and legends exist today.

Just as these tales and stories were not meant to be read, they were not meant to be followed by long question and answer periods which quizzed the listeners. Such quizzing was rarely needed. The storyteller who could not keep the attention of the audience rarely survived. Thus, storytellers sought to tantalize, excite, and involve their listeners. They learned to vary their speech patterns and their voice level, and to use body language to gain and hold the attention of those around them. The good storyteller did not merely repeat what had been memorized. The storyteller both entertained and informed his audience.

In addition to the effectiveness of storytelling over storyreading, another factor alters the effectiveness of telling tales in the modern day world. We often forget that the audiences of the olden-day storyteller had been raised to respect the tales and stories of their culture. Before the printed word, these stories provided one of the major sources of information and history of a people or culture. They included knowledge of what a people valued, enjoyed, and dreamed. They transmitted to younger generations much of what the culture held dear and wanted to remember. Few children in the non-mass media society could resist the excitement, characters, and adventures which these stories contained. Coming from this cultural background, the audience of the storytellers was often aware of many of the stories which were to be told. They would expect each storyteller to grab his audience in his own unique way.

Today, children are not brought up to learn from the stories and tales of past ages. Television and cartoon heroes have replaced those stressed in folk and fairytales. Except for Biblical stories, many children have little real contact with the legends and lore of days past. Instead of oral readings, our youth have been attracted to the audio and visual images of the television and movie screen. The modern storyteller must compete with other media forms for the attention of children.

Besides this competition, readers and tellers of folktales often present their audiences with characters, events, and content from "foreign" cultures. In many cases, the foreign words, phrases, or terms contained in these tales have no meaning for children reared in our contemporary society. In addition, storytellers also deal with "ancient" content and settings. For example, the Age of Chivalry and knights in shining armor are "ancient" in the eyes of space-age children. Stacking the deck even more against the modern teller of stories, the genuine storyteller of the past knew and told the story rather than read a casually understood story from a book.

But all is not lost. Modern tellers of stories and tales can compete effectively for the attention and interests of youthful audiences. They can use tales as a means of informing students about the content, characteristics, and values of other cultures, times and people. They can help children to find the relevance of these tales to their contemporary lives. But to accomplish these outcomes, these tales must be told, not read. It requires that contemporary storytellers become more than good readers. They must learn to fit the image and patterns of the old storytellers (i. e., they must become tellers of tales and stories rather than oral readers).

It is the intent of the remainder of this chapter to describe some skills and procedures to assist the would be storyteller to become more skillful and effective in presenting tales and stories to youthful audiences. Due to space limitations, this section focuses on pre- and post-story factors--especially those which relate to values and values clarification. When these are consciously thought through and practiced, the modern storyteller may well recapture the audiences which used to huddle around the storytellers in the days of yore.

Before you select the tale to be told, assess the age, background, experiences, and knowledge level of your expected audience. Children have different attention spans. Older children have a better understanding of knights, chivalry, fair ladies, etc. than do younger children. The vocabularies of children vary, as does the knowledge they have of peoples and cultures outside their own immediate environment. Never approach the selection of a tale on the premise that "I like it so they should (will) like it too." Approach it from the viewpoint of "What tale would be best suited for this audience at this particular time?" Making proper selections consistently makes your storytelling more effective.

Once your selection is made, no matter how many times you have read the tale before, reread it at least twice more before you tell it. Read it carefully and thoroughly. Don't skim it. If possible, study it so that you can "tell" the story aloud without having to read it to your audience. Don't worry about minor changes in your version as you "spin the tale." Where necessary and appropriate, improvise, invent, and elaborate in order to better fit the tale to your audience. Concentrate on delivering the story and not so much on making sure every single word is remembered or mentioned. In other words, come to know the tale so well that you free yourself to become a storyteller rather than a reader of tales.

When appropriate, inform your audience ahead of time about the tale, its setting, its cultural origin. Try to provide the children with some of the knowledge and vocabulary they need in order to follow and make sense of the story. Children who hear "knight" as "night" can make little sense of a story about King Arthur and his famous (K)nights. In short, prepare your audience for the cultural experience in which they are about to engage. Of utmost importance, don't equate a three- or four-sentence introduction to a tale as being equivalent to an adequate background to the tale. Too frequently story readers assume their audience has basically the same background information about the story as they themselves do. Don't assume too much on the part of your children.

Take time to review some basic information about the tale before you tell it. Use this review as a measuring device to determine how much your audience knows before the tale is told. If children can't answer your preliminary questions, then they don't know information essential to their understanding of the story. For example, if one selected the story, Where Arthur Sleeps,[1] then some pre-story questions to the audience might be:

- What is a staff?
- Where does a Welshman live?
- Who is King Arthur?
- Who are the Cymry?
- According to the legend, when will Arthur awake and return to England?

While telling your tale, revise or eliminate some of the vocabulary to fit the audience. An abundance of Welsh,

Scottish, or Irish terms may "keep the tone" of the tale, but don't keep the "tone" at the cost of half of your audience who won't understand the meaning of what you're saying. Many adults who read some of the available folktales and fairytales have difficulty understanding some of the vocabulary used. You cannot expect younger children who may only hear these terms read aloud to comprehend them. To emphasize this point, below are listed words taken from a published version of the tale, <u>Where Arthur Sleeps</u>: drovers, staff, hazel stick, mottled, matlock, clanger, unbitted, unblinkered, and sonorous. It is doubtful that a story filled with such words would keep the attention of young children--or most adults. So, modify the vocabulary as appropriate.

In telling your tale, use voice inflections to create excitement, suspense, a sense of danger, etc. Add sounds which may be reported in the tale but are not printed in the published form of the tale. Merely raising the volume of your voice can sometimes create a dramatic effect on your audience. The opposite of voice noises is silence. Just as you can use your voice to build different moods and environments, silence can also be used to produce similar and equally dramatic effects. The wise storyteller fluctuates between using voice and silence in diverse ways to create different effects.

Your follow-up questions should be clear and precise. Make sure you plan ahead of time what purpose the follow-up discussion is to serve. Plan your first few questions before you ever tell the tale. Long, drawn-out questions rarely receive answers from young children (or from most adults). Make sure only one question is asked at a time. The average person waits only about one second after a question before either asking another question or making some comment about the original question. People, especially children, need more time than that to think. Each question should seek only one kind of information from the child. And lastly, avoid asking questions that only you could reasonably answer.

Ideally, questions are designed to get information from students about what they know, think, and value. Because children know different kinds of things at different levels of understanding, storytellers need to become skilled in the several kinds of questions they can ask. Because children also have values, make value choices, and react emotionally, storytellers need to touch base with these affective areas as well. Thus, if children are to be helped in framing and

forming their affective receptions and reactions to folk and
fairy tales, then storytellers need to know how to ask question to guide this reaction.

Values clarification discussions are not merely conversations which moralize about a given tale. Such discussions
include segments where participants reveal what they know,
what things mean, what they rate as a value and why, how
they feel, and how they made decisions and choices. Values
clarification then is the process by which students investigate
and reflect upon their values, value choices, feelings, and
the reasons for and consequences of their values and feelings.
Values clarification discussions serve as the medium for
children to express themselves in ways which give evidence
that the process is occurring.

To ensure that values clarification is taking place
within the scope of accurate information and useful under-
standings, the storyteller needs to find out from children
whether or not they know certain specific facts about the story just told. Empirical questions are those which ask for
specific, precise information which has been given or is
available. Sometimes referred to as "recall" questions, these
seek to find out what specific knowledge students have of the
story. Examples of empirical questions (all based on Where
Arthur Sleeps) are:

1. In what country does the story take place?
2. Who is King Arthur?
3. How many times did the Welshman go back to the
    cave for the treasure?
4. What did the Welshman have to do in order to get
    the treasure?
5. What did Arthur do when he awoke and saw the
    Welshman stealing treasure?

While recalled information is important, children must
understand what the information means if it is to be of much
value. Comparative questions provide one means by which
children can express their deeper understanding of the tale.
Comparative questions ask for the identification of how two or
more things are similar or different from one another or how
they relate to one another. Thus, children use "-er" words
(like: taller, faster, bigger, quicker, etc.) or words prefaced
by "more" or "less" (more often, less likely, etc.) to indi-
cate the relative status of one item to another. For instance,
they could reveal how two individuals in a given tale were dif-

ferent from one another. In stating similar qualities, children mention that two items "both have" a given characteristic.
Examples of comparative questions one might ask are:

1.   How does gold differ from silver?
2.   What was the same about the Welshman on each of
     his visits to the cave?
3.   How was the Welshman's third visit to the cave
     different from his first two visits?

Unfortunately, many storytellers focus on just understanding of a tale and leave the child's personal reactions
alone. Valuing questions are designed to get students to express their personal values, preferences, ratings, and choices
while using such terms as "good," "bad," "better," "first,"
"ugliest," "fairest," etc. In answering these questions, students report the value something has for themselves or has
in respect to some standard. In other cases, they may report their own personal preference or liking for an idea, story, action, or person. So, the storyteller needs to learn
how to ask questions that cause the children to use value
terms like those mentioned above in response to a given story. Examples of valuing questions are:

1.   Of the three men in the story, the Welshman, the
     Wise Man, and Arthur, which one did you like
     the best?
2.   Is it good to tell stories about stealing, wars, and
     other bad things?
3.   According to the story, would you label the Welsh-
     man as a bad man?

Just as children have value reactions to stories, they
also react emotionally to them. They get excited, scared,
upset, anxious, happy, sad, and the like as they hear the stories transmitted through various fairy and folk tales. And,
as with values, storytellers need to be able to help children
identify, understand, and reflect upon their emotional reactions to what they experience. Emotive questions ask children to express their emotions in words which signify feelings.
By definition, answers to emotive questions must contain
words like "upset," "happy," "angry," "sad," "mad," "excited," "worried," etc. Remember, if a child's response does
not include a word like that just mentioned, it is not an emotive answer. "I feel that ... " responses are not emotion
answers. Emotive questions seek to help the child put accurate labels on his or her personal feelings as well as assist

them in talking publically about those feelings.   To be most
effective, emotive questions should contain a cue feeling term
within the question itself.   The examples below of emotive
questions illustrate this point:

1. When the Welshman was caught by Arthur, was
    he scared?
2. Would you be afraid of King Arthur?
3. Are you happy that we picked this story to tell?

Too often storytellers (and teachers) talk about helping
students with "affective" or "humanistic" aspects of their self
images, but more often than not, these storytellers are not
skilled in ways likely to produce the results they want.
Value clarification as a process of knowing and thinking about
one's values and feelings is a very worthwhile process for
listeners.   The points brought out in this chapter reveal that
no single factor, even values clarification questions, can work
well without considering other factors which also apply.   For
instance, there's no use asking an excellent emotive question
if the child is not going to be given enough time to think about
a response.   When used in conjunction with one another, however, the points emphasized in this chapter can initiate posi-
tive values clarification thinking in response to your "told"
stories.

Notes

1.   Jones, Gwyn. Welsh Legends and Folk Tales. Walck, 1955.

References

Casteel, J. Doyle & Robert J. Stahl. Value Clarification
      in the Classroom: A Primer. Santa Monica, CA:
      Goodyear, 1975.

_____. _____. Verbal Strategies of Valuing: A Hand-
      book on Values Clarifying Questions. Columbus, MS:
      Mississippi University for Women, 1975 (unpublished
      mimeotext).

Casteel, J. Doyle, Linda Corbett, Wesley Corbett, and
      Robert J. Stahl. Valuing Exercises in the Middle
      School. Resource Monograph No. 11. Gainesville,
      FL: P. K. Yonge Laboratory School, 1974 (ERIC
      Microfiche No. ED 102 034).

NYPL STORYTELLER'S CHOICE AND COMMENTS

Eloise S. Norton

One of my favorite fantasies for the last thirty years has been running something like this:

Whenever I experienced a trying or boring day as a school librarian or library consultant or college professor, I would sit quietly and plan how, in a couple of years, I would chuck it all, head for New York City and tell stories for the New York Public Library. The New York Public Library would welcome me with open arms. This was built into my fantasy. They would put me to work the next day in all the romantic places I loved so well in the fifties, The Metropolitan Museum, The Cloisters, Greenwich Village, Central Park, telling stories to crowds of adoring children. This fantasy has meant a great deal to me all these years and is probably one reason I wrote Marilyn Iarusso, Storytelling Specialist for the New York Public Library. I asked her about the program and the folk literature used from the British Isles, when I became interested in doing this book.

I was interested in learning the twenty-five most frequently told stories by the storytellers during the last ten years in alphabetical order. They were:

"The Cat and the Parrot" by Sara Cone Bryant. In The Last Half-Hour edited by Eulalie Steinmetz Ross. Harcourt.

"The Crab and the Jaguar" by Valery Carrock. In Picture Folk-Tales. Dover.

"Don't Blame Me!" by Richard Hughes. In Don't Blame Me! Harper and Row.

"The Elephant Child" by Rudyard Kipling. In New Illustrated Just So Stories. Illustrated by Nicolas. Doubleday.

"The Golden Arm" by Joseph Jacobs. In English Fairy Tales.
    Dover.

"The Hobyas" by Joseph Jacobs. In More English Folk and
    Fairy Tales. Putnam.

"The Little Rooster and the Turkish Sultan" by Kate Seredy.
    In Good Master. Viking.

"Mr. Miacca" by Joseph Jacobs. In English Fairy Tales.
    Dover.

"Molly Whuppie" by Joseph Jacobs. In English Fairy Tales.
    Dover.

"The Old Witch" by Joseph Jacobs. In More English Folk
    and Fairy Tales. Putnam.

"The Princess on the Pea" by Hans Christian Andersen. In
    Art of the Storyteller by Marie Shedlock. Dover.

"The Pumpkin Giant" by Mary E. Wilkins. In The Harvest
    Feast compiled by Wilhelmina Harper. Dutton.

"The Shoemaker and the Elves" by the Brothers Grimm. In
    More Tales from Grimm, freely translated and illus-
    trated by Wanda Gag. Coward-McCann.

"Sop Doll" by Richard Chase. In Spooks, Spooks, Spooks
    edited by H. Hodes. Watts.

"The Three Billy Goats Gruff" by Peter Asbjornsen and Jor-
    gen Moe. In Time for Old Magic compiled by M. H.
    Arbuthnot. Little.

"Ticky-Picky Boom-Boom" by Harold Courlander. In Anansi,
    the Spider Man: Jamaican Folk Tales told by Philip
    M. Sherlock. Crowell.

"Tikki Tikki Tembo" adapted by Arlene Mosel. In Tikki
    Tikki Tembo. Holt, Rinehart, and Winston.

"The Tinderbox" by Hans Christian Andersen. In The En-
    chanted Book edited by A. Dalgliesh. Scribner.

"The Tinker and the Ghost" by Ralph Boggs and Mary Gould
    Davis. In Anthology of Children's Literature edited
    by E. Johnson. Houghton.

"To Your Good Health" by Marie Shedlock.   In The Art of
the Storyteller.   Dover.

"Tom Tit Tot" by Joseph Jacobs.   In It's Time for Story
Hour edited by E. H. Sechrist.   Macrae Smith.

"Two of Everything" by Alice Ritchie.   In Time for Old Magic compiled by M. H. Arbuthnot.   Little.

"The Witch's Skin" by Ricardo Alegriá.   In The Three
Wishes.   Harcourt, Brace, Jovanovich.

"The Wolf and the Seven Little Kids" by the Brothers Grimm.
In Time for Old Magic compiled by M. H. Arbuthnot.
Little.

"The Yellow Ribbon" by Maria Leach.   In The Rainbow Book
of American Folk Tales and Legends.   World.

When considering the 200 most popular stories of the
New York Public storytellers, the most frequently used sour-
ces seemed to be Jakob and Wilhelm Grimm (especially as
retold by Wanda Gag) and Joseph Jacobs, with the collections
of Harold Courlander, Parker Fillmore, Peter Asbjornsen and
Jorgen Moe closely following.   Next in frequency of use come
Hans Christian Andersen, Richard Chase, Mary Hatch, Pura
Belpré, Rudyard Kipling, Howard Pyle, Eleanor Farjeon, and
Ruth Sawyer.

Many storytellers use Henry Beston, Carl Sandburg,
Richard Hughes, Sorche Nic Leodhas, Walter De La Mare,
Valery Carrick, and Lafcadio Hearn.   Seumas MacManus,
Margery Bianco, Arthur Ransome, Laurence Housman, Marie
Shedlock, Mary Wilkins, and Oscar Wilde were also used as
sources but not as often.   Several popular stories of three
storytellers are used over and over throughout the years,
however.

Concerning the stories from the British Isles, Miss
Iarusso states,

> ... (Joseph) Jacobs is our most popular source
> from the British Isles, with Ruth Sawyer, Seumas
> MacManus and Padriac Colum for Irish tales, and
> Sorche Nic Leodhas for Scottish as runners-up.
> Some of Ruth Manning-Sanders, James Reeves,
> Barbara Picard, Flora Steele, and Amabel Williams-
> Ellis retelling are also chosen.

It was good to learn that, in spite of all the problems and cuts the New York Public Library and New York City have suffered, the storytelling programs have survived.   Miss Iarusso stated,

> We have had a Storytelling Program at The New York Public Library for some sixty years.   By Storytelling we mean stories told by heart to children grade three and up.   Staff cuts have forced us to curtail these to monthly programs during the school year where we have children's librarians. There are occasional special storytelling 'festivals' or seasonal programs in locations which can't sustain monthly programs.   Usually the programs are done by our own librarians though we have occasional special guests.   We still have hundreds of picture book programs a year for children grades K to 2, and an active and ever increasing program of preschool storyhours.

The staff has been reduced considerably resulting in a severe limiting of programs and activities concerning the training.   I was told:

> The training for storytelling was traditionally done as part of our training seminars for new staff, with demonstrations, lectures on techniques and selection standards, and scheduled observations of new storytellers.   The outstanding new storytellers were presented at a Storytelling Symposium each spring.   Last year, in lieu of new staff, we presented some of our top administrators who began as children's librarians and still tell stories in branches on occasion.   This year we will move to a storytelling workshop format until we again have new staff members to present.

Still, one of the outstanding activities has been able to survive this far.   The publication, Stories, a List of Stories to Tell and Read Aloud, has served as a guide for storytellers all over the world.   This list was released in its seventh edition in 1977.   Miss Iarusso reported,

> It was first compiled by Mary Gould Davis, Storytelling Specialist, in 1927.   The over 400 annotated entries in the first edition were selected as editions 'that seemed most helpful both in text and

form to the Story Hour. ' Over the years we've
added subject listings to help storytellers select
tales, and we've included listings of books for the
Storyteller, for reading aloud, poetry collections
and recordings. It's fascinating to see how the
lists have changed and yet how many stories have
been reappearing for five years as endorsed by the
children of New York City.

The storytelling program must survive even if it has
to go commercial and advertise Humble Oil or Maxwell House
Coffee between stories! It has been the model, our example
of excellence in storytelling programs, for many years. In
Paris, one of the leading Children's Service Librarians admitted, "My ideas and feelings about storytelling have been
influenced by the New York Public Library where I trained. "
In Bangkok a librarian stated, "I remember my days as a
storyteller with NYPL with such warmth!" Everywhere I
travel the NYPL is present.

Perhaps the National Endowment for the Humanities
or other foundations might award annual training fellowships,
rather like the Fulbright-Hays grants, and help restore this
program to its former strength. It would be excellent training for children's librarians and school media personnel and
college professors with fantasies. This could be done in
other cities as well.

The librarians would be chosen by the New York Public Library to work for one or two years, be trained, polished, refined, and used as an NYPL storyteller during this
time. Each would return to the library which had granted
leave, a much more valuable children's librarian. The librarian's salary or part-salary could be paid by an industry or
foundation which would receive a tax credit for the sponsor-
ship.

This might be one way of retaining the storytelling
symposium, the much needed workshop, and discovering our
Ruth Sawyers and Frances Clark Sayers of the future as well.

Where are you, storytellers of the world? Shall we
form a Society for the Preservation of NYPL's Storytelling
Program? If Robert and Elizabeth Browning's home can be
preserved in Florence by friends from all over the world,
can't we do as much for NYPL's Storytelling Program?

I believe storytelling for children in grades 3 to 6 must survive in public libraries if it is to survive at all.

I also need my personal fantasy about the New York Public Library and storytelling. It is my comfort, my joy-- I will not allow it to fade away. Someday I really am going to the New York Public Library and tell stories....

APPENDIX A

British Folktales
in the Culture of American Children

Note: See the article by Eloise Norton (pp. 172-189).

Under each culture group, please number in the order of
your choice the five stories you feel are the most important.
Write in if preference is not listed.   Place a check by any
stories you have never heard of.

ENGLAND

_____ Molly Whuppie
_____ Three Little Pigs
_____ Dick Whittington and His Cat
_____ Hare and the Hedgehog
_____ Mr. Miacca
_____ Cock Robin
_____ Three Wishes of a Fox [Error, should read "Three
          Wishes."]
_____ Travels of a Fox
_____ The Old Woman and Her Pig
_____ Story of the Three Bears
_____ Three Sillies
_____ Henny Penny (Chicken-Licken)
_____ Jack and the Bean Stalk
_____ The Cock, the Mouse, and the Little Red Hen
_____ Master of All Masters
_____ Mr. Vinegar
_____ Tattercoats
_____ Tom Tit Tot
_____ Teeny-Tiny
_____ Little Red Hen

SCOTLAND

____ Black Bull of Narroway
____ All in the Morning Early
____ Fairy Flag of Dunvegan
____ Whuppety Stourie
____ Page Boy and the Silver Goblet
____ Wee Bannock
____ Peerifool
____ The Brownie O'Ferne-Den
____ Assipattle and the Giant Sea Serpent
____ Tam Lin

CORNWALL

____ Duffy and the Devil
____ Skerry Werry
____ Skillywidden
____ The Knockers
____ Peter and the Piskies
____ Lyonesse
____ Parson Wood and The Devil

IRELAND

____ The Well of the World's End
____ Children of the Salmon
____ Little Dermot and the Thirsty Stones
____ Peddler of Ballaghhaderseen
____ Connla and the Fairy Maiden
____ King O'Toole and His Goose
____ Children of Lir
____ Bee, the Harp, the Mouse, and the Blum-Clock
____ The Old Hag's Long Leather Bag
____ Billy Beg and the Bull (his bull)
____ Patrick O'Donnell and the Leprechaun
____ Widow's Lazy Daughter

WALES

____ The Man Who Killed His Greyhound (The Hound Gelert)
____ The Quest for Olwen (The Hunting of Twrch Trwyth)
____ The Sigh of Gwyddn Long Shank (The Flooding of the
        Lower Hundred)

___ Where Arthur Sleeps (The Welshman and the Hazel Staff)
___ A Harp on the Water (The Legend of Bala Lake)
___ March's Ears
___ Rhitta of the Beards
___ Lleu and the Flowerface (Blodeuedd and the Slaying of
      Llew)
___ The Dream of Maxen Wledig
___ The Woman of Llyn-y-Fan Fach (The Bride of Llyn-y-
      Fan Fach)
___ The Lad Who Returned from Faerye (Elidorus in Fairy-
      land)
___ Fairy of the Lake

Now please list the ten most important stories drawing from
all cultures above.

APPENDIX B

Added Entries by Participants
Received on Returned Questionnaires

ENGLAND

Mr. Fox
Lazy Jack
Here After This
Jack the Giant Killer 2
Robin Hood 2
History of Tom Thumb 2

Three Wishes
Beowulf
Elsie Piddock Skips in Her
    Sleep
King of the Cats
Golden Arm
Johnny Cake

SCOTLAND

Always Room for One More
Runaway Brownie (Calhoun)
Lass Who Went Out at the
    Cry of Dawn
Loch Ness Monster
MacCordrum of the Seals

Heather and Broom
Women Who Flummoxed the
    Fairies
Changling and the Fond
    Young Mother
The Me Pechs

CORNWALL

Lutey and the Mermaid
Betty Stog's Baby

IRELAND

Deirdre
Sagas of Cuchulain
Hudden and Dudden and Donald
    O'Leary 2
Leprechaun Tales (Green)
Munachar and Manachar
Princess and the Vagabond

Wee Red Cap
Celtic Fairytales (Jacobs)
Shamrock and Spear (Pil-
    kington)
Finn MacCool
Wee Meg Barnileg and the
    Fairies 3

WALES

Arthurian Legends 2
Tales from Welsh Hills (Pugh)
Welsh Legends and Folktales
   (Jones)
Three Jovial Huntsmen

How Trystan Won Esyelt
Dewi and the Devil
Man Who Sold the Winds
Hag of the Mist
Salt Welsh Sea

APPENDIX C

AMGUEDDFA WERIN CYMRU--WELSH FOLK MUSEUM

Y BRENIN ARTHUR/KING ARTHUR

Llyfryddiaeth ddethol--Selected Bibliography

(See further references in many of the books)

ALCOCK, Leslie. Arthur's Britain: History and Archaeolo-
    gy, AD 367-634. London: Allen Lane, the Penguin
    Press, 1971.

ASHE, Geoffrey. The Quest for Arthur's Britain. London:
    Pall Mall Press, 1968.

BROMWICH, Rachel, ed. Trioedd Ynys Prydein. The
    Welsh Triads. Cardiff: University of Wales Press,
    1961.

BROWN, Arthur, C. L. The Origin of the Grail Legend.
    Cambridge, Mass.: Harvard University Press, 1943.

BULLOCK-DAVIES, Constance. Professional Interpreters and
    the Matter of Britain. Cardiff: University of Wales
    Press, 1966.

DAVIES, Jonathan Ceredig. Folklore of West and Mid-Wales.
    Aberystwyth, 1911.

EVANS, J. Gwenogvryn, gol. Y Mabinogion o Lyvvyr Gwyn
    Rhydderch. The White Book Mabinogion: Welsh Tales
    and Romances. Pwllheli: J. Gwenogvryn Evans, 1907.

FOULKES, Isaac. "Cymru Fu," yn cynws hanesion, trad-
    dodiadau, yn nghyda chwedlau a dammegion Cymreigh.
    Wrexham: Hughes and Son, 1862.

GRISCOM, Acton, ed. The Historia Regum Britanniae of
    Geoffrey of Monmouth. London: Longmans, Green
    and Co., 1929.

HARWARD, Vernon J., Jr. The Dwarfs of Arthurian Ro-
    mance and Celtic Tradition. Leiden: E. J. Brill,
    1958.

HOLE, Christina. English Folk-Heroes. London: B. T.
    Batsford Ltd., 1948.

JACKSON, Kenneth. Language and History in Early Britain.
    Edinburgh: Edinburgh University Press, 1953.

JARMAN, A. O. H. Chwedlau Cymraeg Canol. Caerdydd:
    Gwasg Prifysgol Cymru, 1957.

JONES, Gwyn, and Thomas Jones. The Mabinogion. Trans-
    lated. London: J. M. Dent and Sons Ltd., 1949.

JONES, Thomas. A Sixteenth Century Version of the Ar-
    thurian Cave Legend. (Studies in Language and Liter-
    ature in Honor of Margaret Schlough, Warsaw Polish
    Scientific Publications, 1966, pp. 175-185.)

JONES, T. Gwynn. Welsh Folklore and Folk-Custom. Lon-
    don: Methuen and Co., Ltd., 1930.

JONES, W. Lewis. King Arthur in History and Legend.
    Cambridge: Cambridge University Press, 1914.

LOOMIS, Roger Sherman. Arthurian Tradition and Chrétien
    de Troyes. New York: Columbia University Press,
    1949.

_____. The Development of Arthurian Romance. London:
    Hutchinson University Library, 1963.

_____. The Grail: From Celtic Myth to Christian Sym-
    bol. Cardiff: University of Wales Press, 1963.

_____. Wales and the Arthurian Legend. Cardiff: Uni-
    versity of Wales Press, 1956.

_____, ed. Arthurian Literature in the Middle Ages.
    Oxford: Clarendon Press, 1959.

MALORY, Sir Thomas. Le Morte d'Arthur. 2 vols. Lon-
    don: Everyman's Library, 1906.

OWEN, Rev. Elias. Welsh Folklore: A Collection of the

Folk-Tales and Legends of North Wales.   Oswestry:
Woodall, Minshall and Co. , 1896.

REID, Margaret J. C.   The Arthurian Legend: Comparison
of Treatment in Modern and Medieval Literature.
London: Methuen and Co. Ltd. , 1938.

RHYS, John.   Celtic Folklore, Welsh and Manx.   2 vols.
Oxford: Clarendon Press, 1901.

TATLOCK, J. S. P.   The Legendary History of Britain.
Geoffrey of Monmouth's Historia Regum Britanniae
and Its Early Vernacular Versions.   Berkeley: University of California Press, 1950.

TREVELYAN, Marie.   Folklore and Folk-Stories of Wales.
London: Elliot Stock, 1909.

WACE, Robert, and Layamon.   Arthurian Chronicle.   London: Everyman's Library, 1912.

WESTON, Jessie L.   From Ritual to Romance.   Cambridge:
Cambridge University Press, 1920.

WILLIAMS, Ifor.   Hen Chwedlau.   Caerdydd: Gwasg Prifys-
gol Cymru, 1949.

Books on Welsh Folklore Especially Suitable for Children

1.   W. Jenkyn Thomas.   The Welsh Fairy Book.   First
       pub. 1907, re-issued by the University of Wales
       Press, 1952; p. 304.

2.   D. Parry-Jones.   Welsh Legends and Fairy Lore.   Bats-
       ford, 1953; p. 181.

3.   Gwyn Jones.   Welsh Legends and Folk-Tales.   Oxford
       University Press, 1955; p. 270.

APPENDIX D

Places Associated with Arthur

Prepared by Ilid E. Anthony for 1976
Folk Literature of British Isles Study Tour

A. Sites occupied during the "Dark Ages," i. e. Post-Roman,
    5th-9th centuries. They are the correct period for
    the historical figure which may be Arthur.

1. Castle Dore, Cornwall. It stands three miles from
    Fowey, east of the B 3269 from Fowey to Bodmin.

2. Castell Odo, Caernarvon. $\frac{1}{2}$ m West of B 4413 between
    Aberdaron and Nevin in Lleyn Peninsula.

3. Carrgeg-y-Llam, Caernarvonshire. North of B 4417
    between Nevin and Llanaelhaiarn in the Lleyn Penin-
    sula.

4. Carn Boduan, Caernarvonshire. North of B 4417 and
    South of No. 3.

5. Deganwy, Caernarvonshire. On B 5115 between Llandud-
    no Junction and Llandudno.

6. Dinas Emrys, Caernarvonshire. East of A 498 between
    Beddgelert and Penygwryd.

7. Dinas Powys, Glamorganshire. On the A 4055 between
    Cardiff and Barry.

8. Dinorben, Abergele. $\frac{1}{2}$ m Southwest of the A 55 on the
    road between Abergele and Bodelwyddan.

9. Glastonbury, Somerset. A. Glastonbury Abbey. The
    monks in the early Medieval Period claimed to have
    excavated the graves of Arthur and his Queen. B.
    Glastonbury Tor, the Dark Age site above the town.
    On A 39 between Wells and Taunton.

10. <u>Pant-y-Saer, Anglesey.</u>   East of A 5025 from Llangallo.

11. <u>South Cadbury, Somerset-Dorset Border.</u>   South of the
    A 39 near Street, Somerset.

B. <u>Sites associated with Arthur in name and legend.</u>

1. Arthur's Chair, Breconshire.

2. Arthur's Hill-top, Breconshire--the saddle between two
    hills.

3. Arthur's Stone, Gower, Glamorganshire, Cromlech.

4. Arthur's Quoit at Trethewy, Cornwall.   Cromlech.

5. Caerleon on Usk, Monmouth was often supposed to have
    been Camelot.

6. At Valle Crucis, Llangollen there is a pillar dedicated
    to King Eliseg with an inscription tracing his ancestry
    to Vortigern.   This is often associated with Arthur.

7. The Battle of Mons Badonicus has been associated with
    both Liddington Castle, Badbury and Badbury Rings,
    Dorset.

8. Tintagel, Cornwall on B 3263 from Camelford to Tinta-
    gel Head has also associations with Arthur and was
    thought to be the site of Camelot.

C. <u>Sites in Scotland associated with the name of Arthur.</u>
    The historical Arthur was unlikely to have been con-
    sidered.   Aedan, king of Dalriada (Argyllshire) c.
    574 A.D., had a son named Arthur who was killed in
    battle; he may have been the source of the dedications.

1. Arthur's O'en, or Oven near Stirling.

2. Arthur's Seat near Edinburgh.

<u>Books which give descriptions of sites:</u>

Alcock, L. <u>Arthur's Britain: History and Archaeology,</u>
    <u>A.D. 367-634.</u>   London, 1971.

Ashe, G. The Quest for Arthur's Britain. London, 1968.

Lethbridge, T. C. Merlin's Island.

Lindsay, J. Arthur and His Times.

APPENDIX E

Folk Literature of the British Isles
(For Study Tour 1976)

BASIC READING

ALCOCK, Leslie. Was This Camelot? Excavations at Cad-
bury Castle, 1966, 1970. Stein & Day, 1972.
ASHE, Geoffrey. All About King Arthur. London: W. H.
Allen, 1969.
_____. King Arthur: In Fact & Legend. Nelson, 1971.
_____. The Quest for Arthur's Britain. London: Pall
Mall Press, 1968.
BARING-GOULD, William and Ceil. The Annotated Mother
Goose. Potter, 1962.
BRIGGS, Katharine. Fairies in English Tradition & Litera-
ture. University of Chicago Press, 1967.
_____. Personnel of Fairyland: A Short Account of the
Fairy People of Great Britain for Those Who Tell Sto-
ries to Children. (Reprint of 1953 ed.) Gale, 1971.
PICARD, Barbara Leonie. Hero Tales from the British Isles.
(Puffin) Penguin, 1963.
SUTCLIFF, Rosemary. Heroes and History. Putnam, 1965.

GENERAL-BRITISH ISLES

BATCHELOR, Julie F. Superstitious? Here's Why! Har-
court, Brace & Co., 1954.
COLWELL, E. Tales from the Islands. Penguin, 1975.
FINLAY, Winifred. Cap O'Rushes and Other Folk Tales.
Retold by Winifred Finlay; illustrated by Victor Am-
brus. Hale, 1974.
HAZELTINE, Alice I., ed. Hero Tales from Many Lands.
Illustrated by Gordon Laite. Abingdon, 1961.
HODGES, Margaret. The Other World, Myths of the Celts.
Farrar, 1973.
MAYNE, William. William Mayne's Book of Heroes. Dutton.
MILLER, Margaret, ed. Knights, Beasts and Wonders:
Tales and Legends from Medieval Britain. White,
1969.

PALMER, Robin and Pelagie Doane. Fairy Elves. Walck, 1964.
PICARD, Barbara Leonie. Hero Tales from the British Isles. Retold by Barbara Leonie Picard; illustrated by Erie Fraser. Criterion Books, 1961.
RICHARDS, George M. The Fairy Dictionary. Macmillan, 1932.
SAWYER, Ruth. Way of the Storyteller. Rev. ed. Viking, 1962.
SHEDLOCK, Marie. Art of the Storyteller. 3rd ed. Dover, 1952.
SOFTLY, Barbara. Magic People. Holt, Rinehart & Winston, 1967.
UDEN, Grant. A Dictionary of Chivalry. Crowell, 1969.
_____. Hero Tales from the Age of Chivalry: Retold from the Froissart Chronicles. World.
WILLIAMS-ELLIS, Amabel. Fairy Tales from the British Isles. Warne, 1964.

SUPPLEMENTARY REFERENCE SOURCES

ALFORD, Violet. Introduction to English Folklore. Bell, 1952.
ANDREWS, Elizabeth. Ulster Folklore. Dutton, 1919.
BRIGGS, K. M. Folklore of the Cotswolds. Rowman & Littlefield, 1975.
CHAMBERS, E. K. Arthur of Britain. October House, 1967.
CLARKE, Kenneth and Mary. Introducing Folklore. Holt, Rinehart, & Winston, 1963.
CLODD, Edward. Tom Tit Tot, an Essay on Savage Philosophy in Folktale. London: Duckworth & Co., 1898. Reissued by Singing Tree Press, 1968.
CURTIN, Jeremiah. Hero-Tales of Ireland. Gordon Press, 1894.
_____. Myths and Folklore of Ireland. Boston, 1890. (Gale, reprint.)
_____. Tales of the Fairies and of the Ghost-World. Bohn.
GUERBER, Helen A. The Book of the Epic. Lippincott, 1913.
HARRIS, Percy. Truth about Robin Hood. Gale.
JONES, Gwyn and Thomas Jones. The Mabinogion. London: J. M. Dent, 1949.
KENNEDY, Patrick. Legendary Fictions of the Irish Celts. London, 1866. (Gale, reprint.)

KRAPPE, Alexander H.   The Science of Folklore.   Methuen,
     1965.
MOORMAN, Charles.   Book of King Arthur.   University of
     Kentucky Press, 1965.
Ó SÚLLEABHÁIN, S.   The Folklore of Ireland.   Hastings
     House, 1975.
THOMPSON, Stith.   The Folktale.   Dryden Press, 1946.
WILDE, Jane (Lady).   Ancient Legends of Ireland.   London,
     1887.

MOTHER GOOSE

BARCHILON, Jacques and Henry Pettit.   The Authentic
     Mother Goose Fairy Tales and Nursery Rhymes.
     Denver: Swallow, 1960.
BARING-GOULD, S.   A Book of Nursery Songs and Rhymes.
     Singing Tree Press, 1969.
BETT, Henry.   Nursery Rhymes and Tales.   Singing Tree
     Press, 1968.
ECKENSTEIN, Lina.   Comparative Studies in Nursery Rhymes.
     Singing Tree Press, 1968.
FORD, Robert.   Children's Rhymes--Games--Songs--Stories.
     Singing Tree Press, 1968.
GREEN, Percy.   A History of Nursery Rhymes.   London:
     Greening and Co., 1899.   (Reprint, Singing Tree
     Press, 1968.)
HALLIWELL-PHILLIPS, James O.   The Nursery Rhymes of
     England.   Singing Tree Press, 1969.
MONTGOMERIE, Norah.   A Book of Scottish Nursery Rhymes.
     Collected and edited by Norah & William Montgomerie;
     illustrated by T. Ritchie and N. Montgomerie.   Ox-
     ford, 1965.
OPIE, Iona and Peter.   A Family Book of Nursery Rhymes.
     Oxford University Press, 1964.
     _____.   Lore and Language of School Children.   Oxford:
     Clarendon Press, 1967.
     _____.   The Oxford Dictionary of Nursery Rhymes.   Ox-
     ford, 1951.
     _____.   The Oxford Nursery Rhyme Book.   Oxford Uni-
     versity Press, 1955.
The Original Mother Goose.   Singing Tree Press, 1969.
THOMAS, Katherine Elwes.   The Real Personages of Mother
     Goose.   Lothrop and Lee, 1930.

ENGLAND

BRIGGS, Katharine M. and Ruth L. Tongue, eds. Folktales
     of England. (Folktales of the World Series) Univer-
     sity of Chicago Press, 1965.
CAMPBELL, Alfred. Wizard and His Magic Powder: Tales
     of the Channel Islands. Knopf.
COLWELL, Eileen. Round About and Long Ago: Tales from
     the English Counties. Houghton Mifflin, 1972.
CORCORAN, Jean. Folk Tales of England. Bobbs.
CROSSLEY-HOLLAND, Kevin. Callow Pit Coffer. Seabury,
     1969.
_____. King Horn. Macmillan, 1965.
_____. The Pedlar of Swaffham: East Anglian Legend.
     Seabury, 1968.
GARNETT, Richard. Jack of Dover. Vanguard, 1966.
HAVILAND, Virginia. Favorite Fairy Tales Told in England.
     Little, 1959.
JACOBS, Joseph, ed. English Folk and Fairy Tales; Folk
     and Fairy Tales from Many Lands. Illustrated by
     John D. Batten. Putnam, 1904.
_____. More English Folk and Fairy Tales. Collected
     and edited by Joseph Jacobs; illustrated by John D.
     Batten. Dover, 1967.
MANNING-SANDERS, Ruth. Stories from the English & Scot-
     tish Ballads. Dutton, 1968.
NESBIT, E. Old Nursery Tales. London: Brockhampton
     Press.
REEVES, James. English Fables and Fairy Stories. Walck,
     1954.
RHYS, Ernest. Fairy-Gold: A Book of Old English Fairy
     Tales. Dutton, 1939.
STEEL, Flora Annie. English Fairy Tales. Illustrated by
     Arthur Rackham: afterword by Clipton Fadiman.
     Macmillan, 1962.
VANSITTANT, Peter. The Dark Tower: Tales from the
     Past. Crowell, 1969.
WIMBERLY, Lowry. Folklore in the English & Scottish
     Ballads. Dover, 1965.

PICTURE BOOKS (ENGLISH)

BROWN, Marcia. Dick Whittington and His Cat. Scribner,
     1950.
CALHOUN, Mary. The Goblin Under the Stairs. Illustrated
     by Janet McCaffery. Morrow, 1968.

_____. The Pixy and the Lazy Housewife.   Pictures by
        Janet McCaffery.   Morrow, 1969.
CHAUCER, Geoffrey.   Chanticleer and the Fox.   Illustrated
        by Barbara Cooney.   Crowell, 1958.
CONGER, Lesley.   Tops and Bottoms.   Illustrated by Imera
        Gobbato.   Four Winds, 1970.
CROSSLEY-HOLLAND, Kevin.   The Green Children.   Illustra-
        ted by Margaret Gordon.   Seabury, 1968.
DAVIES, Anthea.   Sir Orfeo.   Illustrated by Errol LeCain.
        Bradbury, 1970.
DE LA MARE, Walter.   Jack & the Beanstalk.   Illustrated
        by Joseph Lowe.   Knopf, 1959.
GALDONE, Paul.   Henny Penny.   Seabury, 1968.
_____.   Little Red Hen.   Seabury, 1973.
_____.   Three Bears.   Seabury, 1972.
_____.   Three Wishes.   McGraw-Hill, 1961.
GARNER, Alan.   The Old Man of Mow.   Photographs by
        Roger Hill.   Doubleday, 1967.
GODDEN, Rummer.   The Old Woman Who Lived in a Vinegar
        Bottle.   Viking, 1972.
The History of Mother Twaddle and the Marvelous Achieve-
        ments of Her Son Jack.   Illustrated by Paul Galdone.
        Seabury, 1974.
HOLDSWORTH, William C.   Little Red Hen.   Adapted and
        illustrated by W. C. Hold.   Farrar, 1969.
JACOBS, Joseph.   The Buried Moon.   Pictures by Susan
        Jeffers.   Bradbury, 1969.
_____.   Hereafterthis.   McGraw, 1973.
_____.   Johnny Cake.   Illustrated by Emma L. Brock.
        Putnam, 1967.
_____.   Joseph Jacobs' Lazy Jack.   A picture book by
        Barry Wilkinson.   Bodley Head, 1969.
_____, ed.   More English Folk and Fairy Tales.   Col-
        lected and edited by Joseph Jacobs.   Illustrated by
        John D. Batten.   Putnam, 1904.
JEFFERS, Susan.   Three Jovial Huntsmen.   Adapted and il-
        lustrated by Susan Jeffers.   Bradbury, 1973.
LINES, Katherine.   Dick Whittington.   Illustrated by Edward
        Ardizzone.   Walck, 1970.
MOORE, Eva.   Dick Whittington and His Cat.   Retold by Eva
        Moore.   Pictures by Kurt Werth.   Seabury, 1974.
NESS, Evaline.   Mr. Miacca: An English Folk Tale.   Holt,
        Rinehart, and Winston, 1967.
ROCKWELL, Anne.   The Three Bears and Other Stories.
        Hamilton.
SEWALL, Marcia.   Master of All Masters.   Little, 1972.
Three Little Pigs.   The Story of the Three Little Pigs with
        drawings by L. Leslie Brooke.   Warne, 1934.

Three Little Pigs.   The Three Little Pigs in Verse (author
    unknown).   Illustrated by William Pene du Bois.   Vi-
    king, 1962.
Tom Tit Tot.   Tom Tit Tot, an English folk tale.   Illustrated
    by Evaline Ness.   Scribner, 1965.
WIESNER, William.   Tom Thumb.   Walck, 1974.
WILKINSON, Barry.   The Diverting Adventure of Tom Thumb.
    Adapted and illustrated by Barry Wilkinson.   Harcourt,
    1969.

CORNWALL

MANNING-SANDERS, Ruth.   Peter and the Piskies.   Roy,
    1958.
TREGARTHEN, Enys.   The Doll Who Came Alive.   Day,
    1972.
_____.   Piskey Folk, A Book of Cornish Legends.   Ar-
    ranged by Elizabeth Yates.   Day, 1960.
_____.   The White Ring.   Harcourt, 1949.

PICTURE BOOKS (CORNISH)

CALHOUN, Mary, adapter.   The Witch's Pig: A Cornish Folk-
    tale.   Illustrated by Lady McCrady.   Morrow, 1977.
ZEMACH, Harve.   Duffy and the Devil: a Cornish Tale Retold.
    Pictures by Margot Zemach.   Farrar, Straus, 1973.

IRELAND

BENNETT, Richard.   Little Dermot and the Thirsty Stones,
    and Other Irish Folk Tales.   Coward, 1953.
COLUM, Padraic.   The Boy Who Knew What the Birds Said.
    Macmillan, 1918.
_____.   The Children Who Followed the Piper.   Macmillan,
    1938.
_____.   The Fountain of Youth.   Macmillan, 1940.
_____.   The Frenzied Prince.   Heroic Stories of Ancient
    Ireland.   McKay, 1943.
_____.   The Girl Who Sat by the Ashes.   Illustrated by
    Imero Gobbato.   New York: Macmillan, 1968.
_____.   The King of Ireland's Son.   Illustrated by Willy
    Pogany.   New York: Macmillan, 1962.
_____.   The Stone of Victory and Other Tales by Padraic
    Colum.   Foreword by Virginia Haviland; illustrated by
    Judith Gwyn Brown.   McGraw, 1966.

_____, ed. A Treasury of Irish Folklore; the Stories, Traditions, Legends, Humor, Wisdom, Ballads and Songs of the Irish People. Rev. ed. Crown, 1962.

DANAHER, Kevin. Folktales of the Irish Countryside. D. White, 1970.

DILLON, Ellis. Wise Man on the Mountain. Illustrated by Gaynor Chapman. Atheneum, 1970.

EVSLIN, Bernard. The Green Hero: Early Adventures of Finn McCool. Four Winds Press, 1975.

GREEN, Kathleen. Leprechaun Tales. Illustrated by Victoria de Larrea. Lippincott, 1968.

_____. Philip and the Pooka and Other Irish Fairy Tales. Illustrated by Victoria de Larrea. Lippincott, 1966.

JACOBS, Joseph, ed. Celtic Folk and Fairy Tales. Selected and edited by Joseph Jacobs; illustrated by John D. Batten. D. Nutt, 1891.

MAC MANUS, Seumas. The Bold Heroes of Hungry Hill and Other Irish Folk Tales. Retold by Seumas Mac Manus; illustrated by Jay Chollick. Farrar, Straus, 1951.

_____. Donegal Fairy Stories. Doubleday, 1939.

_____. Hiberian Nights. Macmillan, 1963.

_____. Rocky Road to Dublin: Autobiography of Irish Storyteller.

_____. The Well O' the World's End. Macmillan, 1939.

O'FAOLAIN, Eileen. Irish Sagas and Folk-Tales. Retold by Eileen O'Faolain; illustrated by Joan Kiddell-Monroe. Walck, 1954.

PICARD, Barbara Leonie. Celtic Tales; Legends of Tall Warriors and Old Enchantment. Retold by Barbara Leonie Picard. Criterion Books, 1965.

PILKINGTON, Francis M. Three Sorrowful Tales of Erin. Walck, 1966.

PILKINGTON, R. M. Shamrock and Spear: Tales and Legends from Ireland. Harcourt and Brace, 1968.

SAYERS, Peig. Peig: Biography of a Storyteller. Syracuse University Press, 1974.

STEPHENS, James. Irish Fairy Tales. Illustrated by Arthur Rackham. Macmillan, 1968.

YEATS, U. B., ed. Fairy and Folk Tales of Ireland. Macmillan, 1973.

YOUNG, Ella. The Tangle-Coated Horse and Other Tales. McKay, 1968.

_____. The Unicorn with Silver Shoes. Longmans, 1949.

_____. The Wonder Smith and His Son: a Tale from the Golden Childhood of the World. Illustrated by Boris Antzbasheff. McKay, 1957.

PICTURE BOOKS (IRISH)

BODEN, Alice. The Field of Buttercups. Adapted and il-
lustrated by Alice Boden. Walck, 1974.
CALHOUN, Mary. Hungry Leprechaun. Illustrated by Roger
Duvoisin. Morrow, 1962.
JACOBS, Joseph. Munachar and Manachar. Pictures by
Anne Rockwell. Crowell, 1970.
_____. Hudden and Dudden and Donald O'Leary. Illus-
trated by Doris Burn. Coward, 1968.
MICHEL-DANSAC, Monique. Peronnique: An Old Tale.
Adapted and illustrated by Monique Michel-Dansac.
Atheneum, 1970.
O'FAOLAIN, Eileen. The Little Black Hen. Illustrated by
Aldren Watson. Random House, 1940.

SCOTLAND

BENDICK, Jeanne. My Story of Loch Ness Monster. Mc-
Graw Hill, 1976.
CAMPBELL, J. F. Mouth of the Night: Gaelic Stories.
Macmillan, 1976.
HAVILAND, Virginia. Favorite Fairy Tales Told in Scotland.
Little, 1963.
HUNTER, Mollie. The Ferlie. Funk & Wagnalls, 1968.
(Fiction)
_____. Thomas and the Warlock Funk. Harper, 1967.
(Fiction)
_____. Walking Stones. Harper, 1970. (Fiction)
MAC DONALD, Alex. Story & Song from Loch Ness Side.
(Norwood Folklore Series). Norwood, PA.
NIC LEODHAS, Sorche. Twelve Great Black Cats, and
Other Eerie Scottish Tales. Dutton, 1971.
_____. By Loch and by Lin. Holt, Rinehart, and Win-
ston, 1967.
_____. Claymore and Kilt. Holt, Rinehart, and Winston,
1967.
_____. Gaelic Ghosts. Holt, Rinehart, and Winston,
1967.
_____. Ghost Go Haunting. Holt, Rinehart, and Winston,
1965.
_____. Heather and Broom. Holt, Rinehart, and Winston,
1960.
_____. Sea Spell & Moor Magic. Holt, Rinehart, and
Winston, 1968.
_____. Thistle and Thyme. Holt, Rinehart, and Winston,
1962.

SCOTT, Sir Walter. Tales of a Grandfather. (Reprint)
        London: Black, 1963.
SHEPPARD-JONES, Elizabeth (told by). Scottish Legendary
        Tales. Nelson and Sons, 1962.
WILSON, Barbara Ker. Scottish Folk-Tales and Legends.
        Walck, 1960.

PICTURE BOOKS (SCOTTISH)

ARMSTRONG, Gerry and George. Magic Bagpipe. Albert
        Whitman & Company, 1964.
HUGHES, Ted. Nessie the Mannerless Monster. Pictures
        by Gerald Rose. Faber, 1964.
NIC LEODHAS, Sorche. Always Room for One More. Il-
        lustrated by Nanny Hogrogian. Holt, Rinehart, and
        Winston, 1965.

WALES

ALEXANDER, Lloyd. Black Cauldron. Harcourt, 1965.
        (Fiction)
_____. Book of Three. Harcourt, 1964. (Fiction)
_____. Castle of Llyr. Harcourt, 1966. (Fiction)
_____. Coll and His White Pig. Harcourt, 1965. (Fic-
        tion)
_____. The Foundling and Other Tales of Prydain. Har-
        court, 1973. (Fiction)
_____. King's Fountain. Dutton, 1971.
_____. Taran Wonderer. Harcourt, 1967. (Fiction)
BOWEN, Qwen. Tales from the Mabinogion. Vanguard,
        1974.
COLUM, P. Island of the Mighty; Being Hero Stories of
        Celtic Britain Retold from the Mabinogion. Macmil-
        lan, 1924.
GARNER, Alan. Owl Service. Walck, 1968. (Fiction)
GRIFFITH, W. Adventures of Pyrideri: Taken from the
        Mabinogion. Verry, 1962.
GUEST, Lady Charlotte. The Red Book of Hergast. 1849.
HOLBROOK, Sabra. Foundling and Other Tales of Prydain.
        Farrar, 1973.
_____. High King. Farrar, 1968.
_____. Sir Tristan of All Times. Farrar, 1970.
JENKY, Thomas W. More Welsh Fairy and Folk Tales.
        Verry, 1957.

JONES, Gwyn. King Beast and Heroes. Oxford University
       Press, 1972.
_____. Welsh Legends and Folk Tales. Retold by Gwyn
       Jones; illustrated by Joan Kiddel-Monroe. Walck,
       1955.
LANG, Andrew. King Arthur: Tales of the Round Table.
       Schocken, 1967.
PARRY-JONES, D. Welsh Legends and Fairy Lore. London:
       Batsford, 1953.
PUGH, Ellen. More Tales from the Welsh Hills. Illustrated
       by Joan Sandin. Dodd, Mead, 1971.
_____. Tales from the Welsh Hills. Dodd, Mead, 1968.
SHEPPARD-JONES, Elizabeth. Welsh Legendary Tales.
       Nelson, 1960.
TREVELYAN, Marie. Folklore and Folk Stories of Wales.
       British Book Center, 1974.

PICTURE BOOKS (WELSH)

ALEXANDER, Lloyd. King's Fountain. Dutton.
JACOBS, Joseph. Jack, the Giant-Killer. Illustrated by
       Fritz Wegner. Walck, 1970.
ROBBINS, Ruth. Taliesin and King Arthur. Adapted and il-
       lustrated by Turth Robbins. Parnassus, 1970.
THOMPSON, Harwood. The Witch's Cat. Illustrated by
       Quentin Blake. Addisonian, 1975.

HEROES, LEGENDS, AND EPICS

England

ALFRED THE GREAT, 849-901
    HELM, Peter J. Alfred the Great. Crowell, 1965.
    HODGES, C. Walter. Namesake: A Story of King Al-
       fred. Coward, 1964.
    JOHNSON, David. Alfred the Great (Jackdaw # 89.)
       Grossman, 1969.
    JOHNSON, Eleanor N. King Alfred the Great. West-
       minster, 1966.
    MAPP, Alfred J., Jr. The Golden Dragon: Alfred the
       Great and His Times. Open Court, 1974.
    TREASE, Geoffrey. Escape to King Alfred. Vanguard,
       1958. (Fiction)

ARTHUR, 5th Century A.D.
    FRASER, Antonia. King Arthur and the Knights of the
        Round Table. Knopf, 1970.
    GREEN, Roger L. King Arthur (Puffin) Penguin, 1974?
    HIBBERT, Christopher and Charles Thomas. Search for
        King Arthur. American Heritage, 1970.
    HIEATT, Constance. The Castle of Ladies. Crowell,
        1973.
    _____. The Joy of the Court. Crowell, 1971.
    _____. Knight of the Court. Crowell, 1969.
    _____. Knight of the Lion. Crowell, 1969.
    _____. The Minstrel Knight. Retold by Constance
        Hieatt; illustrated by James Barkley. Crowell,
        1974.
    _____. Sir Gawain and the Green Knight. Crowell,
        1967.
    _____. The Sword and the Grail. Crowell, 1972.
    JEWETT, Eleonore M. Hidden Treasure of Glaston. Vi-
        king Press, 1946. (Fiction)
    KNOWLES, James. Legends of King Arthur. Warne,
        1958.
    LANG, Andrew. King Arthur: Tales of the Round Table.
        Schocken, 1967.
    McLEOD, Mary. The Book of King Arthur and His Noble
        Knights. (5-7).
    MALORY, Sir Thomas. The Boy's King Arthur. Edited
        by Sidney Lanier; illustrated by N. C. Wyeth.
        Scribner, 1917.
    MAYNE, William. Earthfast. Dutton, 1967. (Fiction)
    NEWSTEAD, Elaine. Bran the Blessed in Arthurian
        Romance. A. M. S. Press, 1939.
    NYE, Robert. Taliesin. Hill & Wang, 1967.
    PICARD, Barbara Leonie. Stories of King Arthur and
        His Knights. Walck, 1966.
    PYLE, Howard. The Story of the Champions of the
        Round Table. Scribner, 1905.
    _____. The Story of King Arthur and His Knights.
        Scribner, 1903.
    _____. The Story of the Grail and the Passing of Ar-
        thur. Scribner, 1933.
    _____. The Story of Sir Lancelot and His Companions.
        Scribner, 1907.
    ROBBINS, Ruth. Taliesin and King Arthur. Parnassus
        Press, 1970.
    SCHILLER, Barbara. Eric and Enid. Illustrated by Ati
        Forberg. Dutton, 1970.

_____. The Kitchen Knight. Holt, Rinehart, and Winston, 1965.

SERRAILLIER, Ian. Challenge of the Green Knight. Walck, 1967.

SKORPEN, Liesel. Old Arthur. Harcourt, 1972.

STERNE, Emma G. and Barbara Lindsay. King Arthur and the Knights of the Round Table. Golden Press, 1962.

SUTCLIFF, Rosemary. Tristan and Iseult. Dutton, 1971.

TENNYSON, Alfred. Idylls of the King. Airmont, 1968. (Poetry)

TROUGHTON, Joanna. Sir Gawain and the Loathly Damsel. Dutton, 1972.

TWAIN, Mark. Connecticut Yankee in King Arthur's Court. Harper and Row, 1889. (Fiction)

WHITE, Terence. Sword in the Stone. Putnam, 1939.

WILLIAMS, Jay. The Sword of King Arthur. Illustrated by Louis Glanzman. Crowell, 1968.

BEOWULF, 7th Century

CROSSLEY-HOLLAND, Kevin. Beowulf. Farrar & Strauss, 1968.

HOSFORD, Dorothy. By His Own Might: The Battles of Beowulf. Saxon.

NYE, Robert. Beowulf, a New Telling. Hill & Wang, 1968.

SERRAILLIER, Ian. Beowulf the Warrior. Walck, 1961.

SUTCLIFF, Rosemary. Beowulf. Dutton, 1962.

CARACTACUS, 1st Century

SHORE, Maxine. Captive Princess: Fiction Account of Caractacus in England. McKay, 1952.

HAVELOK THE DANE, before 13th Century

CROSSLEY-HOLLAND, Kevin. Havelok the Dane. Dutton, 1965.

SERRAILLIER, Ian. Havelok the Dane. Walck, 1967.

HEREWARD THE WAKE, 11th Century A.D.

KINGSLEY, Charles. Hereward, the Wake.

ROBIN HOOD (William Fitzooth), 12th Century

COOKE, D. E. Men of Sherwood. Harcourt, 1961.

FRASER, Antonia. Robin Hood. Knopf, 1971.

GILBERT, Henry. Robin Hood. David McKay Co.

GREEN, Roger L. Adventures of Robin Hood. (Puffin)
    Penguin, 1956.
MCGOVERN, Ann. Robin Hood of Sherwood Forest.
    Crowell, 1968.
MCSPADDEN, J. Walker. Robin Hood and His Merry
    Outlaws. Illustrated by Louis Slobodkin; with an
    introduction written by May Lamberton Becker.
    World Publisher, 1946.
MALCOLMSON, Ann. Song of Robin Hood. Houghton,
    1947.
OMAN, Carola. Robin Hood. Dutton, 1951.
PYLE, Howard. Some Merry Adventures of Robin Hood
    of Great Renown in Nottinghamshire. Scribner,
    1954.
SERRAILLIER, Ian. Robin and His Merry Men. Walck,
    1970.
_____. Robin in the Greenwood; Ballads of Robin
    Hood. Walck, 1968.
VANCE, Eleanor. Adventures of Robin Hood. Random,
    1953.

WILLIAM 1st, the Conqueror (1027-1087)
    COSTAIN, Thomas B. William the Conqueror (World
        Landmark).
    HODGES, C. Walter. Norman Conquest: Story of
        Britain. Coward, 1966.

Ireland

CUCHULAIN, I. A. D.
    GREGORY, Lady. Cuchulain of Muithemhe: Story of the
        Men of the Red Branch of Ulster. (5th ed.) Oxford
        University Press.
    HULL, Eleanor. The Boy's Cuchulain. Crowell, 1910.
    _____. Cuchulain: The Hound of Ulster. Crowell.
    NUTT, Alfred T. Cuchulain, the Irish Achilles (Reprint
        of the 1900 ed.) A. M. S. Press.
    SUTCLIFF, Rosemary. The Hound of Ulster. Dutton,
        1963.

FINN MCCOOL, 2nd and 3rd Century A. D. (Finn Mac Cumaill)
    EVSLIN, Bernard. The Green Hero: Early Adventures
        of Finn McCool. Four Winds Press, 1975.
    SUTCLIFF, Rosemary. The High Deeds of Finn McCool.
        Dutton, 1967.

Scotland

FLORA MCDONALD, 1722-1790
    VINING, Elizabeth. Flora: a Biography. Lippincott,
        1966.

MONTROSE, 1612-1650
    IRWIN, Margaret. Bride: Story of Louise & Montrose.
        Dufour, 1962.
    WEDGWOOD, C. V. Montrose. (Makers of History
        Series) Archon, 1966.

ROB ROY (Robert MacGregor) 1671-1734)
    SCOTT, Sir Walter. Rob Roy. (Everyman) Dutton.

ROBERT I, King of Scotland, 1274-1329
    BAKER, Nina. Robert Bruce. Vanguard, 1948.
    BARROW, G. W. S. Robert Bruce. University of Cali-
        fornia, 1965. (Adult)
    STEPHENS, Peter J. Outlaw King: Story of Robert the
        Bruce. Atheneum, 1964.

WILLIAMS WALLACE, 1272-1305
    (In Sutcliff: Heroes & History and Other Hero Collec-
        tions)

Read About These British Saints:

England: St. George of England
         St. Oswald of Northumbria
         St. Augustus
Ireland: St. Patrick
Wales: St. David

INDEX